READERS' GUIDES TO ESSENTIAL CRITI

CONSULTANT EDITOR: NICOLAS TREDELL

Published

Forthcoming

Readers' Guides to Essential Criticism
Series Standing Order ISBN 1–4039–0108–2
(outside North America only)

You can receive future titles in this series as they are published by placing a standing order. Please contact your bookseller or, in the case of difficulty, write to us at the address below with your name and address, the title of the series and the ISBN quoted above.

Customer Services Department, Macmillan Distribution Ltd, Houndmills, Basingstoke, Hampshire RG21 6XS, England

---

Contemporary Scottish Literature

MATT McGUIRE

Consultant editor: Nicolas Tredell

palgrave
macmillan

First published 2009 by
PALGRAVE MACMILLAN

Palgrave Macmillan in the UK is an imprint of Macmillan Publishers Limited,
registered in England, company number 785998, of Houndmills, Basingstoke,
Hampshire RG21 6XS.

Palgrave Macmillan in the US is a division of St Martin's Press LLC,
175 Fifth Avenue, New York, NY 10010.

Palgrave Macmillan is the global academic imprint of the above companies
and has companies and representatives throughout the world.

Palgrave® and Macmillan® are registered trademarks in the United States,
the United Kingdom, Europe and other countries.

ISBN-13: 978-0-230-50669-5 hardback
ISBN-10: 0-230-50669-0 hardback
ISBN-13: 978-0-230-50670-1 paperback
ISBN-10: 0-230-50670-4 paperback

This book is printed on paper suitable for recycling and made from fully
managed and sustained forest sources. Logging, pulping and manufacturing
processes are expected to conform to the environmental regulations of the
country of origin.

A catalogue record for this book is available from the British Library.

A catalog record for this book is available from the Library of Congress.

10 9 8 7 6 5 4 3 2 1
18 17 16 15 14 13 12 11 10 09

Printed and bound in China

Dedicated to my mother and father, Geraldine and Kieron McGuire
And, of course, Maree

CONTENTS

Nation and Nationalism

This Chapter examines claims by Douglas Gifford that recent Scottish literature constitutes a 'real' Literary Renaissance. It asks whether cultural vitality in Scotland emerged as a reaction and response to certain disappointments in the political arena, particularly the failed devolution referendum of 1979?. Peter Kravitz contests such notions, foregrounding the lengthy gestation of seminal texts such as Alasdair Gray's *Lanark*, published in 1981 but three decades in the making. Besides the issue of renaissance, several critics assert that Scottish literature provides a unique artistic space in which the politics of national identity are keenly played out. They include Cairns Craig, Alan Riach and Carla Sassi. In contrast Christopher Whyte insists that nationalist criticism serves to distort, delimit and detract from the signifying possibilities of Scottish literature. In this Chapter the national question forms a conduit to examining criticism of Alasdair Gray and his groundbreaking novel *Lanark*.

Language

This Chapter focuses on the politics of language and its particular relevance within Scottish literature. It includes discussion of writing in Scots, Gaelic and in vernacular forms of English. We begin by revisiting Edwin Muir's famous claim of the 1930s that the Scottish writer is somehow maimed or disabled by the country's fractured linguistic inheritance. In contrast, critics like Rory Watson argue that this is in fact one of Scottish literature's most enabling characteristics. Contemporary Scottish writing is seen to be enlivened by an acute awareness of the linguistic terrain upon which it travels. J. Derrick McClure's book *Language, Poetry and Nationhood* (2000) is used to explain the historical evolution of Scotland's various languages. In discussing the role of urban vernacular we consider critical reactions to the poetry of Tom Leonard. The continuing crisis confronting literature in Gaelic is also examined in detail.

CHAPTER THREE   62

Gender

One of the most important transformations within contemporary Scottish literature has concerned the influence and visibility of women's writing. Marilyn Reizbaum and Joy Hendry argue that Scottish women's writing has traditionally suffered from a form of double marginalization; this on account of questions of gender and its locus within a minor literary culture. For Aileen Christianson the enduring problem is nationalism, a patriarchal ideology that has historically sidelined and subordinated women's experience. The 1990s saw the publication of several weighty anthologies of Scottish women's writing which sought to redress this historical imbalance. This chapter examines reactions to the work of two important female writers of the period, the poet Liz Lochhead and the novelist Janice Galloway.

CHAPTER FOUR   92

Class

For Christopher Whyte the flourishing of literary talent during the 1980s, described by some as a national renaissance, was, in fact, the overdue arrival of working-class voices within the literary domain. Douglas Gifford reads these contemporary innovations in the context of the Glasgow history novel. For Cairns Craig there has always been a particularly proletarian bias at the heart of literary endeavor in Scotland. In contrast for poet and critic Douglas Dunn, the preponderate influence of working-class/Glasgow fiction represents a distorted and narrow view of late twentieth-century Scottish culture. The second half of this Chapter features a discussion of critical responses to the work of James Kelman.

CHAPTER FIVE   118

Postcolonialism

This Chapter begins with the outright exclusion of Scotland from what has been proposed as a canon of postcolonial cultures, a point argued in the seminal study *The Empire Writes Back* (1989). Scotland occupies an unusual position as a country that has both suffered and benefited from the British imperial adventure. Critics like Craig Beveridge and Ronald Turnbull employ an explicitly postcolonial framework and read Scottish culture through Frantz Fanon's concept of 'inferiorisation'. Berthold Schoene on the other hand is hesitant regarding any outright assertion of Scottish postcoloniality. For Schoene, such narratives reveal an internal friction and the country's problematic history of exploiting its own marginal groups like the rural peasantry and the urban working-class. This Chapter examines critical responses to the work of Irvine Welsh. It also features discussion of the film version of Welsh's groundbreaking novel *Trainspotting* (1993).

Postmodernism

This chapter features arguments by three critics on the relevance of postmodern theory to Scottish literature. For the critic Eleanor Bell postmodernism provides a welcome antidote to the immuring effects of cultural nationalism on our understanding of Scottish writing. Randall Stevenson concurs, arguing that postmodern thinking averts a worrying tendency toward parochialism within Scottish criticism. He claims that Scotland's ideological heritage – Calvinism, the Enlightenment, and the industrial revolution – make it particularly conducive to the challenges posed by postmodern theory. For Cairns Craig, Scottish literature can actually lay claim to be the inventor of postmodernism. He argues that the roots of many postmodern concepts can be found in Scottish Romantic writing, particularly the work of Sir Walter Scott and James Hogg. This Chapter also considers critical responses to the work of two influential contemporary writers: Muriel Spark and A. L. Kennedy.

Acknowledgements

I am grateful to the series editor, Nicolas Tredell, Sonya Barker, Felicity Noble, Vidhya Jayaprakash and all the team at Palgrave Macmillan for their help, support and guidance during the writing of this book. Their patience and effort is greatly appreciated. I would also like to thank the following friends, colleagues, peers and teachers for their continuing support over the years: Alistair Braidwood, Rhona Brown, Sarah Carpenter, Gerry Carruthers, John Coyle, Cairns Craig, Seamus Deane, Joyce Dietz, Sarah Dunnigan, Martin Edwards, Theo van Heijnsbergen, Douglas Gifford, Alan Gillis, Jane Goldman, Joseph Hughes, Craig Hughson, Aaron Kelly, Paddy Lyons, Chris Montgomery, John McBurnie, Kirsteen McCue, Robin Mukherjee, Colin Nicholson, Alan Riach, David Salter, Beth Schroeder, Kenneth Simpson, Jeremy Smith, Randall Stevenson and Ronnie Young.

Finally, this book is for my family and is dedicated with love to Geraldine and Kieron McGuire, Claire and Stuart Platt, and of course Maree.

Introduction

The latter decades of the twentieth century witnessed a dramatic transformation in the public profile and critical esteem afforded to Scottish literature. The high regard for contemporary Scottish writing is born out in the number of awards its authors have received. *A Disaffection*, by James Kelman (born 1946), won the world's oldest literary prize, the James Tait Black, in 1989, while Kelman became the first Scottish author to win the Booker Prize in 1994 with his novel *How Late It Was, How Late*. Kelman's fellow Glaswegian and close friend Alasdair Gray (born 1934) had received the Whitbread Prize for his novel *Poor Things* in 1992. Around this time A.L. Kennedy (born 1965) was named one of Granta Magazine's 'Twenty Best Young British Novelists'. Remarkably Kennedy would make this top 20 again, ten years later, in 2003. In poetry the accolades were equally thick on the ground. Don Paterson (born 1963) won the T.S. Eliot Prize in 1997 and 2003, the only poet ever to have done so twice. While in 1996 and then again in 2000 Kathleen Jamie (born 1962) was awarded the Geoffrey Faber Memorial Prize for two of her own poetry collections.

Coinciding with such literary recognition Scottish writing also began to enjoy an unprecedented degree of success in more popular genres. This was most notable perhaps in the detective fiction of Ian Rankin (born 1960) and Alexander McCall Smith (born 1948) and the science-fiction of Iain M. Banks (born 1954). A radical fusion of the popular and the literary, few books of the 1990s deserve the accolade 'publishing phenomenon' more than *Trainspotting* (1993) by Irvine Welsh (born 1958). Depicting a group of junkies scheming their way through the heroin subculture of the 1980s Edinburgh, the novel acted as a shot in the arm for a flagging publishing industry. *Trainspotting* would go on to sell over a million copies in the UK alone (most debut novels do well to sell a few thousand copies). Welsh's book was a cultural landmark, a provocative and transgressive novel which saw the traditional boundaries between the literary and the non-literary openly and deliberately flouted. *Trainspotting* was at the vanguard of a spectacle where books were increasingly appearing in new places, such as the shelves of record shops. It inaugurated a paradigm shift which saw mainstream youth culture (drugs, music, football) becoming the everyday fodder of literary fiction. During the 1990s Welsh himself wrote for the popular 'lad's' magazine *Loaded*.

The 'Trainspotting effect' as it is often dubbed found its way into the veins of the British film industry. The film adaptation by Danny Boyle (born 1956) was an overnight box-office smash and did much to raise the profile of Welsh's already successful novel. Boyle's film brought Scottish literature to the attention of an international audience, in many cases for the first time, and will also be considered in Chapter Five of this Guide. Like Welsh's main protagonist Mark Renton, movie directors began to scour the pages of Scottish fiction searching for 'one more hit', a novel ripe for adaptation and with the same intensity and appeal as *Trainspotting*. The film versions of *Morvern Callar* (2002) based on the book by the Oban writer Alan Warner (born 1964) and *Young Adam* (2003) by the Scottish counterculturalist Alexander Trocchi (1925–84) are perhaps the most notable examples of this trend.

In light of this success we can begin to understand why the Irish writer and critic Colm Toíbín (born 1955), in his introduction to *The Penguin Book of Irish Fiction* (2001), would cite contemporary Scottish writing as something of a literary benchmark:

> ■ [C]ompare the calmness of contemporary Irish writing with the wildness of contemporary Scottish writing. It is as though the legacy of Sterne and Swift, Joyce, Beckett and Flann O'Brien had taken the Larne-Stranraer ferry; in the writings of James Kelman, Alasdair Gray, Irvine Welsh, Janice Galloway and Alan Warner there is political anger, stylistic experiment and formal trickery.[1] □

Toíbín suggests that current Scottish authors are the heirs of a distinguished literary lineage which stretches from the eighteenth-century novelist Laurence Sterne (1713–68) and the satirist and poet Jonathan Swift (1667–1745) to the innovative twentieth-century writers James Joyce (1882–1941), Samuel Beckett (1906–89), and Flann O'Brien (1911–66. Such flattering comparisons pervade the criticism of contemporary Scottish literature. As never before late twentieth-century Scottish writing began to revel in a rich variety of global influences. These include Russian, American and French literature; science-fiction; existential philosophy; and the postmodern innovations of the *nouveau roman*. The *nouveau roman* was a highly experimental form of writing pioneered in the 1950s by French novelist Alain Robbe-Grillet (1922–2008). The latter decades of the twentieth century would see Scottish writing confront and overcome historical accusations of cultural parochialism. Sir Walter Scott (1771–1832) and his romantic noble highlander seemed a far cry from the urban squalor and the gothic landscapes of the contemporary Scottish imagination. In the film of *Trainspotting*, when Tommy takes Sick Boy, Spud and Renton into the highland heart of tourist Scotland, our anti-hero can only rage against the escapist fantasy embedded in such scenic sentimentalism: 'I hate being Scottish. We're the lowest of the low. The Scum of the fucking earth. The most wretched, servile, miserable, pathetic trash that was ever shat into creation.'[2] In the literary life of the nation, recent Scottish writing can be seen as marking a definitive break with the past. The immuring clichés of Scotland's yesteryear have been irrefutably cast aside. Unsurprisingly perhaps, this explosion of creativity provoked an unprecedented level of interest from literary critics both within Scotland and from much further afield. This book is a thematic guide to the essential criticism produced in response to the profusion and eclecticism of Scottish writing in recent years. The aim of the introduction is to provide an overview of the key literary developments and anticipate the discussion of the themes that are dealt with in subsequent chapters.

Thinking about contemporary Scottish literature in terms of a movement is a profitable, though not altogether unproblematic, critical enterprise. Formed in the early 1970s, the Glasgow writers' group is often regarded as the point of origin for what would eventually become a remarkable literary flourishing. The group was established by Philip Hobsbaum (1932–2005), then a lecturer in English Literature at the University of Glasgow. Hobsbaum had created similar groups before; first in London and then in Belfast, where writers like Seamus Heaney (born 1939), Michael Longley (born 1939) and Bernard MacLaverty (born 1942) would meet and discuss their latest work. Among the Glasgow group were a number of writers who would go on to achieve significant degree of literary success. They included Alasdair Gray, James Kelman, the poet Tom Leonard (born 1944), poet and dramatist Liz Lochhead (born 1947), and the Gaelic poet Aonghas MacNeacail (born 1942). Reading the Glasgow group as a cauldron of cross-fertilising creativity has been a popular critical strategy. However, one must be cautious of such convenient and cosy interpretation, and resist mistaking consequence for what is often, at best, merely coincidence. It is worth noting that attendance at the group by many of these writers was at best patchy, with some rarely present at all. Having said this, the legacy of these individuals for Scottish literature in both practical and aesthetic terms cannot be underestimated. Once they themselves had broken through, this generation would be instrumental in bringing the work of emerging local talent to the attention of the publishers for the first time. Scottish writers who received a hand up from their literary forbears in this way included Janice Galloway (born 1956), Duncan MacLean (born 1964), Jeff Torrington (born 1935) and Agnes Owens (born 1926). Whilst the writers of the Glasgow group had radically different ideas about how they each wanted to write, they shared an almost militant belief in the right to create art out of their own experience and with whatever voice they chose. James Kelman's much publicised and highly political acceptance speech at the 1994 Booker Prize can be read as something of an artistic manifesto for many of his contemporaries. Against media accusations of literary vandalism the author defiantly declared: 'my language and my culture have a right to exist.'[3] A sense of camaraderie was also present in Kelman's winning novel which contained the following dedication: 'Alasdair Gray, Tom Leonard, Agnes Owens and Jeff Torrington are still around, thank Christ.'[4] In terms of aesthetics, the enduring influence of these individuals lies in their stubborn refusal to bow to establishment expectations about what 'good' literature ought to be. Later Scottish writers would directly acknowledge this subversive and iconoclastic *esprit de corps* and its effect on their work. Irvine Welsh credits Kelman with 'setting the whole thing out so that people like myself can have more fun.'[5] Whilst A. L. Kennedy has said that people like Tom Leonard and James Kelman 'made my generation of writers possible [...] gave us permission to speak.'[6]

So contemporary writing marks a radical departure in the historical evolution of Scottish literature. Developments in the creative sphere have been accompanied by, and in many cases provoked, a substantial debate in which a number of commentators have attempted to reconstitute the critical agenda for Scottish literature. Questions of nationalism and the Anglo-Scots relationship, whilst they remain relevant, have been incorporated within a broader theoretical discussion. This increasingly includes a host of other issues like the nature of post-industrial society, the politics of sexual and ethnic minorities, and the advent of globalisa-tion with its attendant late capitalist consumer culture. Nowhere is this sea change more clearly demonstrated than in the visibility and critical profile afforded to women's writing. Chapter Three of this Guide, on Gender, examines this terrain in detail but it is worth highlighting these advances at the outset. Historically, Scottish literature has always been something of a boys' club, built on the foundation of an exclusively male canon that includes Robert Burns (1759–96), Sir Walter Scott and Robert Louis Stevenson (1850–94). Writing by women has traditionally been subordinated and sidelined within the debates that have surrounded the work of their male contemporaries. Since the 1970s, developments within feminist studies have sought to expose the elliptical nature of such patriarchal traditions. It is the poet and dramatist Liz Lochhead who is generally regarded as having broken the mould for Scottish female writers during the 1970s. In her wake followed a host of female authors, seeking to write from and about specifically female perspectives. This recent outpouring has been matched by critical attempts to recover and reassess the importance of women writers in Scottish literary history, a development that will be addressed in more detail in Chapter Three of this Guide.

Returning to the Glasgow group, just as this idea has been some-what exaggerated, the role of another figure remains dramatically under-acknowledged within more generalised accounts of Scottish writing in this period. That person is Peter Kravitz (birth date unavailable). Born in London, Kravitz attended Edinburgh University during the 1970s and upon graduation worked as a commissioning editor for Polygon, the publishing house set up by students of the university in the 1960s. From here Kravitz was instrumental in championing the work of a number of previously unpublished Scottish writers. Polygon were the first UK publishers to take an interest in James Kelman, producing his collection of stories *Not Not While the Giro* (1983) as well as his first two novels, *The Busconductor Hines* (1984) and *A Chancer* (1985). They would also publish debut novels by A. L. Kennedy, Janice Galloway, Agnes Owens and Leila Aboulela (born 1964) and in the 1990s would produce work by both Ian Rankin and Alexander McCall Smith. In 1984 Kravitz also became editor of the distinguished literary journal the *Edinburgh Review*, which dated back as far as 1802. Kravitz radically revitalised the journal, turning it into an important outlet for this emerging generation of literary *provocateurs*. The journal epitomised the spirit of internationalism and self-entitlement that became a hallmark of Scottish writing during this period. In his debut editorial Kravitz announced:

■ The motto from now on will be 'to gather all the rays of culture into one whole'. This does not just mean the complete range of arts and crafts, but culture in its widest possible sense as shown in our logo drawn by Alasdair Gray. Culture as something that is not *either* Dostoevsky and Charles Rennie Mackintosh *or* a Guinness in your local and a football match, but BOTH.[7] □

It is this emphasis on redefinition, and on redrawing the boundaries, which characterises much of the writing featured in this Guide. A similar ethos of radical renewal constantly emerges from the pages of Scottish fiction during this period. It is in this spirit of cultural inclusion, symbolised by Kravitz's *Edinburgh Review*, that the seeds of Irvine Welsh's fiction, and its dramatic fusion of the popular and the literary, were originally sown. Writing about the lived realities of working-class experience, James Kelman has commented that a similar premise can be seen to underpin his own work:

■ Apart from direct experience I have access to other experiences, foreign experience, I have access to all the areas of human endeavor, right back from the annals of ancient history; in that sense Socrates or Agamemnon is just as much a part of my socio-cultural background as the old guy who stands in the local pub.[8] □

Kravitz's fascinating insider's perspective on this period forms the introduction to *The Picador Book of Contemporary Scottish Fiction* (1997) and is featured in Chapter One of this Guide. He depicts the emergence of this post-war generation as effecting a paradigm shift within the secondary criticism devoted to Scottish literature: 'The publication of work by Alasdair Gray, James Kelman and others in the early 1980s rendered the [critical] volumes that had excluded them obsolete almost as soon as they were published. In retrospect they were marking the end of a former era in Scottish literature and the beginning of a new one.'[9] If one is searching for a precise date for such beginnings then arguably 1981 offers itself as the most suggestive year zero. This year witnessed the publication of Alasdair Gray's epic novel *Lanark*. Brimming with artistic bravura, *Lanark* was an experimental book of biblical proportions. And, similar to the Bible, it was not a single book, but rather several volumes packaged as one. *Lanark* featured a daring blend of naturalism, fantasy and postmodern *legerdemain* ('sleight of hand'). It confronted Scotland with its past and its present, whilst also offering a nightmare vision of its potential future. A book of encyclopaedic proportions, *Lanark* wore its influences like a badge of honour. In actual fact Gray reprinted them in the book's own audacious 'index of plagarisms'. Key sources of reference included the Romantic poet and painter William Blake (1757–1827); John Bunyan (1628–88), author of *The Pilgrim's Progress* (1678–84); Thomas Carlyle (1795–1881), historian, essayist and cultural critic; Lewis Carroll (the pseudonym of Charles Lutwidge Dodgson (1832–98)), author of *Alice's Adventures in Wonderland* (1865); and the poet, critic and philosopher Samuel Taylor Coleridge (1772–1834). The list goes on. According to Gavin Wallace *Lanark* detonated a 'cultural time bomb' that had been ticking away inside Scotland for years.[10] In the words of novelist and critic Anthony Burgess (1917–93) 'Scottish literature at last had its *Ulysses*'.[11]

The vigorous flowering of Scottish literature during this period coincided with its consolidation as a formal subject of inquiry within the academy. In 1971 the University of Glasgow established the Department of Scottish Literature and began offering an honours degree in the subject. In subsequent decades the quantity and quality of the secondary material devoted to Scottish literature developed dramatically. Previously, Scottish criticism tended to favour the general survey, offering more aerial perspectives. Critics tended to look down from a great height and attempt to offer broad brush accounts of the nation's literary history. Maurice Lindsay's *The History of Scottish Literature* (1977), Francis Russell Hart's *The Scottish Novel: From Smollet to Spark* (1978) and Alan Bold's *Modern Scottish Literature* (1983) are all notable examples of this model. The other predominant inclination was to lean toward cultural nationalism, distinguishing and defending

Scottish literature from the assimilating energies of English Literature. Published in 1983, Alan Bold's *Modern Scottish Literature* described a nation that remained ensconced in familiar prejudices, still looking over its shoulder at the Auld Enemy, England:

> ■ Scotland is still fighting old battles, still obsessed by the past, still trying to convert defeat into victory. Scotland is a country uniquely haunted by history. With so many defeats to contend with the Scots have gradually come to regard themselves as born losers.[12] □

One of the fundamental characteristics of contemporary Scottish literature is the degree to which both writers and critics have begun to move beyond such reactionary politics. The thematic scope of the chapters in this Guide (nation, language, gender, class, postcolonialism and postmodernism) evince the alternative questions that have come to preoccupy the Scottish imagination in recent decades. If we read *Lanark* as something of a year zero in terms of the creative imagination, then arguably the four-volume *History of Scottish Literature* (1987) signalled a similar turning point in the evolution of Scottish criticism. Edited by Cairns Craig, the history contained 40 essays covering Scottish literary development from the sixth century to the present day. A useful comparison can be made between a similar project published 20 years later, the three-volume *Edinburgh History of Scottish Literature* (2007). Containing over 100 essays, the *Edinburgh History* illustrates the degree to which the interrogation of Scottish literature prospered and developed in the intervening decades. In practical, but also in ideological and theoretical terms, the 1990s saw a great transformation in critical approaches to Scottish writing.

In recent years several critics have hailed the dynamism and exuberance of contemporary Scottish writing as something of a literary renaissance. This is a term with an important history in Scottish literature. From the French *renaître* (literally 'to be born again'), renaissance was originally used to denote a European wide revival of learning that lasted from the fourteenth to the seventeenth century. Beginning in Italy, The Renaissance looked to antiquity and the culture of Greece and Rome for its inspiration. A period of dramatic development in the sciences and the arts, the renaissance produced such famous works as the Mona Lisa by Leonardo da Vinci (1452–1519) and the painted ceiling of the Sistine Chapel by Michelangelo (1475–1564). In terms of Scottish literature, the word renaissance was first coined by French poet and scholar Denis Saurat (1890–1958) in his article 'Le Groupe de la Renaissance Écossaise' published in 1924. The term was used to delineate a group of writers that emerged during the early 1920s. Alongside the towering figure of Hugh MacDiarmid (pseudonym of

Christopher Murray Grieve (1892–1978)), the Scottish renaissance included figures like Lewis Grassic Gibbon (pseudonym of James Leslie Mitchell (1901–35)), Edwin Muir (1887–1959), Willa Muir (1890–1970), Naomi Mitchison (1897–1999), Catherine Carswell (1879–1946) and Neil Gunn (1891–1973). One of the defining features of this movement was a desire to recover and resituate the place of Scottish culture. For many of these writers, Scottish literature was in a moribund state, having endured centuries of marginalization within the Anglo-centric system of cultural value embedded within the British state. As we shall see below, a central preoccupation for many renaissance writers was how to represent specifically Scottish voices and experiences on the page of the literary text. For many writers of the 1920s these cultural aspirations were intimately bound up with the politics of nationalism. It is worth noting that the National Party of Scotland, forerunner to the modern Scottish National Party (SNP), was founded in 1928 by, among others, Hugh MacDiarmid. In claiming that contemporary Scottish writing signals yet another renaissance, critics are implicitly invoking many of the aesthetic and political ideologies championed by this original 1920s group. Chapter One of this Guide will examine whether recent writing can be justifiably located within this type of critical context.

One of the most significant developments in Scottish Studies in recent years has been a concerted interest shown by critics from outside Scotland. More than ever before the study of Scottish literature has begun to assume the appearance of a truly international discipline. Critics in the United States have begun to interrogate the subject from a number of interesting and original perspectives. One of the areas where this development has been most apparent has been in the field of Romantic studies. Critics like Ian Duncan (Berkeley), Katie Trumpner (Yale), Caroline McCracken Flesher (University of Wyoming) and Leith Davis (Simon Fraser University) have all brought their energies to bear on this important period in Scotland's literary history. Reflecting this development, this Guide features work from a number of people that might be termed 'critical outsiders'. These include from Germany Berthold Schoene, from Italy Carla Sassi, from the United States Mary McGlynn, and from Ireland Aaron Kelly. A more cosmopolitan critical terrain is symptomatic of the sheer diversity and range of writing that constitutes contemporary Scottish literature. Reflecting the globalised nature of late twentieth-century experience, Scottish writing is more ethnically and culturally diverse than ever before. It now includes writers like: Suhayl Saadi, born in 1961 and raised in Glasgow by parents of Afghan-Pakistani origin; the Sudanese writer Leila Aboulela, who lived in and wrote about Aberdeen in her novel *The Translator* (1995); and the Canadian Alistair MacLeod, born in Nova Scotia in 1936, but writing about the Scottish Gaelic diaspora in his book *No Great Mischief* (1999), which won the IMPAC Dublin Literary Award in 2001.

Another driving force transforming Scotland's literary landscape has been the local publishing industry. Whilst the vast majority of British publishing happens in London, a number of small Scottish presses rose to prominence during the 1980s and 1990s. In 1987 the Edinburgh publishing house Canongate launched the Canongate Classics series. Subsidised by the Scottish Arts Council, the plan was to reissue classic Scottish texts in affordable paperback editions. In time the series would include such luminaries as James Boswell (1740–95), biographer and diarist; Sir Walter Scott, novelist and poet; Margaret Oliphant (1828–97), novelist and biographer; and Sir Arthur Conan Doyle (1859–1930), novelist and detective fiction writer. The Canongate Classics series also brought to the attention of the reading public a host of minor Scottish writers whose work had been out of print for decades. 2002 saw the publication of the one hundredth Canongate Classic. In terms of our current study it is highly significant that this was a re-issue of Alasdair Gray's seminal *Lanark*; 20 years after its initial publication, the novel was already a modern classic.

A number of political, social and economic contexts inform the background to this explosion of creative and critical energy within Scotland. One of the most significant was, and in fact still is, the national question. A referendum in 1979 had seen Scotland come within a hair's breadth of devolved self-governance. Despite the majority of voters voting 'yes' for devolution, a last minute clause added by Westminster required 40per cent of the *total* Scottish electorate to come out in favour. In the end voter turnout had not been sufficient and devolution was averted, if only in the short term. The 'debacle' of 1979, as it came to be known, forced a general election in Britain. When voters returned from the polls they welcomed in a Conservative Government under the leadership of Britain's first ever female Prime Minister, Margaret Thatcher (born 1925; Prime Minister 1979–90). This important moment in British history was to have dramatic consequences for Scotland in the coming decades. Presiding over a Britain that simply wasn't working, to quote the Tory election slogan, Thatcherism set about rolling back the Welfare State. In an attempt to cure the country of its economic lethargy Thatcher looked towards the ruthless application of free market economics. A Tory government, crucially one with almost no electoral mandate north of the border, set about dismantling the remnants of British heavy industry. The result was devastating levels of unemployment with some of the most acute effects felt within working-class communities of Scotland. Whilst the city-boys of the south-east flourished under the deregulation of the financial sector, working-class communities across Britain slowly imploded. By the time the 1990s rolled around the national question in Scotland was once again back on the political agenda. In 1997 the country had had enough and New Labour swept to power in an historic election victory. An important part of their mandate had been the promise of devolution referendums in both Scotland and Wales. This time there was no mistake. In 1997 the Scottish Parliament, suspended since 1707, was voted back into existence, albeit with limited powers of self-governance. One of the most hotly contested issues in recent years has been the relationship between this story and the kind of writing produced in Scotland at the time. This issue will be addressed in due course in this Guide. The final chapter of T.M. Devine's best-selling history, *The Scottish Nation: 1700–2000* (1999), provides a highly readable account of these events. Devine draws direct correlation between developments within the literary scene and the growing self-confidence of the country at large:

■ There was also a new vitality in many aspects of Scottish culture which helped to underpin the growing interest in Home Rule. Research into Scottish history, literature, politics and society expanded as never before. Novelists such as James Kelman, Alasdair Gray and William McIlvanney [born 1936], Iain Banks, and later Irvine Welsh enjoyed enormous international success with works grounded in the gritty realities of urban Scotland often written in the working-class vernacular [...] Political scientists have drawn attention to the 'Quiet Revolution' which occurred in Quebec in the 1960s. They see this as an increase in cultural activity which helped to heal some of the breaches in the community and enabled a more unified movement towards self determination among the Quebecois. Something akin to this cultural awakening took place in Scotland in the 1980s and helped to infuse the crusade for Home Rule with a new impetus and confidence. However, it is important to recognize that in fields like literature at least the revival was part of a vibrant and continuing tradition that stretched back to the era of MacDiarmid and the 'Scottish Renaissance' of the 1920s.[13] □

For Devine the rise of Scottish nationalism during the 1980s was infused and invigorated by concurrent developments in cultural and intellectual fields. This argument is part of a tradition whereby critics have long maintained the heightened significance of Scottish cultural politics. In the wake of the Act of Union (1707), when Scotland lost its political autonomy, it was cultural institutions – the church, the law, the education system – that were regarded as the bastions of a distinct national identity. The poet and critic Robert Crawford (born 1959) argues: '[I]n countries such as Scotland [...] a lack of democratic control over the nation's own affairs means that, in the absence of political institutions, cultural institutions are often regarded as the custodians of national distinctiveness.'[14] Christopher Whyte describes how in Scotland, literary representation has functioned as something of a substitute for political representation: 'in the absence of an elected political authority [within Scotland] the task of representing the nation has been repeatedly devolved to its writers.'[15] If Scottish culture has historically preserved a distinct national identity, for Cairns Craig contemporary culture has been a galvanising and enabling force, one that helped revive the political fortunes of Scottish nationalism:

■ [T]he 1980s proved to be one of the most productive and creative decades in Scotland this century – as though the energy that had failed to be harnessed by the politicians flowed into other channels. In literature, in thought, in history, creative and scholarly work went hand in hand to redraw the map of Scotland's past and realign the perspectives of its future.[16] □

The validity of these arguments is addressed in Chapter One of this Guide. Whilst questions of national identity *are* integral to Scottish literature, there coexists another reading in which contemporary writing can be seen deliberately to distance itself from the ideological baggage and theoretical wranglings of cultural nationalism. Despite claims by Craig and others, it is not always easy to locate this renewed cultural confidence among the misfits and rejects that populate the pages of recent Scottish writing. We might think back to Renton's vitriolic outburst in the film of *Trainspotting* and its total decimation of any enduring national pride. It is this type of contradiction that we will begin to tease out in the pages that follow.

This Guide to Essential Criticism of Contemporary Scottish Literature is divided into six chapters. The first half of each chapter addresses one of the predominant themes within recent Scottish criticism. The six key areas of debate are nation, language, gender, class, postcolonialism and postmodernism. The second half of each chapter will focus on critical responses to the work of specific authors. For example, Chapter One addresses questions of nation and nationalism before considering critical responses to the work of Alasdair Gray. Subsequent chapters will assess the critical reaction to the work of the following authors: Tom Leonard, Liz Lochhead, Janice Galloway, James Kelman, Irvine Welsh, A. L. Kennedy and Muriel Spark (1918–2006). The choice of these writers is by no means arbitrary. In part it reflects the sheer volume of critical commentary devoted to their work and by implication their importance within the canon of contemporary Scottish writing. Any critical book of this sort must be selective. Whilst each chapter focuses on the work of one or two authors, we will in passing draw attention to the work of other writers. This Guide does not attempt to offer a definitive theory of contemporary Scottish Literature. Nor does it seek to cement or imprison the work of writers within particular critical paradigms. Many of these writers could, and in fact have been, discussed under a number of our chosen chapter headings. For example, whilst Alasdair Gray is considered in Chapter One alongside the question of nationalism, his work is often assessed in terms of its postmodern aesthetics or its enduring relevance to questions of class. Rather than offering an exhaustive account, as its title suggests, this is a Guide to the *essential* criticism of contemporary Scottish literature. At the same time it endeavours to suggest promising avenues of further critical inquiry. A substantial bibliography of the secondary literature is included at the end of this book.

CHAPTER ONE

Nation and Nationalism

A real literary renaissance?

Some of the most enduring preoccupations of Scottish literary and cultural criticism during the twentieth century derive from the politics of nationalism. Should Scotland strive towards outright political autonomy and national sovereignty, or are its best interests served through continued incorporation within the British state? More recently the question has altered slightly: how should we read the devolution settlement in 1997? A halfway house on the road to independence? Or the final fix of a British Government attempting to shore up a crumbling union? In our introduction we saw T. M. Devine argue for a sense of causality, between the invigorating energy of contemporary Scottish literature on the one hand and the revived fortunes of post-1979 nationalism on the other. This type of link, between culture and politics, has been endorsed on a number of occasions by various critics. In an essay published in 1996 Ian A. Bell claims: 'the tremendous outpouring of fiction from Scotland in the last twenty years can be seen as offering a radical literature of resistance and reclamation.'[1] Exactly what this literature was resisting and reclaiming remains open to debate. Liam McIlvanney assumes a similar tone: '[B]y the time the Parliament arrived [in 1999], a revival in Scottish fiction had been long underway [...] Without waiting for the politicians, Scottish novelists had written themselves out of despair.'[2] In his survey of post-war writing Douglas Gifford argues that the 1980s signalled a decisive shift in the literary landscape of Scotland. For Gifford the experimental nature of Scottish fiction became a standard bearer for a cultural devolution, one which saw Scotland increasingly disassociating itself from mainstream British values. Scottish fiction provided the locus for a variety of voices concerned with articulating a more confident and independent set of identities:

■ After 1980, and while still containing a great deal of urban-centred dystopian scepticism, the fiction attempts a more positive vision of

Scotland, increasingly working in new genres, mingling these in a detrimental contemporary eclecticism which simultaneously exploits older Scottish cultural and fictional traditions and breaks with them. It is tempting to see this change in confidence as somehow related to the 1979 Devolution referendum and the growing assertions of Scottish identity and its varieties that emerged almost in defiance of that quasi-democratic debacle. With this new confidence, Scottish fiction approached the millennium as a standard bearer for Scottish culture, arguably even supplying the most successful explorations of changing Scottish identities, in a rich variety of voices and genres. The new complexities in novelistic vision relate dynamically to the changes taking place in Scottish society at large, not only reacting to them, but influencing the framework of thought in which they took place.[3] □

There is, however, another school of thought, one which does not read literature as intimately bound up with the politics of cultural nationalism. In his groundbreaking study *The Break-Up of Britain* (1977) Tom Nairn (born 1932) argued that culture had little real bearing on what he called the emergence of 'neo-nationalism' amongst Britain's peripheral regions: 'Politically speaking the key to these neo-nationalist renaissances lies in the slow foundering of the British state, not in the Celtic bloodstream [...] [In the Scottish case] this is overwhelmingly a politically orientated separatism, rather exaggeratedly concerned with problems of state and power, and frequently indifferent to the themes of race and cultural ancestry.'[4] Nairn's analysis of a political separatism, with culture playing little real part, is directly contradicted by Michael Gardiner's book *The Cultural Roots of British Devolution* (2004). For Gardiner the concept of Britishness is itself enshrined in the culture of the eighteenth century and in particular the expansion of the British Empire. Devolution is the last stage in a process of a century long decolonisation which has seen the British Empire gradually dismantled from within. Rather than a resurgent nationalism, Gardiner reads recent literary developments in Scotland as symptomatic of 'the growing ambivalence deep in the British management of culture.'[5] This cautious approach toward assertions of a rejuvenated cultural nationalism finds support in the comments of several Scottish writers during this period. Whilst *The Guardian* newspaper would christen Alasdair Gray the 'Founding Father of the Scottish Renaissance', the author himself remained highly sceptical of such overt labelling: 'Rather than a sudden explosion of literary creativity in the early eighties, the "Scottish Renaissance" in truth denoted a change in publication policy and adjusted the critical view of Scottish writers: the proliferation of Scottish works on the literary market had more to do with changes in the market than with a sudden emergence of literary talent and/ or cultural self-awareness.'[6] Gray evoked fellow Glaswegian writer

Tom Leonard in his dismissal of such terms of reference. Leonard was cynical about any ideas of renaissance, remarking that in contemporary Scotland there still weren't any Sistine Chapels to boast of.[7] In an ironic twist, Gray's own debut novel *Lanark* would feature a young Glaswegian artist, Duncan Thaw, spending months on his back painting an epic mural on the ceiling of a condemned chapel. Moreover, during his own career as a muralist Gray himself has painted the ceilings of several chapels in Scotland. As we shall see, the deliberate blurring of boundaries between reality and fiction would become one of the hallmarks of Gray's idiosyncratic artistic vision.

The current chapter begins with the work of two critics: Gavin Wallace and Douglas Gifford. Both attempt to employ the term 'renaissance' as a way of thinking about the profusion and eclecticism of recent Scottish fiction. This type of theoretical framework also features in a number of studies of contemporary Scottish poetry. The most obvious example is the anthology *Dream State* (1994), edited by Donny O'Rourke. O'Rourke introduces the collection with the assertion that it was the poets rather the politicians that dreamed alternative states, in both the metaphysical and political sense, for Scotland. The current chapter will seek to interrogate the claim implicit in O'Rourke's highly suggestive title. Having considered questions of nationalism we will turn to the related issue of national identity and its treatment within contemporary Scottish literature. A dominant strain within recent criticism asserts that the literary text provides a unique artistic space, one in which debates about national identity are most keenly and imaginatively played out. A number of wider theoretical debates, most notably Benedict Anderson's seminal work on the nation as an 'imagined community' are crucial here. Key figures in the Scottish context include Cairns Craig, Alan Riach and the Italian critic Carla Sassi. In marked contrast Christopher Whyte argues that this critical bias, towards the politics of national identity, is a symptom of a problematic reductionism within the dominant paradigms surrounding Scottish literature. For Whyte it inevitably forecloses on the variety of signifying possibilities inherent in the literary text. Alternative critical debates about Scottish literature are seen to be halted before they ever really get off the ground. Having examined these various positions, we will look at critical responses to Alasdair Gray's *Lanark*. *Lanark* is the novel most regularly identified as heralding a sea change within the Scottish literary imagination. Nationalist and nation-centred readings of *Lanark* will be considered alongside a number of other perspectives on Gray's highly original text.

Critical anthologies are highly formative in shaping how we think about individual texts, groups of writers and periods of literary history. Often the scope of the anthology itself, rather than the content of particular essays, is the overriding factor here. One of the most important collections of contemporary Scottish criticism is *The Scottish Novel Since the Seventies* (1993). Edited by Gavin Wallace and Randall Stevenson, *The Scottish Novel Since the Seventies* sought to highlight and interrogate the abundance of innovative fiction that appeared on the Scottish literary scene during the 1980s. Implicit in the title is the assumption that Scottish fiction of this period constitutes a discrete object of critical interest. The book contains a number of seminal essays on key novelists including William McIlvanney, Alasdair Gray, James Kelman, Janice Galloway and Iain Banks. It also features an essay by best-selling crime writer Ian Rankin on the fiction of Muriel Spark. Rankin had been writing a Masters thesis on Spark at the University of Edinburgh during the 1980s when he began to turn his hand to the murky world of detective fiction. The extract below is taken from Gavin Wallace's introduction to *The Scottish Novel Since the Seventies*. In it he argues that the quality and quantity of post-'79 fiction renders 'the Scottish novel' a distinct and meaningful term. Writing in 1993, Wallace juxtaposes the vitality of recent fiction with the enduring frustration felt by many regarding the country's political status. The devolution debacle of 1979 and the long decade of Thatcherism, he claims, fostered a reactionary energy that manifested itself in the radical experimentalism that pervaded Scottish writing of the period. As Wallace's co-editor Randall Stevenson argued elsewhere, what politics refused, literature and culture provided.[8] Like Douglas Gifford, Wallace uses the term 'renaissance' as a way of describing the vitality of the Scottish writing scene in the late eighties. For Wallace contemporary fiction might usefully be considered in terms of the aesthetic assumptions which underpinned the original Scottish renaissance in the 1920s. Importantly though, he argues that recent fiction evinces both a sense of continuity and a definitive break with the past. Whilst contemporary writers are increasingly seen to oppose 1920s preoccupations with 'myth, archaism and symbolic ancestral historicism', continuity persists in a mutual interest in questions of 'language, nation and community':

■ It has become commonplace to observe that the past two decades have become the most productive and challenging period in Scottish literary culture since the Scottish Renaissance of the 1920s and 1930s. Indeed, the profusion and eclecticism of creative talent across all genres and all three of the nation's languages has led some to speak not simply of revival, but of a new – perhaps even more 'real' – Scottish Renaissance. Such declarations of confidence have also been made possible through equally major achievements in literary criticism, scholarship and Scottish cultural studies throughout the same period which have restored the long-eroded intellectual context in which past cultural achievements can be satisfactorily retrieved and appraised, present trends reflected, and future developments fostered and encouraged.[9] ☐

For Wallace the accomplishments of recent years have been significant enough to prevent the kind of appropriation which, in the past, often characterised the critical reception of Scottish fiction:

■ 'So thorough have these achievements proved that few, other than the most eccentric, would now gainsay the category of the 'the Scottish novel' as a distinctive literary force or as a viable critical concept. The days when a *Sunday Times* reviewer could applaud [Greenvoe (1972), by George Mackay Brown (1921–96)] as a novel 'in the great tradition of English social realism' seem long distant; echoes of the time when understandable extremes of apology and defence seemed prerequisite critical reflexes for protecting Scotland's claim to cultural autonomy against the forces of assimilation to an English or British continuum. Objective, confident debate, both critical and popular, about Scottish fiction has flourished as the laments which dominated the early 1980s for traditions immured in ignorance and neglect – unpublished, unread, untaught – have faded.'[10] ☐

For Wallace the most influential figures within this narrative of national re-awakening are Alasdair Gray and James Kelman. A crucial aspect of his argument is the fact that many of the technical and thematic innovations in recent Scottish fiction are the product of an avowedly international set of influences. More than at any time in its history, Scottish fiction is seen to be undeniably global, both in its frame of reference and in its ideological significance. It draws on a number of aesthetic developments including the *nouveau roman* and postmodern meta-fiction, a term denoting a level of self-awareness, a tendency for novels to be aware of and question their own status as fictional texts, and as a consequence the relationship between art object and external world:

■ A movement of fictional innovation, led by the Glasgow writers Alasdair Gray and James Kelman, suddenly emerged, indebted to the parameters of working-class urban realism established in the preceding decades, but simultaneously transcending them. What had come to be felt as the stultifying restriction of a defeatist realism was redefined and redeemed by awareness of movements within a wider experimental context, such as the French *nouveau roman* or postmodernism and meta-fiction.[11] ☐

Without doubt for Wallace the shift in the tectonic plates of Scotland's literary landscape is represented by the publication of Alasdair Gray's *Lanark* in 1981 which he links with innovative work by an international range of writers such as the Argentinian Jorge Luis Borges (1899–1986), the Colombian Gabriel García Márquez (born 1928), the English-Indian Salman Rushdie (born 1947), the German Günter Grass (born 1927) and the American Thomas Pynchon (born 1937):

■ The considerable impact of this bold enlargement of Scottish creative potential remains symbolized by the publication in 1981 of Alasdair Gray's novel *Lanark* [...] Here was an epic, formally adventurous, thematically profound novel synthesizing realism and fantasy, in ways made familiar by – and with much of the dexterity of – writers such as Borges, Marquez, Rushdie, Grass, Pynchon et al.; yet remaining wholly faithful to a specifically Scottish tradition. And to Scottish places, or one place in particular: Gray's science-fictional and naturalistic projection of Glasgow/Unthank marked a culmination of the creative nucleus which Glasgow, and the urban west of Scotland, had provided for novelists for much of the century, as well as providing new points of departure. The author's almost Joycean treatment of locality led some critics to suggest that perhaps the Scottish novel at last had something resembling its *Ulysses*. Complemented on the visual plane by his powerful graphics and artwork, Gray's novel detonated a cultural time-bomb which had been ticking away patiently for years, even if many believed after 1979 that the mechanism had seized up for good. London publishers were jolted into a better-informed awareness of Scottish writing, becoming eager to seize on the commercial promise of a rejuvenated literary tradition that might conform to the dictates of a new and lucrative 'fashion': a marketable efflorescence of the Scottish imagination.[12] □

Wallace's suggestion that contemporary writing constituted not just a new, but somehow a more 'real' Scottish renaissance was an idea first articulated by Douglas Gifford. Gifford had argued that 1979, or rather the reaction to it, had a discernible impact on the creative imagination in Scotland: '[S]omething [...] changed in contemporary Scottish literature. Somewhere in the '80s a new mood, and a new perspective, entered into the work of novelists, poets and dramatists [...] By the '90s the moods and possibilities of the fiction had changed profoundly. An eclectic restlessness was linked to the need to find a fresh starting-point, or to find different aspects of Scottish tradition as inspiration.'[13] The extract below is taken from Gifford's seminal essay of 1990 where he asked if contemporary fiction did not represent 'At Last – the Real Scottish Literary Renaissance?' Again we see the tendency to read political and cultural narratives as being irrevocably intertwined, initially in an inhibiting and subsequently in an enabling fashion: 'It has taken a decade to recover from the depression which the debacle of the referendum on Scottish devolution induced. But there's no mistaking the present revival of hopes in the political and cultural scene. There's much of the heady atmosphere of the thirties, in the years of John McCormick (birth date unavailable) and Hugh MacDiarmid, when our poetry and fiction offered folk epics and Scottish mythology to remind us of our roots and ancient separateness.'[14] What is different about Gifford's argument is that he encourages us to adopt a longer historical perspective. He associates the current literary rejuvenation not just with the 1920s, but with a series of Scottish cultural revivals stretching back as far as the eighteenth century and the work of men like Robert Burns and the Scottish poets Allan Ramsay (1686–1758) and Robert Fergusson (1750–74). Scottish literature, it would seem, has always been characterised by sporadic periods of revival and cultural reassertions of its own distinct identity.

■ And before [the 1920s] there was revival of a different kind, of Celtic awareness, in the eighteen-nineties, when Patrick Geddes and 'Fiona McLeod' [pseudonym of William Sharp (1855–1905)] tried soulfully to place us in a creative twilight, in which our national destiny was to be the mysterious periphery of Europe, the Tir-nan-Og which would relieve the world's guilty materialism. And the eighteen-fifties, the eighteen-twenties, and the later eighteenth century all in their time offered variants of revived national identity – each of which, from the vernacular wit of Ramsay, Fergusson and Burns, to the affected Anglicisation of the 'decent mirth and sober joy' of the snobbish *Literati* of polite Edinburgh, is now perceived along with all the others as failing to speak to a 'whole' Scotland because of its obsession with a single aspect – be it the historical part, the country part, or that part of the Scottish mind which so readily prefers escapism and consoling romantic or rural delusion to industrialised social reality.[15] □

For Gifford the problem with previous revivals has always been their failure to speak for a 'whole Scotland'. In contrast he highlights the degree to which the likes of Kelman and Gray look outwards beyond Scotland, how their work is influenced by and seeks to address a host of international contexts. Contemporary Scottish literature speaks about and emerges from a more global set of circumstances than that of earlier generations. Gifford describes a protean Scottish literature, one that is engaged in a number of dialogues, both with its own native traditions and those of the wider world:

■ So what's new about our present revival? Is it in its turn going to be seen as energetic, interesting, but short-lived, and unrepresentative if a 'whole' Scotland? Is it even a Scottish revival at all, when so much of its product can be read in the context of British and American culture? Is James Kelman not rather working from a European existential tradition, in which his outsiders, his bus conductors, chancers and disaffected teachers are alienated from world materialism, world city planning, and world-wide breakdown of community? And is Alasdair Gray's vision of Glasgow being exploited by distant planners in Lanark not rather an example of how any decaying industrial conurbation in Europe can expect to be handled by

anonymous Brussels institutions? Perhaps we should adopt another perspective entirely and see hope for a newer kind of Scottish consciousness
in the very maturity of outlook that repudiates Scottish historicism for a
modern awareness of international similarity.[16] □

The description of James Kelman, as someone working in a European
existential tradition, will be picked up in more detail in Chapter Four
of this Guide. For Gifford this new internationalism does not signal
the dissolution of a distinct national identity within the country's
literature. Instead it points towards a more confident, less reactionary engagement between Scottish culture and the world beyond its
borders: 'Are we losing Scottish tradition in all this new internationalism? Should we regret the move away from a folk-supernatural and an
introspective communalism? Perhaps the answers to both questions
are yes *and* no [...] The strength of the new revival seems to me to lie
in its unselfconscious readiness to write about imagined and surreal
cities, or to satirise the South of England, or to recreate the fairy tales
of the Brothers Grimm, and darker legends of Europe, as well as work
in the home territory.'[17]

As Wallace alluded to above, the renaissance within contemporary
Scottish literature is by no means limited to developments in the novel.
Drama and poetry have played key roles in any purported narrative of
national reawakening. Also edited by Wallace and Stevenson, *Scottish
Theatre Since the Seventies* (1996) offers a similar framework for think-
ing about the development of the Scottish stage during this period.
In terms of poetry Donny O'Rourke's anthology *Dream State: the New
Scottish Poets* is an important text which sought to politicise recent
Scottish writing. O'Rourke's anthology features poets born since the
end of World War II and whose work first began to emerge during the
1980s. They included people like John Burnside (born 1955), Carol Ann
Duffy (born 1955), Jackie Kay (born 1961), Don Paterson and Kathleen
Jamie. In his introduction O'Rourke argues that Scottish poets were
amongst the most courageous and creative respondents to the political
despair that arose out of the disappointments of 1979. He begins with
a quote from Glaswegian poet Edwin Morgan. Whilst not strictly part
of this 'new' generation – born in 1920 and publishing since 1938 –
Morgan is nonetheless a vital figure. He himself has spoken about how
Sonnets from Scotland (1984) came out of a feeling of disappointment
with the political vacuum of the early eighties:

■ Normally it ought to be enough to be called a poet, *tout court*, but I feel
the present moment of Scottish history very strongly and want to acknowledge it, despite the fact that my interests extend to languages, genres, and
disciplines out with Scotland or its traditions. Much modern Scottish poetry

differs from poetry in the rest of the British Isles by being written in Gaelic or in some form of Scots, but my point would be even if it were written in English it may be part of a hardly definable intent in the author to help build up the image of poetry which his country presents to the world. If Scotland became independent tomorrow, there is no guarantee that it would enter a golden age of literary expression. Yet I am sure I am not mistaken in sensing, even among those who are less than sympathetic to devolutionary or wider political change, an awareness of such change which in subtle ways affects creative endeavour, suggesting a gathering of forces, a desire to "show" what can be done.[18] □

Like both Wallace and Gifford, Donny O'Rourke describes the passing of a torch between an older generation of Scottish writers, here represented by Morgan, and the group of younger writers that emerged during the 1980s:

■ In the verve and variety of his verse, the insight and generosity of his teaching and in the copious modernity of his imagination, Morgan is very much this anthology's presiding spirit. Writing in 1979 in the magazine *Aquarius*, he was responding to the coming to power of the Thatcher government and Scotland's powerlessness after a rancorously-contested, listlessly-enacted referendum had failed to secure even limited self-government.[19] □

For O'Rourke, the vigorous nature of contemporary writing emerged out of and in defiance of the despair that characterised Scotland under Thatcherism.

■ Most of the writers in this book felt a similar need to 'acknowledge the moment.' For some, the Thatcher election was the first in which they had been eligible to vote. Our inability as a nation to opt in sufficient numbers for the constitutional expression of what had long been culturally obvious did not for the most part propel young writers into political activity. Disillusionment with party politics tended to find expression in cultural commitment. Of course, some explicitly political poetry was written then, and since. And yet a kind of queasy quietism does seem to have prevailed as far as day-to-day dialectics were concerned. The 1980s saw poem after poem present and represent this new Scotland. Or (more exactly) *Scotlands*. For the poetry was characterised by a vigorous pluralism as ideas and ideals of nation and nationhood were explored, and Scots and Gaelic took on new impetus [...] Often it seemed that the poets, more confidently than the politicians, were dreaming a new state.[20] □

This extract from O'Rourke's anthology risks creating something of a false impression. While some Scottish writers were propelled by failures in the political arena it is important to recognise that others were not. Whilst Alasdair Gray would later pamphleteer on the virtues of Scottish independence in *Why Scots Should Rule Scotland* (1992), he was also sceptical of binding the creative impulse to the national question in such overt and deliberate ways. Gray compares the situation for Scottish writers with those living in London, making the point that one's proximity to the centre of political power does not necessarily produce better literature:

■ There is no evidence that the local experience of Royal Home Counties writers gives them worthier subject matter or more intelligent dictions. Why should it? Does the proximity of a thing called government inspire a finer class of thought? It might, if the government was fostering peaceful employment and social equality. It doesn't, so all it fosters is the wealth of the rich and a false sense of self-importance [...] the best London-based writers show lives as unblessed by government as Scotland is.[21] □

In his introduction to *The Picador Book of Contemporary Scottish Fiction* Peter Kravitz is also circumspect about the idea of a contemporary Scottish renaissance. Kravitz denies that the emergence of writers like Gray and Kelman was inspired by a reaction to the political events of 1979. Instead, he argues that their work has much deeper roots, located in the early 1970s, if not long before:

■ The sudden appearance in print of many of these writers has been called a boom by many commentators. In reality, however, it was more the result of a process: Alasdair Gray, Jeff Torrington, Bill Douglas (1943–91) and James Kelman wrote for more than a decade before being published in book form in Scotland or England [...] Gray had been working on *Lanark* since the 1950s.[22] □

What *is* significant though is that through publishers like Canongate and Kravitz's own work at Polygon, and journals like the *Edinburgh Review* and *Cencrastus*, the 1980s witnessed a transformation in the potential outlets for new Scottish writing. The importance of 1979 and the issue of a thwarted nationalism remains widely debated within Scottish criticism. More recently Catherine Lockerbie, Director of the Edinburgh International Book Festival, commented on the stifling effect of nationalist preoccupations on the ways in which Scottish writers have chosen to write. Following the success of 1997 she claimed that, with the advent of devolution, writers did not have to prove that they were Scottish anymore and that the days of the 'quasi-political' Scottish novel were over.[23] However, there is a sense in which such criticism would wrongly bind contemporary Scottish literature to the national question. It is misleading to regard Gray, Kelman and others as pathologically obsessed with this single issue. Kelman for one is highly sceptical that nationalism offers a panacea for the kind of social alienation his work is interested in: 'This idea that the interest of the country at large can be expressed irregardless of political and economic difference is very suspect indeed.'[24] This aspect of Kelman's work will be returned to in detail in Chapter Four of this Guide. The relationship between contemporary Scottish writing and the politics of devolution remains unsettled. Even though Scotland now has its own parliament and a form of self-government, it remains to be seen what effect, if any, this will have on the literary imagination. Closely related to the politics of cultural nationalism is the issue of how the literary text allows us to think about the nation as a concept, and what it might mean for an individual to possess and be moved to affirm a national identity. These questions have preoccupied a number of Scottish critics who have sought to interrogate the modern nation state as a particular kind of imagined community.

The nation as imagined community

Several critics have argued that Scottish literature provides a unique artistic space in which the nature and significance of national identity is most fully articulated and explored. Such perspectives are far from unique to the criticism of Scottish literature. Several critics have linked the historic development of the novel during the eighteenth century with the emergence of the nation state as *the* political unit of the modern world. *Imagined Communities* (1983) by Benedict Anderson (born 1936) contains the most influential articulation of this thesis. For Anderson the nation is not merely a sociological construction, a political tool for administering a particular group of individuals with shared interests. Instead, it exists as an 'imagined community'. It is part of the cultural fabric peculiar to a specific people living in a specific place. Anderson argues that historically speaking, the novel has been a fundamental tool in enabling disparate people, with little direct experience of one another, to imagine themselves as part of the wider community that is the nation. It is culture as much as a political, legal or economic framework which binds individuals together and forms allegiance to the nation. Moreover, the novel has been of paramount importance in consolidating the single language state as the ideal form of the modern nation. In his essay 'The national longing for form' (1990) the critic Timothy Brennan provides a succinct summary of Anderson's thesis:

■ It was the novel that historically accompanied the rise of nations by objectifying the 'one, yet many' of national life, and by mimicking the structure of the nation, a clearly bordered jumble of languages and styles. Socially, the novel joined the newspaper as the major vehicle of the national print media, helping to standardize language, encourage literacy, and remove mutual incomprehensibility. But it did much more than that. Its manner of presentation allowed people to imagine that special community that was the nation.[25] □

Brennan's article is part of a collection of essays edited by Homi Bhabha (born 1949) entitled *Nation and Narration* (1990). Bhabha is specifically interested in what he describes as the cultural compulsion of nationalism and its roots in narrative discourse. We might ask, if Scotland ceased to exist as a fully functioning nation state after 1707, what effect might this have had on the development of the Scottish novel? One of the critics consistently interested in this question has been Cairns Craig. In *Out of History* (1996) Craig outlines the historic marginalisation of Scottish writing within the larger canon of English Literature. Following from this, his book *The Modern Scottish Novel* (1999) explores the ways in which contemporary Scottish writers build on the legacy of their modernist predecessors and seek to re-examine, through their fiction, the construction of national identity. The quotation below is taken from the opening section of *Out of History*. Here Craig laments the sense of cultural inferiority he regards as having characterised the historical reception of Scottish literature.

■ *Parochial*: the word has haunted discussion of Scottish culture; it damns us before we start because we must leap in desperation to join 'the world'; condemns us when we finish with having been no more than ourselves. Politics, literature, education, art: they are all constantly threatened by the infection of the parochial; brief flourishes of an apparently healthy vitality only make more evident the usual condition of the patient, dragging out a half-hearted imitation of life as it is lived by others [...] Where, we ask, are our masterpieces of literature (substitute: theatre, music, art, political thought) to compare with (insert: Shakespeare, Joyce, etc.), and the answer can only be that they are flawed. Scottish culture has cowered in the consciousness of its own inadequacy recognising the achievements of individual Scots simply as proof of the failure of the culture as a whole. Succeed, and you are no longer Scottish (not really Scottish) – you are like David Hume [1711–76] or Muriel Spark, someone who has leapt beyond the bounds set by Scottishness; be Scottish and your achievement is necessarily local, you have immured yourself – as MacDiarmid said of Neil Gunn – in Scottshire.[26] □

For Craig achievements within Scotland, scientific, philosophical and cultural, have been historically stripped of the national context in which they occurred:

■ Not having a culture or a history which is shaped exactly like those of a major European culture (whose are, except the major cultures?), not having conformed to the pattern of those cultures whose 'progress' is taken to define progression itself, we are only the echo of real events, real achievements, real creations that have already occurred somewhere else – somewhere that is by some magical transformation also the world. Or, as in the case of the Scottish Enlightenment, or Scottish achievements in science and engineering, they are presented as having nothing to do with being Scottish: success is in spite of rather than because of their cultural environment and so they do not count as part of the culture.[27] □

The central term upon which Craig builds his analysis of this situation is 'tradition'. Can Scotland, deprived of its nationhood since 1707, be said to have an identifiable and meaningful literary tradition? Craig begins by re-visiting a review by the American-born and English-based poet, dramatist and critic T. S. Eliot (1888–1965) of the famous book *Scottish Literature: Character and Influence* (1919) by G. Gregory Smith (birth date unavailable). Smith's was the first piece of criticism to argue at length for the existence of a literature that could be said to be distinctly Scottish. Smith used the term Caledonian Antisyzgy, meaning a union of opposites, to describe what he regarded as *the* defining characteristic of Scottish literature. This has remained one of the most enduring definitions of Scottish literature throughout the twentieth century. For Smith it outlines the way in which Scottish writing was replete with contradiction and self-division, Enlightenment rationalism and folk supernaturalism, the overarching symbol being 'the gargoyle grinning at the elbow of the kneeling saint.'[28] Eliot's review of Smith's book flatly denied there was any such thing as Scottish literature. Instead, he claimed Scottish literature was merely an appendage, a constituent part of the wider body of writing identified as 'English Literature'. Eliot's review first appeared in the literary journal *The Athenaeum* in 1919 where he argued:

■ [W]hen we assume that a literature exists we assume a great deal: we suppose that there is one of the five or six (at most) great organic formations of history. We do not suppose merely 'a history', for there might be a history of Tamil literature; but part of History, which for us is the history of Europe. We suppose not only a corpus of writings in one language, but writings and writers between whom there is a tradition [...] We suppose a mind which is not only the English mind of one period with its prejudices of politics and fashions of taste, but which is a greater, finer, more positive, more comprehensive mind than any mind of any period. And we suppose to each writer an importance which is not only individual, but due to his place as a constituent of this mind.[29] □

Craig locates Eliot's thesis in the context of his most famous critical essay 'Tradition and the Individual Talent' (1919). Here Eliot argued that the significance of an individual work of art is not its unique aesthetic qualities, but rather its place within an identifiable literary tradition. The foundation for such tradition is writing in a single language. Scotland, with writing in three languages (Gaelic, Scots and English), is regarded as anomalous and cannot therefore be said to possess a distinct literary tradition of its own.

■ This review was written in the same year as Eliot's 'Tradition and the Individual Talent' which asserts, with a more positive object, the same doctrine: the value of a work of literature is dependent on its having a place within a comprehensive tradition, a tradition both local and European. No writer can achieve real significance, 'maturity', unless he has the weight of a developed tradition on which to draw. The consequence of Eliot's view is that no literature which fails to sustain a continuous development can be a significant literature, and no work within that literature can be a great work: for Eliot, all literature exists on the edge of an abyss, continually threatened by the extinction of continuity and the possibility of plunging the future into the new dark age in which the creation of great works is impossible because all contact with tradition has been lost.[30] □

In this sense the Scottish writer is bereft, they assume the status of a literary orphan, adrift, cut off from their aesthetic roots. This type of analysis appears elsewhere in Scottish criticism. Douglas Gifford claims:

■ The dilemma of the Scottish writer [...] seems to consist in the fact that he exists – from Ramsay and Burns to [James] Hogg [1770–1835] and Scott to Stevenson and the Renaissance writers – in a literary environment which fails to inform him [...] There is a Scottish fictional tradition, *but that tradition is precisely about the writer's repeated sense of their being no tradition.*[31] □

James Kelman has described his own situation as a writer in remarkably similar terms: 'There were no literary models I could look to from my own culture. There was nothing whatsoever. I'm not saying these models didn't exist. But if they did I could not find them.'[32] So what is Craig's response to this argument? His reply is to reject Eliot's definition of what a so-called organic literary tradition actually looks like.

■ Such a view damns all peripheral cultures and all writers within peripheral cultures with the rigor of a Calvinist predestination. Nineteenth-century notions of organic cultures were always hortatory rather than descriptive, but few cultures were less fitted to receive the accolade of being pronounced 'organic' than Scotland. The internal division between Scots and Gaelic deprived it of that fundamental unity which Eliot requires and on which cultural nationalism throughout Europe was based – 'writings in one language'; in addition, the decay of Scots in the face of encroaching English among the educated, was compounded at the other end of the social scale by mass immigration, in large measure from Ireland but also from central Europe. At no time in its history could Scotland have been described as an 'organic' or 'unified' culture: it could never have been described as one 'comprehensive' mind transcending the 'prejudices of politics and fashions of taste' of particular periods; therefore it could not qualify as a tradition or as a literature.[33] □

Craig goes on to make the important point that 'The Great English Tradition' as expounded by the critic F. R. Leavis (1895–1978) is in fact an appropriation of a number of peripheral, non-English cultures. It conspicuously includes not only the English authors Jane Austen (1775–1817) and George Eliot (1819–80) but also the American Henry James (1843–1916) and the Polish novelist Joseph Conrad (1857–1924). As a result Scottish literature should not be regarded as a uniquely anomalous body of writing. Instead it can be shown to suffer the same form of cultural assimilation that characterises the writing of other peripheral states:

■ [Eliot's theory] was a gift to the dominant [English] culture, which could use this conception of tradition to incorporate writers from other cultural areas into the body of its own organism. F. R. Leavis was to use Eliot's theory in precisely this way: Leavis influential *The Great English Tradition* opens with the assertion, 'The great English novelists are Jane Austen, George Eliot, Henry James and Joseph Conrad': – English? An American expatriate and a Polish seaman whose first foreign language was French?[34] □

Having identified the circumspect nature of 'The Great English Tradition', Craig goes on to offer an alternative account of what a Scottish literary tradition might actually look like. Rather than some falsely imagined unitary or organic formation, Scotland's literary tradition is a heterogeneous one. It is defined by multiplicity rather than homogeneity. The history of Scottish writing is not a *unified* tradition, but rather 'a dialectic of traditions'. The insistence by Scotland's writers on moving between various traditions is what constitutes the specific intellectual and artistic space of the nation. The lack of unity is not failure as certain commentators have labelled it. Instead, Craig argues, it is a unique and enabling condition. Scottish literature becomes indicative of a globalising energy that, for several centuries, has defined the experience of cultural modernity. It is not anomalous, but rather a paradigm example of this process. The correspondence between Craig's thesis and postcolonial theorisations of cultural hybridity will be addressed in Chapter Five of this Guide.

Craig's attempt to re-establish a meaningful dialogue between contemporary Scottish writing and that of the past is most fully articulated in *The Modern Scottish Novel*. Here he locates contemporary writers (Spark, Gray, Kelman, Kennedy, Welsh) as part of a specifically Scottish tradition of novel writing, one that reaches back to the formal innovations of early twentieth-century like John Buchan (1875–1940), Lewis Grassic Gibbon and Neil Gunn. *The Modern Scottish Novel* can be seen as a more detailed working out of the 'contemporary renaissance' thesis articulated by Gifford and Wallace earlier in this chapter. It draws a series of correspondences between contemporary writing and the artistic preoccupations of early twentieth-century Scottish writers. In the quotation below Craig constructs a pliant and fluid notion of the novel as a literary text. Rather than a straightforward declaration of nationhood or a partisan polemic, the novel is offered as a form of 'embodied argument'. This idea can be read as a variation of Benedict Anderson's notion of an imagined community. The novel becomes a site in which the various discourses that constitute the intellectual life of the nation come into fruitful contact with one another.

■ The novel is an 'embodied argument' which both carries forward a tradition as an inheritance from the past and projects a path for tradition by defining or redefining the *telos* [ultimate aim] towards which the tradition is directed [...] 'Tradition' is a term which has been used as an insistence on inner unity, but like proponents of standardized languages such unity is in fundamental conflict with the very nature of the processes of tradition-making and tradition-receiving: traditions are heteroglossic [made up of many different voices], every tradition is a combination [...] Nations are not undone because they adopt modes of life or modes of discourse from elsewhere: the nation is a space in which those influences are put into play with the inheritance which is specific to that particular place. The nature of a national imagination, like a language, is an unending series of interactions between different strands of tradition, between influences from within and without, between the impact of new experiences and the reinterpretation of past experiences: the nation is a series of ongoing debates, founded institutions and patterns of life whose elements are continually changing but which constitute, by the nature of the issues which they foreground, and by the reiteration of elements of the past, a dialogue which is unique to that particular place. The national imagination is not some transcendental identity which either survives or is erased: it is a space in which a dialogue is in process between the various pressures and inheritances that constitute the particularity of human experience in a territory whose boundaries might have been otherwise, but whose borders define the limits within which certain voices, both past and present, with all their centripetal and centrifugal implications, are listened for, and others resisted, no matter how loud they may be.[35] □

For Craig it is a fundamental error to seek out authentic or essentialist notions of Scottishness or some real Scotland contained within the
pages of the nation's literature. Such entities are inevitably more fluid
and dynamic than previous theoretical models have allowed:

■ The tradition of the modern Scottish novel [...] is not an 'expression'
of a national "geist" [spirit], nor a singular founding principle to which any
work must conform to be "Scottish": the tradition is a space of debate, a
dialogue between the interacting possibilities of a medium shaped by the
conditions of those living in Scotland – its languages and its economic
and social circumstances – and within the institutions which give shape
to its national imagining. It is an attempt to identify a national tradition of
the novel in Scotland, not as an essence which will exclude or include various writers as the 'truly Scottish', but as a dialogue between the variety of
discourses which, in debating with each other, constitute the space that
is the imagining of Scotland and Scotland's imagination. That there is a
tradition of the Scottish novel is also, however, an index of the continuity
of the nation and the national imagining to which it contributes.[36] □

Whilst both Anderson and Craig consider the nation to assert itself
most fully in the literary form of the novel, other critics have maintained that it is in poetry that this communal voice can be most clearly
identified. Craig's analysis of the novel finds critical kinship in Alan
Riach's work on Scottish poetry. Riach maintains that it is in poetry
that questions about Scottish national identity have been and continue
to be most meaningfully articulated. The anthology *Scotlands: Poets and
the Nation* (2004), edited by Gifford and Riach, is a key book in this
debate. Its underlying premise is that throughout its history one of
Scottish poetry's defining features has been its continued fascination
with questions of nationhood:

■ Scotland is a major theme in the poetry of Scotland. This might appear
self-evident, yet it is the most obvious that is most easily overlooked,
and this theme is a distinctive and differentiating feature of Scottish literature. The comparisons make this clear. In the literature of the United
States, the frontier, 'lighting out for the territories' or the idea of the man
alone, outcast individualism set against society's pressures to conform,
are main themes; in West Indian literature, notions of hybridity and mul-
ti-faceted identity are prominent; in New Zealand and Australian literatures, different experiences of indigenous peoples and colonial encounters open into different social worlds; and nothing in English literature
compares in consistency and continuity with the theme of the matter of
national identity in the poetry of Scotland.
    Comparison with Ireland may be particularly instructive. The feminised
nation, Kathleen ni Houlihan or Mother Ireland, is an idea so potent that

many songs were made, and motives forged, that would send men and women to martyrdom for it. Scotland too shares some of that, particularly in its Jacobite legacy, but the modernising trend towards imagining Scotland as a possible state (a 'Dream State' perhaps) is a recognition of the pluralism the country is capable of encompassing, not a call for constricting uniformity. And yet the idea of national identity remains sustaining. As Cairns Craig has said, no matter how Anglicised Scots become, they do not become English. On the evidence of the poems collected here, Scottish nationality nourishes many differences within itself – and after all, recognition, understanding and celebration of difference is the principal work of culture and the arts.[37] □

If critics such as Riach, Craig and Gifford have read literature as an extended meditation on the nation, for other critics this represents *the* most highly problematic aspect of Scottish criticism.

Escaping the nation ... ?

Not all critics agree with the kind of nation-centred approach espoused above. Marshall Walker begins his survey *Scottish Literature since 1707* (1996) with the following caveat: 'when allied to a political conviction the creative urge does not simply march to a flag.'[38] The same year that *Scotlands: Poets and the Nation* was published, Christopher Whyte's *Modern Scottish Poetry* (2004) also appeared. Dividing the post-war period into decades, Whyte sought to examine the work of 20 Scottish poets that had emerged during the second half of the twentieth century. He maintains that the nationalist preoccupations of certain critics have only served to distort the ways in which we are encouraged to think about literature in Scotland. For Whyte Scottish poetry represents a highly eclectic and varied body of work, one that only intermittently turns its gaze towards questions of national identity. His opening gambit is that the critical study of Scottish poetry has been imbalanced and as a consequence is in urgent need of re-evaluation.

■ Can it be validly argued that the Scottishness, presumed or otherwise, of Scottish poetry should take precedence over any other feature in our readings? Possibly yes, and possibly no. After an interregnum lasting for close on three centuries, a national parliament was finally convened in Edinburgh in 1999, thanks at least in part to a campaign for political autonomy dating back to the 1920s and beyond. Should we assume that poetry written during the same period will automatically fall into a coherent narrative pattern echoing that process? That individual poems will act like iron filings, leaping into place when the appropriate magnet (the appropriate historical or political narrative) is applied beneath the paper they are scattered across?[39] □

Whyte picks up on the critical tendency to read the underlying energies of contemporary Scottish literature as somehow culminating in the successful devolution referendum of 1997:

> ■ How realistic is it to expect that, if we were to bring together the most significant works of Scottish poetry from the last sixty years, they would dutifully reflect a growing desire for and progress towards national autonomy? Or might the preoccupations that emerge be of a different, even an unrelated nature? It is not possible for the present to offer definitive answers to these questions, and it may never be so. But there can be little doubt that, however dominant it has been so far in readings of Scottish poetry, Scottishness and the drive for institutional autonomy are only two among many possible filters through which such poetic material can be viewed. Or that, as critical instruments, both are in urgent need of balancing and contextualisation.[40] □

Whyte does not contend that poetry in Scotland is entirely uninterested in the politics of nationalism. Instead, what he seeks is a change in emphasis. By temporarily shifting our focus away from questions of national identity he argues that the work of contemporary Scottish poets can begin to be read as poetry first and foremost:

> ■ Reclaiming such autonomy means that both history and politics must renounce any privileged status as tools for the interpretation of Scottish literature. Surely it is best that those whose prime concern is history should study history, and those whose prime concern is politics, politics. The position the present study takes up regarding nationalist ideology and, more particularly, the 'question about Scottishness', might best be defined as 'agnostic'. Hopefully it can be acceptable to set aside, for the moment, issues of national identity, searching for it, constructing it, reinforcing it, along with the allusion that the primary function of poetic texts lies in identity building, and that they are capable of resolving identity issues. There is an urgent need to approach Scottish texts from a range of different and complementary perspectives. As with the study of both history or politics, the becoming of a nation is only one among many considerations which compete for our attention.[41] □

One of the most articulate and thoughtful answers to the type of objection voiced by Whyte comes from a non-Scottish critic, the Italian scholar Carla Sassi. In her book *Why Scottish Literature Matters* (2005) Sassi argues that the close affinity between literature and national identity is a product of the very nature of the literary text. Literature does not delineate or seek to fix identities in a problematic or essentialist way. Instead, it opens up a space for debate. Again the resonance with the work of Benedict Anderson and Cairns Craig can be detected here. The operating mode, to adopt computer-speak, of literature is the conditional. Literature functions by way of tentative assertion, by allusion and inquiry, rather than by strict adherence to dogma:

■ Literature, in Scotland as elsewhere, has always been a privileged site for this debate [about national identity], and has certainly contributed towards the elaboration and the diffusion of ideas. Furthermore, even a 'conservative' literary text which aims at representing nationhood will tend to do so in a problematic rather than a prescriptive way, unlike say, a historical or political treatise. It is not in the nature of a literary text, in fact, to set unequivocal definitions and to draw definitive borderlines; even when an author purports to portray nationhood according to current definitions, or is animated by a specific ideology, the layered structure of the text will end up problematising and even contradicting his/her original plan.[42] □

For Sassi a vibrant and healthy literature is inevitably a site of ideological contestation. Literary texts remain an important locus for exploring how national communities relate, both to themselves and the external world.

The thematic nature of the chapters that make up the rest of this Guide – language, gender, class, postcolonialism, postmodernism – testify to the expanded terms of debate in which the discussion of Scottish literature is now conducted. At the beginning of this chapter we identified Alasdair Gray's *Lanark* as a foundational text within the so-called 'renaissance theory' of contemporary Scottish fiction. We will now consider this and some of the other critical interpretations that have been applied to Gray's groundbreaking novel.

Alasdair Gray

Like most of Alasdair Gray's work, *Lanark* is a playfully allusive and deliberately subversive piece of art. The novel is as a conglomeration of four books which juxtapose a realist story on the one hand (books one and two) with a fantasy narrative on the other (books three and four). The realist sections present the childhood and adolescence of Duncan Thaw as he grows up in Glasgow, attends art-college and struggles to find love and meaning on the socio-economic margins of post-war society. This semi-autobiographical section of Gray's novel has been described by several critics as a portrait of the artist as a young Glaswegian an illusion to Joyce's *A Portrait of the Artist as a Young Man* (1916). The Joycean reference is more than merely witty critical copy. As we mentioned earlier, the artistic ambition and epic scope of Gray's novel encouraged many critics to suggest Lanark did for Glasgow what

Joyce's *Ulysses* did for Dublin back in 1922. Steeped in despair and alienation, Thaw's narrative climaxes with the main protagonist committing
suicide by drowning himself. He awakes at the beginning of book three
in the fantasy world of Unthank, a nightmarish projection of some
future Glasgow. With no memory of his former existence he christens
himself Lanark and spends the rest of the novel seeking redemption in
this surreal and often frightening landscape. Anticipating the kind of
formal trickery that would become the hallmark of Gray's later work,
the books of *Lanark* are not presented to us in sequential order. We begin
in medias res – in the middle of things – at the start of book three with
Lanark in Unthank and read them in the following order – three, one,
two, four. The Thaw narrative is sandwiched between the Lanark sections and we are invited to make connections between the hellish world
of Unthank and the decaying landscape of post-industrial Glasgow. The
title of the novel ironically evokes ideas of social utopianism and the
quest for ameliorative alternatives to the exploitations of industrial capitalism. New Lanark is a real village located 30 miles from Glasgow near
the source of the river Clyde. In the early nineteenth century it was
the site of a radical social experiment conducted by industrialist and
philanthropist Robert Owen (1771–1858). Owen envisioned an alternative society to the one he saw burgeoning in the industrial heartlands
of Britain. In the cotton mill at New Lanark he outlawed a number of
practices including the use of child labour and the administration of
corporal punishment for the workers. In the shadow of the mill he set
up a very different kind of village for his employees. The workers in the
mill enjoyed decent housing, schools for their children, evening classes,
free healthcare and affordable food. This idyllic social experiment is
offered as a symbolic counterpart to Gray's nightmarish vision of unfet-
tered capitalism in Unthank, where civilisation is described as the pie
that bakes and eats itself.

Gray's novel has received a significant amount of critical attention
both within and beyond Scotland. As Phil Moores testifies: 'Gray's
influence upon British writing in general, and Scottish writing in particular, is significant. In an age of small-scale novels of manners, he is
writing huge state-of-the-nation addresses that deal with love, politics,
war, death, childhood, religion and disease, sometimes all at once.'[43]
Novelist and commentator Will Self (born 1961) is similarly enthusiastic: 'Gray is in my estimation a great writer, perhaps the greatest living in this archipelago today [...] a creative polymath with an inte-
grated politico-philosophic vision.'[44] Excluding Muriel Spark (who had
been publishing since the 1950s) Gray became the most written about
Scottish writer of recent years. A number of useful monographs exist
on his work with Stephen Bernstein's *Alasdair Gray* (1999) and Gavin
Miller's *Alasdair Gray: the Fiction of Communion* (2005) being the most

notable examples. Beside these, several essay collections have been devoted exclusively to the author's work – *The Arts of Alasdair Gray* (1991) edited by Robert Crawford, and *Alasdair Gray: Critical Appreciations and a Bibliography* (2002) edited by Phil Moores. Gray's work has also been examined at length in the context of more general discussions about postmodern literature. Brian McHale's *Postmodernist Fiction* (1987) and Simon Malpas's *The Postmodern* (2005) are the most accomplished examples of this strategy. Whilst questions of postmodernism are considered more fully in Chapter Six of this Guide, there is a brief extract from Randall Stevenson's discussion of Gray's postmodernity below. If proof were needed of the growing reputation of Scottish writing abroad we need look no further than the international reception of Gray's work. A number of European critics have written at length about his fiction including Beat Witschi in *Glasgow Urban Writing and Postmodernism* (1991), Dietmar Böhnke in *Shades of Gray* (2004) and Johanna Tiitinen in *"Work as if You Live in the Early Days of a Better Nation"* (2004).

The extract below comes from the publisher and critic Kevin Williamson (born 1961). Williamson founded Rebel Inc. in the early 1990s, the independent press which was the first to publish work by Irvine Welsh. The punk attitude of the press was captured in their slogan 'F*** the mainstream' with their self-professed mission: 'to take a sledgehammer to the literary establishment.'[45] Williamson's comments illustrate the monumental impact *Lanark* had on the Scottish literary scene of the early 1980s. They establish an important link between the ambitious and iconoclastic nature of Gray's work and the efforts of later Scottish writers. Indeed, we might think of Gray, Williamson and Welsh as forming a kind of triangulation within contemporary Scottish writing –artistically daring, formally innovative, overtly iconoclastic. In a highly memorable phrase Williamson describes *Lanark* as 'an alarm clock going off, a wake up call to another place':

■ The idea of Scottish science fiction tickled me back then. The Scotland I knew has hills and glens, fishermen and farms, dole queues a mile long, high rise slums, alcohol coming out of every pore, and football supporters who were aff their heids. Scotland didn't seem to be the raw material of science fiction. It was a place that seemed more preoccupied with the past than the future. [...] So the sun was shining, people were starving, and Scotland was being royally screwed by faceless bureaucrats, flag-waving warmongers, and arrogant rich assholes. Same as it ever was. People knew the score, but at the time there seemed to be a state of punch-drunk disbelief as unemployment more than trebled, in only a few short years, as the heart was being ripped out of Scotland's ancient ability to produce things. That's the way it was back in the summer of '82, and *Lanark* connected with all of this.[46] □

For Williamson there is an explicit link between the publication date of *Lanark* and the political climate inaugurated by Thatcherism:

■ The timing of the publication of *Lanark* could not have been better. Scottish writing needed a *Lanark*. Scotland needed a *Lanark*. Hell, writing needed a *Lanark*. Somebody, somewhere, *had* to articulate some of the concerns, fears and aspirations of ordinary folk in Scotland. But do so in such an entertaining, interesting and unique way that it made people sit up and think.[47] □

If Scotland and Scottish writing needed a *Lanark* as Williamson asserts, other critics have taken this point further and read Scotland as *the* crucial aspect in the genesis of Gray's novel. For Robert Crawford the innovations of *Lanark*, its penchant for doubles and parallel worlds, emerges out of a specifically Scottish tradition. *Lanark*'s interest in dualism and duality can be traced back to Robert Louis Stevenson's *The Strange Case of Dr Jekyll and Mr Hyde* (1886) if not before:

■ Gray's writing is widely indebted to Scottish tradition. In literature, his love of plain style may owe something to the novels of [John] Galt [1799–1839] and Stevenson; his genre-busting, footnote-crammed texts have an antecedent (as he has pointed out) in the Carlyle of *Sartor Resartus* [1833–34]; his love of doubling, whether in Lanark/Thaw, in 'The Spread of Ian Nichol', or in Monboddo's 'bilocation' surely owes something to that love of doubles [which] is so strong in the Scottish tradition of Hogg and Stevenson. The very names of Gray's characters – Monboddo, Lanark, Kelvin, and innumerable others – help anchor his work in a Scottish cultural and political milieu.[48] □

Lord Monboddo, or James Burnett (1714–99), was a famous eighteenth century Scottish judge and scholar of language. Originally from Belfast, Baron Kelvin, or William Thompson (1824–1907), was a mathematical physicist and engineer who pioneered studies in thermodynamics and electricity at the University of Glasgow. The Glasgow Museum along with its nearby river and park are all named after this illustrious figure. In such readings of Gray's work we might detect the influence of Cairns Craig, specifically the attempt to reclaim a specifically Scottish tradition within the novel. If Gray's text is part of a national tradition, several critics read *Lanark* as the detonating charge igniting an explosion within the contemporary Scottish imagination. For Craig the novel forms the opening volley in what would be a sustained 'effort to redefine the nature of Scottish experience and the Scottish tradition.'[49]

■ [A]t no time in the past fifty years has the 'schizophrenic' view of Scotland seemed to have more justification than in the aftermath of the failure of the political movement if the 1970s and the irresolute outcome of the vote in

the Referendum of 1979. The importance of *Lanark* when it was first published in 1981 was that it seemed directly to confront these cultural and
literary issues: with its protagonist split between the lives of two entirely
separate characters it took on the burden of the self-division of the Scottish
tradition; with part of the novel in an urban realist mode and part in a fantasy style, it directly faced the division of the Scottish novel into two oppos-
ing strands; and its political concerns addressed the concerns of Scottish
government and society in a context where the political debate seemed to
have foundered.[50] □

For Craig *Lanark* symbolises a moment of vital resuscitation in a culture that appeared moribund and beyond reclamation:

■ By the scale of its ambition and its apparent eccentricity, *Lanark* pro-
claimed the vitality and originality of a culture which, to many, seemed to
be close to exhaustion, if not extinction, and was the first statement of
what was to dominate Scottish writing throughout the 1980s – the effort
to redefine the nature of Scottish experience and the Scottish tradition,
both to account for past political failure and to begin to build a Scottish
culture which would no longer be disabled by a lack of confidence in its
own cultural identity.[51] □

Craig addresses the novel's division into four books and its highly
wrought narrative framework. Like Crawford, he locates this aspect
of Gray's work within a particularly Scottish tendency toward duality
and doubleness. This way of thinking about the national psyche is, of
course, indebted to Gregory Smith's original theory of the Caledonian
Antisyzgy. The hellish vision of Unthank provides a metaphor for the
alienation and despair that defines existence in twentieth-century
Glasgow:

■ Thaw's story is enclosed within Lanark's; while, at the same time, Lanark's
voyage through a fantasy world that is part science fiction, part medieval
romance is at once a commentary upon Thaw's life in history and a repetition of it that allows him to be released from the dead-end world in which he
has been trapped. It is a journey which takes Thaw-Lanark not only through
parodies of many other literary works – turning *Lanark* into a compendium of
the modern mind – but through many different kinds of society, so that the
novel is also a compendium of human histories, and of the societies that
humanity has envisaged as the ends to which it aspires.
[...]
The 'thaw' which art brings to the iced-up world of Glasgow is as short-
lived and has as little impact on the total system as the New Lanark experiment by which Robert Owen had attempted to melt the harshness of capitalism. Thaw and Lanark divide between them the possibilities of transforming

life by art and politics – another dualism of the modern condition sundering the aesthetic from the practical – only to discover that they live in a nightmare world in which every escape route that they take leads straight into the maw of another monstrous head on the hydra of a system in which one is either the exploiter or the exploited, in which one is almost inevitably both at the same time.[52] □

Craig is also alert to the epic scope of *Lanark* and the consequent magnification of the novel's signifying possibilities. Gray's ironic 'index of plagiarisms' contains, among others, William Shakespeare (1564–1616), Ben Jonson (1572–1637) and James Joyce. As a result the novel transcends the possibility of a critical reductionism which would delimit it as merely a Scottish book about the state of Scotland. Instead we might note that the novel is described as a 'compendium of the modern mind'. *Lanark* represents a work of Scottish fiction asking questions of universal importance, questions about hope and despair; capitalism and consumerism; technology and art. From a specifically Scottish vantage point, the book can be seen to interrogate the contours, contradictions and confinements that constitute the dark heart of western civilisation.

For Douglas Gifford *Lanark* succeeded in a crucial way in which previous Scottish novels had failed. Along with diagnosing the fragmentation associated with the experience of modernity, it represented an epic search for 'a whole Scotland'. Gifford frames the novel in terms of its symbolic effect as a wake-up call to the nation. In contrast to small-scale fictions of local intent, *Lanark* incorporates the entire country within the scope of its artistic vision:

■ *Lanark* represents Duncan Thaw as witness to the loss of holistic awareness of Scotland. Nevertheless, Gray's panoramic illustrations of factories, oil refineries and rigs, cities and glens, bens and seascapes, together with the exploration of recognisably Scottish institutions, from art college to infirmary, from crumbling church to empty factory or shipyard, show the matter to be Scotland as it has developed through history till now [...] Thaw represents the beginning of Gray's quest for a new and whole Scotland.[53] □

The influence of European and American literature on the text is symptomatic of the breadth of Gray's vision for a modern Scottish literature, one which is a part of and can speak about a global form of experience. For Gifford *Lanark* can be read as an attempt to rewrite T. S. Eliot's Modernist poem *The Waste Land* (1922), with Glasgow at the dark core of a crumbling western civilisation. Scotland is not a mere cultural curio. It belongs to a dystopian nightmare of global proportions; a greed-driven society where people trample one another in their march to the top. Scotland is revealed as both a particular and a universal in this narrative of social trauma: 'Gray has made his picture of Glasgow and the west of Scotland in decline his *Waste Land* – with its exaggerated images of sterility and decay thus becoming the images of the decline of the bigger West; the barren city of failures of Europe and the world beyond.'[54]

If *Lanark* provoked a serious debate about the state of Scotland, it was equally important in bringing a host of other themes to the fore. Randall Stevenson reads the novel in the terms of its thematic preoccupations with modernism and, more latterly, postmodernism. Postmodern analysis has been highly popular in the critical inter-pretation of Gray's work although it is worth noting the author's own scepticism regarding such ostensibly trendy discourses: 'I have been perplexed by the adjective *post-modern*, especially when applied to my own writing, but now decided that it is an academic substitute for *con-temporary* or *fashionable*. Its prefix honestly announces it as a specimen of intellectual afterbirth.'[55] Such cynicism may be attributed to the general vagueness and, perhaps more problematic, the political rela-tivism which is often associated with postmodern theory. This point will be picked up on in more detail in Chapter Six of this Guide. In the extract below Stevenson addresses the non-sequential presenta-tion of the various books in *Lanark*. He aligns this deliberate disorder with a general scepticism characteristic of much modernist writing of the early twentieth century. For writers like Virginia Woolf (1882–1941), D. H. Lawrence (1885–1930) and James Joyce such scepticism was, in part, a reaction to the increasing regimentation of external life enthroned by industrialisation:

■ A feature of modernism, nearly as distinctive as its invention of new registers for dramatising thought, is its abandonment of conventions of chronological narrative arrangement. Long histories of personal develop-ment in Victorian fiction are replaced in *Ulysses* (1922) or *Mrs Dalloway* (1925) by concentration within a single day of consciousness, into which past events are randomly inserted by memory. Time and history grow less and less conceivable by means of the logical, measured progress of clock and calendar. Shredding and slicing life, in Woolf's view, or menac-ing it with madness, in Lawrence's, clocks provide for modernist fiction more of a threat than a plausible, realisable sense of order.[56] □

The development of the assembly line by American industrialist Henry Ford (1865–1947) and the acceptance of *The Principles of Scientific Management* (1911) by Frederick Taylor (1856–1915) saw a search for greater industrial efficiency lead to a highly regimented workplace, symbolised by the activity of clocking in and clocking out. In reaction modernist writers increasingly championed a literary aesthetic which favoured subjective 'time in the mind' as opposed to objective notions of 'time on the clock'. Stevenson's account also highlights *Lanark's* concern with questions of control and the alienation of human experience under the forces of industrial capitalism:

■ Alasdair Gray's writing, particularly in *Lanark*, obviously shares this sense of a fragmented, incoherent, even apocalyptic history. With its individual books ordered Three, One, Two, Four; a prologue inserted between Books One and Three; and an epilogue somewhere towards the end of Book Four, *Lanark* thoroughly challenges serial form – its author, or his spokesman, explaining 'I want *Lanark* to be read in one order but eventually thought of in another.

[...]

Lanark also provides some evidence of *why*, since modernism appeared early this century, the clock has continued to seem such an unreliable, even invidious instrument. Modernism's new chronologies are often critically assessed – sensibly enough – as a response to the collapse of a coherent history in 1914. Contemporary views of time, however, were also pervasively influenced by developments reaching Britain at least a decade earlier. By the 1890s, technology had become available to ensure that employees had to 'clock in' and 'clock out' of their place of work. Around the same time the theories of Frederick Taylor began to disseminate ideas of 'scientific management' – ways of minutely controlling the labour force, devoted to repetitive mechanical tasks whose value and duration were established by 'time and motion study' [...] Gray, throughout *Lanark*, concerns himself with what is only a later, expanded version of the industrialised capitalism which horrified Lawrence. The differences between the two visions mostly follow from the ways technology has enlarged possibilities for establishing 'a great and perfect system'; for consolidating new orders 'strict, terrible, inhuman'. *Lanark* expands these possibilities still further, into nightmare and fantasy. Technology enables 'the creature' – 'a conspiracy which owns and manipulates everything for profit' to make entirely literal what used to be only metaphors of commodification and consumption: men and women, in the Institute, are actually turned into food and eaten.[57] □

Stevenson's desire to widen the frame of reference resonates with Gray's own assertions that despite being set in Scotland, he wrote a novel that he hoped would appeal to an international readership. Questions of nation and nationalism are of particular relevance to Scottish writing during this period. However, as Gray's novel demonstrates, they remain only one point of possible signification within the literary text. The rest of this Guide might be considered an exploration of the themes which constitute those other layers of meaning. One of the issues which has particular relevance to contemporary Scottish literature, and to the assertion of a distinctive national tradition, is the question of language and it is this theme that the next chapter is specifically concerned with.

CHAPTER TWO

Language

A liberation of the voice?

A sense of verbal dexterity and the use of linguistic innovation are among the most defining characteristics of contemporary Scottish literature. Cairns Craig has argued that the literary revival outlined in the previous chapter, if traced back to its source, begins in what he calls a radical 'liberation of the voice.'[1] He claims that, initially influenced by developments on the Scottish stage, a sustained interest in the artistic possibilities of vernacular speech brought a new intensity to both poetry and fiction in Scotland:

> ■ What happened in Scotland in the 1960s and 1970s, and what laid the foundation for the enormous creative achievements of the 1980s, was the liberation of the voice. The Scottish voice declared its independence and sustained it in a way that the brief fad for regional accents initiated by the Beatles failed to do in England. The liberation of the voice was at first an acceptance of and an assertion of the vernacular; it happened most obviously in the theatre, where the lack of a narrator allowed characters' speech to stand forth undeflected by 'standard' forms of speech.[2] □

It is this 'liberation of the voice' that this chapter aims to chart and interrogate.

As a prelude we might begin by noting various strategies and effects recent writers have realised in their attempts to articulate an identifiably Scottish voice. Winner of the T. S. Eliot Prize in 2005, Carol Ann Duffy is a poet not normally associated with Scotland. She was, however, born in Glasgow in 1955 and lived there for five years before moving to England. Duffy recalls: 'My family moved to England in the early 1960s and I spent most of my childhood in Stafford, feeling very much an outsider and trying to change my accent to sound like the English kids.'[3] It is this heightened awareness of the differences in Scottish speech that adumbrates much of the discussion that follows. In her poem 'The Way My Mother Speaks' (1990) Duffy fondly recalls hearing expressions in Scots like *'The day and ever'* and *'What like is it?'* and confesses to being 'homesick, free, in love/with the way my mother speaks'.[4] It is through the sound of words, the grain and texture of language, that the poet as a young girl sought to counteract feelings of alienation, estrangement and despair. The tenderness of Duffy's poetry stands in sharp contrast to the ways in which other Scottish writers have been emboldened by the politics of language. James Kelman won the 1994 Booker Prize for *How Late It Was, How Late*, a novel written almost entirely in working class Glaswegian. His victory provoked outrage from certain sections of the mainstream media which focused in particular on the novel's language and its liberal use of swear words. In his acceptance speech Kelman was characteristically combative and defended his right to create art using whatever diction he chose: 'my language and my culture have a right to exist.'[5] This specific episode will be considered alongside the discussion of class in Chapter Four of this Guide. Elsewhere Kelman has written: 'language is your culture – if you lose your language you've lost your culture, so if you've lost the way your family talk, the way your friends talk, then you've lost your culture.'[6] This unswerving commitment to language in all its forms can be detected in the work of a number of contemporary Scottish writers including Tom Leonard, Liz Lochhead and Irvine Welsh. Welsh's *Trainspotting* employs a distinctive phonetic narrative in its portrait of the heroin subculture of 1980s Edinburgh. Much of the novel is narrated in the highly stylised voice of its main character Mark Renton. The book opens: 'The sweat wis lashing oafay Sick Boy; he wis trembling. Ah wis jist sitting thair, focusing oan the telly, trying no tae notice the cunt. He wis bringing me doon.'[7] Crucially though, *Trainspotting* is no one-trick pony. Like much Scottish writing of this period, it is not concerned with the mere realistic representation of vernacular speech. Some of the novel's most memorable scenes derive from characters abilities to code shift and manipulate language. In court, on trial for shoplifting, Renton adopts the polite register of the judicial system in order to dupe the magistrate with the veneer of genuine repentance:

■ Thank you, your honour. I'm only too well aware of the disappointment I've been to my family and friends and that I am now wasting valuable court time. However, one of the key elements in rehabilitation is the ability to recognize that the problem exists [...] I'm no longer indulging in self-deception. With god's help, I'll beat this disease.[8] □

In this scene Renton's articulacy earns him a reprieve, whereas his co-defendant, the less expressive Spud, receives a custodial sentence. For the critic Aaron Kelly: 'Renton is able to subvert the language of power, to expose it as merely one discourse amongst others, and he makes a mockery of its claims to truth, justice, objectivity.'[9] Alongside Scots and urban dialect, the minority language of Gaelic continues to be a vital, although highly threatened, corner of the Scottish literary landscape. Critical reactions to the recent fortunes of Gaelic will also be addressed in due course.

Whilst Kelman and Welsh's work are significantly different, they might be characterised in terms of their shared interest in the artistic possibilities of working-class speech. Their work seeks to validate the experience of those who have been historically marginalised within mainstream society, with a group who have been silenced and sidelined within the pages of traditional literary fiction. However, as the example from *Trainspotting* illustrates, there is more at work here than simply the authentic representation of vernacular speech. The 1980s and 1990s saw Scottish literature embrace and celebrate its status as a linguistic melting pot like never before. Regional accents and local dialects stepped out of the wings and increasingly took centre stage in the literary life of the nation. Previously, in the 1920s, the language question had for the most part been conducted in terms of the impingement of English on the Scots language. In the late-twentieth century, the profusion and eclecticism of languages within Scottish writing signals the growing emergence of new forms of politics, of narratives which have sought to deconstruct more familiar nationalist rivalries. Suhayl Saadi's novel *Psychoraag* (2004) is one of the most original examples of this polyphonic style of writing. Set in contemporary Glasgow, the book is a fusion of a number of languages including demotic Glaswegian, Urdu and late-twentieth century street slang. A 'rag' being the jazz term for a form of music played off the regular beat, Saadi's novel plunges the reader into a new and previously unwritten territory, a multi-generational, multi-national experience that rethinks the parameters of what it might mean to live in twenty-first century Scotland. This interest in the experience of ethnic groups can be read as part of a much wider phenomenon within British literary culture. It is a process which has seen a number of authors including Monica Ali (born 1967), Zadie Smith (born 1975) and Hari Kunzru (born 1969) achieve remarkable critical acclaim. These developments mark a break from the renaissance of the 1920s, where the language question was primarily framed in terms of an opposition between English and Scots. Scots was regarded as the original language of the nation, displaced and marginalised by English as part of over 400 years of cultural subordination. The history of this evolving linguistic landscape will be outlined in due course. We will begin by considering how easily such binary oppositions might be incorporated within the type of nationalist criticism outlined in Chapter One of this Guide. At the same time it is worth thinking about how a contemporary writer like Suhayl Saadi forces us to reset the cultural co-ordinates of such obvious binary oppositions.

Edwin Muir's book *Scott and Scotland: the Predicament of the Scottish Writer* (1936) was one of the first attempts to theorise the relationships between language and literature in Scotland. In terms of our contemporary focus it is worth noting that the Edinburgh based publisher Polygon reissued this book in 1982. In *Scott and Scotland* Muir argued that the Scottish writer is maimed as a result of his country's fractured and uneven linguistic inheritance. Whilst in the 1930s the Scots language may have still been the common tongue of the masses, it had long ceased to function as the language of politics, law and education. Muir used a metaphor to illustrate the effects of this situation – if Scots was the language of the heart, he argued, English was the language of the head. What exactly Muir meant by this will be returned to in due course. For now we might note that contemporary writing has compelled a decisive shift in the ways in which critics have sought to interpret Scotland's linguistic terrain. The language question can no longer be lumped into convenient dichotomies juxtaposing English and Scots. The linguistic politics of recent writing asks us to consider a set of alternative concerns such as class, ethnicity, gender, region and so on. Late twentieth-century Scottish writers celebrate rather than lament their lack of linguistic homogeneity. Difference rather than harmony has become the watchword of the day. For the critic Roderick Watson such linguistic free-play interrupts the kind of reductive nationalist thinking about Scottish literature that we saw in the previous chapter:

> ■ [Q]uestions of language and identity still haunt the work of contemporary Scottish writers. One might even argue that the linguistic pluralism inherent in Scottish cultural identity – in the continuing interplay between Scots, English and Gaelic – has made writers especially sensitive to how subjectivity is simultaneously constructed and undone in the precisions and imprecisions of language and in the tangled translations and transitions (and the political and social complexities) between utterance and reception. Such questions, however, are less likely today to be framed in terms of a national identity or as part of a literary enterprise claiming continuity with and the revivification of an ancient literary tradition. If identity is an issue among contemporary Scottish writers, it is more likely now to be a matter of personal, political, sexual or existential being.[10] □

The current chapter is divided into three sections, addressing in turn issues pertaining to Scots, vernacular forms of English and Gaelic. The first task is to outline the historic evolution of these languages over the past four centuries. This is a crucial part of understanding the nature of the choice confronting the contemporary Scottish writer. Having retold this story we will consider the extensive use of urban vernacular within contemporary Scottish writing. Critical responses to the work of Glasgow poet Tom Leonard will be used to illustrate the impassioned and highly political nature of this debate. The final section is concerned with the role of Gaelic writing within contemporary Scottish literature. A minority language operating at the margins of a minority literature, Gaelic writing continues to defy the odds and stare down the barrel of its own threatened extinction.

The history of Scots

Since the Union of the Crowns in 1603, and the conjoining of the English and Scottish thrones, the Scots language has witnessed a catastrophic decline in its fortunes. This has coincided with a dramatic rise in the importance of English in almost every aspect of Scottish life. Prior to the seventeenth-century Scotland existed as an autonomous nation state, one with a flourishing cultural life and a series of intimate relationships with the great powers of continental Europe. The 'Auld Alliance', for example, refers to the close affinity that existed between Scotland and France prior to the Reformation. During the medieval period the majority of people in Scotland spoke either Gaelic or Scots. Gaelic was primarily the language of the highlands and islands, whereas Scots was the common parlance of the lowlands, where the nobility would also have had some knowledge of English. The official parlance of the royal court, Scots was a separate language rather than merely a dialect of English, as later commentators would argue. It was the language of politics, law, commerce and art. Under royal patronage the court poets, or 'Makars' as they are known – Robert Henryson (c.1450–c.1505), William Dunbar (c.1460–c.1530), Gavin Douglas (c.1474–c.1522) and David Lindsay (c.1486–1555) – wrote some of the finest European poetry of the day in Scots. Gavin Douglas translated Virgil's Roman epic *The Aeneid* into Scots, illustrating the degree to which it was a language capable of the most sophisticated and sublime poetry. Beginning in the sixteenth-century, several key events were to have disastrous impacts on the role and status of the Scots language. According to the critic J. Derrick McClure the key aspects of this narrative include the Protestant Reformation, the Union of the Crowns (1603) and the Act of Union (1707). The Protestant Reformation has its origins in 1517 in Wittenberg ,Germany where the monk and priest Martin Luther (1483–1546) famously nailed his *95 Theses* to the door of the town Church in 'protest' against the sale of indulgences by the Catholic clergy. In terms of language and literacy, one of the key doctrines of the newly formed Protestant religion was that individuals must participate in a direct relationship with God. The priest was no longer the interpreter and mediator of God's will. Individuals must learn to read the Bible for themselves which as a result was translated from Latin into almost every European vernacular. Crucially, in Scotland the first vernacular Bible was not written in Scots but in English. In the quotation below McClure outlines the disastrous effect these events had on the linguistic landscape of post-reformation Scotland:

> ■ The Reformation not only had the effect of flooding Scotland with English theological works and placing an English translation of the Bible in every Scottish household above a certain income level; it replaced France by England as Scotland's strongest political connection and principal cultural model among European powers [...] [The seventeenth century] saw a steady decline in literary creativity in Scotland; the abolition of Parliament in 1707 led to the extinction of Scots as a language carrying social or political prestige [...] Scots, that is, was prevented by the entire course of the nation's history after the Reformation from fulfilling its early potential of becoming the recognised national language of Scotland [...] a well-known feature of Scottish intellectual life in the eighteenth century was a strong revulsion against the tongue and a desire to replace it with the London–Oxford–Cambridge standard of literary English: a desire which its proponents saw as entirely compatible with an enduring belief in a Scottish national identity and profession of Scottish pride.[11] □

Throughout the subsequent centuries the key institutions of the state (the Church and the monarchy) would be at the forefront of the increasing Anglicisation of Scottish public life.

In order to gain access to England's expanding Empire, Scotland renounced its political sovereignty in 1707 and acceded into full political union in a British state. The gravitational centre of the country shifted irrevocably southward, and to London in particular. The 'strong revulsion' against the Scots tongue which McClure mentions formed a key part of the cultural terrain of the subsequent eighteenth-century. As the scientific age of the Enlightenment swept throughout Europe, empirical observation and rational thought gradually began to replace superstition and inherited belief as the dominant ideological force. Scotland produced several Enlightenment thinkers who would have a definitive impact on the shape of the modern world: these included the philosopher David Hume; economist and moral philosopher Adam Smith (1723–90), author of *The Wealth of Nations* (1776); geologist James Hutton (1726–97); and the engineer and inventor of the steam engine James Watt (1736–1819).

This period is of central importance for Robert Crawford's argument in his book *Devolving English Literature* (1992). In the extract below Crawford claims that the eighteenth-century witnessed an exacerbation of negative perceptions of the Scots language. Emanating from London, a disdain for Scots would become increasingly evident amongst the more educated and aspirant members of Scottish society. Middle-class Scots took speech lessons, often from Irish actors, in an effort to rid themselves of their 'Scotticisms', or identifiable Scottish speech habits. Crawford argues that it was these circumstances that led to the invention of English Literature as a University subject. Developed in the 1750s by Adam Smith at the University of Glasgow and Hugh Blair (1718–1800) at the University of Edinburgh, classes in 'Rhetoric and Belles Lettres' were designed to teach young Scottish men how to use English correctly. The curriculum saw the enthronement of a canon of English literary texts as paradigm examples of proper language usage. In the wake of the Act of Union, London was increasingly regarded as the gravitational centre of the new British state. If middle-class Scots were to forge a place for themselves in this new Britain, they would have to do so in English. Although poets such as Allan Ramsa, Robert Fergusson and Robert Burns continued to make use of Scots in their verse, every significant work of the Enlightenment, in philosophy, history and economics, was written in English. If Scots continued to survive as a language of the poetic imagination, it was rapidly disappearing from the intellectual and political life of the nation. It is here that Edwin Muir's division between the language of the heart (Scots) and the language of the head (English) originates. Crawford comments:

■ In Scotland the general eighteenth-century concern with linguistic propriety was particularly intense because it was bound up with a conflict between the urge to treasure the language of Lowland Scotland – Scots – in which most of the greatest popular and learned poetry of Scotland, from Gavin Douglas to the ballads, had been created, and a contrary impulse to develop a Scotland which would take complete advantage of the 1707 Act of Union by playing its part in the newly united political entity of Britain. To play a full part, Scottish people would have to move from using Scots to using English, an English which was fully acceptable to the dominant partner in the political union. This English, it was argued, both had to replace Scots and had to be purged of what we would now call 'markers of Scottish cultural difference', purged of Scotticisms. The growing wish for a 'pure' English in eighteenth-century Scotland was not an anti-Scottish gesture, but a pro-British one. If Britain were to work as a political unit, then Scots should rid themselves of any elements likely to impede their progress within it. Language, the most important of bonds, must not be allowed to hinder Scotland's intercourse with expanding economic and intellectual markets in the freshly defined British state.[12] □

During and after the Enlightenment era, ambitious Scots would become increasingly Anglicised in their speech habits. Here we can begin to detect a class element emerging in the various ways of speaking within Scotland. Scots is in the process of becoming identified as the language of the uneducated, lower orders of society. The Victorian era would see this elitist and Anglocentric value system made law through the Scottish Education Act (1872) which made it illegal for Scottish children to speak Scots in the classroom. Rather than a separate language with a distinguished literary heritage, Scots was seen as an aberration, a deformed or poor man's English. If it had been worthy of *The Aeneid* 300 years before, by the late Victorian era Scots was a language not even fit for a child's school lesson. In *Devolving English Literature* Crawford uses this historical narrative to inform his analysis of contemporary writing, particularly the use of dialect in the work of writers like Tom Leonard and James Kelman. He employs the discourse of postcolonial theory to describe the power relations that exist between Scots and English. Received Pronunciation (R. P.) English is contrasted with the 'barbarian' tongues that emanate from the peripheral regions of the British Empire. Cairns Craig has made similar claims about the imperial nature of the language question as it is played out in Scottish culture: 'It is not by our colour, of course, that we have stood to be recognized as incomplete within the British context, it is by the colour of our vowels.'[13] James Kelman would also claim that his work, set amongst the disenfranchised and disaffected of contemporary Glasgow, belongs to a 'literature of decolonisation'. These and other issues pertaining to postcolonial readings of Scottish literature will be returned to in Chapter Five of this Guide.

During the twentieth-century the role and status of the Scots language remained a central preoccupation for many writers. At the heart of the 1920s renaissance was Hugh MacDiarmid's belief that political independence would follow from a renewed affirmation of Scotland's unique cultural identity. MacDiarmid had already seen this strategy reap substantial rewards in Ireland, where the Celtic Revival helped foster a sense of cultural separateness that ultimately contributed to Irish independence in 1922. For MacDiarmid the spiritual source of Scottish poetry was not Robert Burns, but William Dunbar. In epic poems like *A Drunk Man Looks at the Thistle* (1926) MacDiarmid sought to resurrect and restore the Scots language to its former glory, imbuing it with an artistic intensity not seen since medieval times. His goal was to undo 400 years of linguistic displacement and denigration. MacDiarmid used John Jamieson's *Etymological Dictionary of the Scottish Language* (1808) by John Jamieson (1759–1838) to create what he called 'synthetic Scots' or Lallans. This new language provided the poet with a deep linguistic well from which to draw words, sounds and images in order to construct his poetic vision. Despite MacDiarmid's achievement, the crucial fact remained that many of the words in Jamieson's dictionary had completely fallen out of use among the majority of Scottish people. Unlike the songs of Burns, MacDiarmid's was a highly wrought, modernist poetic, one with extremely limited popular appeal. He would later acknowledge the contradictory nature of his aesthetic and political vision in the poem 'Second Hymn to Lenin': 'Are my poems spoken in the factories and fields,/In the streets o' the toon?/Gin they're no', then I'm failin' to dae/What I ocht to ha' dune.'[14]

Fellow renaissance writer Lewis Grassic Gibbon was similarly interested in the problem of writing Scottish fiction through the medium of Standard English. For Gibbon there was an underlying sense of estrangement beneath the Scottish writer's use of the English language: '[U]nfortunately it is not English. The English reader is haunted by a sense of something foreign stumbling and hesitating behind this smooth façade of adequate technique; it is as though the [Scottish] writer did not write himself, but translate himself.'[15] Edwin Muir's *Scott and Scotland* can be read as a reaction against the resuscitation of vernacular Scots advocated by MacDiarmid and others. Muir maintained that Scotland needed a language capable of expressing *both* the emotional and intellectual life of the nation. Even if MacDiarmid was able to create a highly wrought poetry in Scots, the language of politics, commerce and education remained resolutely English. Muir saw this divided linguistic inheritance through the prism of Gregory Smith's Caledonian Antisyzgy. Scotland's split personality, its Jekyll and Hyde-ness, was made manifest in the nation's language. Estranged from themselves, Scotsmen were condemned to think in one language and feel in another. It was this problematic situation that Muir termed 'the predicament' of the Scottish writer:

■ Every genuine literature, in other words, requires as its condition a means of expression capable of dealing with everything the mind can think of or the imagination can conceive. It must be a language for criticism as well as poetry, for abstract speculation as well as fact, and since we live in a scientific age, it must be a language for science as well. A language which can serve for one or two of those purposes but not for the others is, considered as a vehicle for literature, merely an anachronism. Scots has survived to our time as a language for simple poetry and the simpler kind of short story [...] all its other uses have lapsed, and it expresses therefore only a fragment of the Scottish mind. One can go further than this and assert that its very use is proof that the Scottish consciousness is divided. For, reduced to its simplest terms, this linguistic division means that Scotsmen feel in one language and think in another; that their emotions turn to the Scottish tongue, with all its associations of local sentiment, and their minds to a standard English which for them is almost bare of associations other than those of the classroom [...] The curse of Scottish literature is the lack of a whole language, which finally means the lack of a whole mind.[16] □

For Muir the solution for the Scottish writer lay in abandoning Scots altogether and to writing in English. However, if MacDiarmid's attempt to revive Scots was not as successful as he would have wished, a similar statement could also be made regarding Muir's attempts to dismiss the language. Muir's analysis, that Scotsmen feel in one language and think in another, has been disproved by successive generations of writers who have sought to write a highly sophisticated, cerebral literature in a variety of Scots. In the wake of the 1920s renaissance a number of poets would continue to pursue the project inaugurated by MacDiarmid including William Soutar (1898–1943), Robert Garioch (1909–81), Douglas Young (1913–73) and Sydney Goodsir Smith (1915–75). In the contemporary period several poets continue to champion the use of Scots within their work including Robert Crawford, W. N. Herbert (born 1961) and David Kinloch (born 1959). All three of these poets also teach at Universities, an interesting point bearing in mind the problem of elitism inherent in MacDiarmid's original revival of Lallans. In prose a number of contemporary writers continue to interrogate the artistic potential of Scots including Matthew Fitt (born 1968) in his novel *But n Ben A-Go-Go* (2000) and Des Dillon (born 1960) in books such as *Itchycooblue* (1999).

Whilst poetry and prose are important to the enduring relevance of Scots, it is arguably on the stage where the language has been most originally and consistently redeployed. In accounting for the 'liberation of the voice' within contemporary literature we might recall Cairns Craig's claim that it was the theatre where the seeds of this radical deliverance were first sown. In his introduction to *Scottish Theatre Since the Seventies* (1996) Randall Stevenson supports such claims. For Stevenson, Scots as a spoken language, in contrast to the written word is able to connect with the audience in an immediate and meaningful way:

■ Divisions between the Standard English used for most official purposes and the roguish, marginal existence enjoyed by Scots have of course been much discussed by students of Scottish affairs, Hugh MacDiarmid included, as have their contributions to splits and antisyzygies in the Scottish imagination and soul. In the theatre, however, the use of Scots has little to do with splitting and everything to do with solidarity – with a collective cocooning of stage and audience in a community of speech which often includes, by implication, a sense of shared outlooks, values and emotions.[17] □

Stevenson maintains that the use of Scots on stage during the 1970s helped foster a stronger sense of communal identity. At the same time it greatly contributed to revitalising the possibilities for non-standard speech among other literary genres.

■ Scots in the theatre does indeed have a peculiar hold over the emotions, a power to 'faddom the hert' of audiences and draw them into complicity with stage action, almost independently of what the 'sense' or direction of that action is itself [...] It is not authenticity, but difference – difference from Standard English in particular – which gives this language its power to communicate a distinctively Scottish experience.[18] □

Significantly, when Scots appeared on the stage during the seventies it was often infused with the rhythms and syntax of working-class speech. *The Hard Man* (1977) by Tom McGrath (born 1940) and *The Slab Boys Trilogy* (1978) by the artist and playwright John Byrne (born 1940) are among the most notable examples of this. Moreover, it is interesting to note the number of Scottish writers – Morgan, Gray, Kelman, Lochhead – better known for poetry or fiction, that have also written for the stage during their careers.

The rise of urban vernacular

As the opening scene from Irvine Welsh's *Trainspotting* illustrated, urban vernacular speech has formed one the most energising currents in Scottish writing of the last three decades. However, it is far from clear whether this particular aesthetic trajectory could ever have been anticipated. During the 1930s some of the most ardent defenders of Scots regarded the working-class vernacular of Glasgow as an affront to an ancient and prestigious literary language. The *Scottish National Dictionary* of 1936 carried the following condemnation in its preface: 'Owing to the influx of Irish and foreign immigrants in the industrial area near Glasgow the dialect had become hopelessly corrupt.'[19] Similarly excoriating, in 1933 Paisley Grammar School teacher T. D. Robb (birth date unavailable) wrote *Deletiae Poetarum Scotorum,* or 'The Destruction of Scots Poetry':

■ For what has the Doric of the populous centres of the country become? It is not Scots at all, but a thing debased beyond tears. It is a mongrel patois due to lower class immigration from Ireland, from Lancashire mills, and the meaner streets of Glasgow. Traditional vernacular has gone. The streets are sibilant with 'huz yins', 'wis youse', 'wee wis'; ungrammatical with 'I seen', 'I done'.[20] □

There is a heavy irony in the type of attitude displayed by Robb. Scots language defenders can be seen to adopt the same prejudice toward working-class speech that they themselves experienced from the advocates of Standard English. Such contradictions expose the underlying tension between nationalism and more class orientated politics. The contemporary use of vernacular speech questions the presumptions of bourgeois Scottish nationalism. The language of the industrial proletariat within Scotland can be seen to partake in a form of double marginalisation. It is an anathema to both the 'proper English' brigade as well as those who champion more literary forms of Scots. This antagonism between Scots and more working-class dialects anticipates the resistance toward prevailing ideologies, particularly nationalism, which is present in writers like Kelman and Welsh. An enduring characteristic of contemporary Scottish literature is a tendency towards non-conformity, with writers increasingly interested in emancipatory projects premised on questions of class, gender, ethnicity, sexuality and so forth. A highly diverse body of literature, writing from Scotland can no longer be readily subsumed within the critical straitjacket of cultural nationalism. Both the quotations above are taken from an essay by the poet and critic Tom Leonard entitled 'Literature, Dialogue, Democracy'.[21] Emerging during the 1960s, Leonard was one of the first people to champion the so-called 'mongrel patois' of the urban proletariat and their right to a voice within the field of literary culture.

Tom Leonard

The Glasgow poet Tom Leonard is one of the most important figures in the explosion of creativity surrounding the use of urban dialect. For a time he was part of the Hobsbaum group at Glasgow University that included James Kelman, Alasdair Gray and Liz Lochhead. The impact of his work on subsequent generations of Scottish writers cannot be underestimated. Kelman comments: 'Tom Leonard: his voice, his expression of voice, his commitment to the expression. He was the first British writer whose work struck into me: he is always present.'[22] Similarly Alasdair Gray writes: 'Readers who choose to learn about Tom's work [...] will discover a range of thought and feeling too great for the glib classifications learned in classrooms.'[23] From his very first publication *Six Glasgow Poems* (1969) Leonard could be seen to be taking the language of the street into a whole new territory. The 'mongrel patois' of Glasgow is revealed to be a form of utterance capable, not just of angry invective, but of the most sublime poetic expression.

One of Leonard's most famous poems 'The Good Thief' illustrates the linguistic and aesthetic strategies that underpin much of his writing. Written in phonetic Glaswegian, the poem imagines the words spoken by one of the thieves that were crucified alongside Christ. Again, like Kelman and Welsh who came after, Leonard is not merely interested in the realistic representation of working-class speech. The language of the poem presents the reader with a number of metaphysical questions about the nature of religion, culture and community. Derrick McClure describes, 'the almost opaque, quasi-phonetic transcription of the short, disjointed phrases, pronounced with a high degree of ellipsis of unstressed syllables, characteristic of uneducated Glasgow speech: *yawright* "are you all right?", *ma right insane* "am I right in saying", *yirwanny uz* "you're one of us".'[24] What is clear is that whatever language the good thief is speaking it is neither Standard English nor the kind of Scots advocated by MacDiarmid: 'going to' is written as 'gonny'; 'all right' is 'awright'; 'one of' is 'wanny'. Through this strategy Leonard achieves a highly original, phonetic transcription of Glasgow speech. Christ is referred to by the all-purpose Glasgow appellation 'Jimmy' in the poem's opening gambit, 'heh Jimmy'. At the same time we are reminded that the thief does not actually know who Christ is, both in a literal and metaphysical sense. As such his compassion and camaraderie are revealed to be all the more poignant. McClure draws out the radical assumptions underpinning Leonard's use of language. He is particularly interested in the exclusion of working-class experience as a form of language worthy of literary utterance.

■ [There is] the plethora of clichés and banalities, woefully realistic as a representation of actual speech but wholly unlike the sparkling imaginative richness of Scots poetry until then: *still wayiz* ('still with us', i.e. still alive), *wanny uz*, *ma right insane* ('Am I right in saying ...' is a sadly overused phrase from television quiz shows), *see it nyir eyes*. And finally, the truly shattering realization – which readers are liable to experience some time after their initial acquaintance with the poem, and which (as Leonard observed) some of them miss altogether – of the significance of the poem's title: the persona is that of one of the thieves crucified along with Christ. A link, hinted at by the reference to 'the gemm' but not overtly mentioned is that Parkhead, Celtic's football ground and the scene of annual tussles at which violent brawls used to occur with deadly regularity, is nicknamed 'Paradise' (*today shalt thou be with me in Paradise*) – and according to an ancient Church tradition, the death of Christ occurred at three p.m., the hour of afternoon kick-off.[25] □

Leonard's poem imbricates the crucifixion of Christ with the working-class ritual of the Saturday football match. When the thief has to repeat himself ('gonny miss the GEMM jimmy'), shouting the word 'GEMM', we are reminded that he is in fact speaking to a man who is on the cusp of death. 'nearly three a cloke thinoo/dork init/good jobe they've gote thi lights' refers to the floodlights of the football match. It also recalls Christ's death at three o'clock and a moment when a sudden darkness spread across the land. In terms of language, the phonetic transcription of Glasgow speech encourages us to re-evaluate who exactly Christ was: son of a carpenter; the Lord made flesh; an ordinary man. The poem becomes a meditation on the nature of both religious and cultural elitism. At the same time it evinces the artistic potential of working-class speech and its ability to foster abstract philosophical thought. McClure highlights the underlying tension between Leonard's work and the nationalist bias of previous language debates in Scotland. In Chapter One we saw Wallace and Gifford argue that contemporary writing represented a more 'real' Scottish literary renaissance. The militant and class aspects of much dialect writing disrupt any straightforward narrative of national revival. Leonard's poetry calls into question the project of the 1920s renaissance and the attempt by certain writers to employ language as a foundation for nationalist cultural politics. Leonard's characters are the spokespersons for an underclass, their voices are those that in the past have been marginalised within nationalist histories of Scottish literature. McClure comments:

> ■ Leonard's achievement has been to establish in modern Scottish writing a register which directly challenges literary Scots as much as it does English [...] The political implications of Leonard's medium are also decidedly unlike those of MacDiarmid and his successors: Leonard is not concerned to use his language as a weapon in the cause of Scottish political and cultural independence. His field of concern is the class system within Scotland rather than the country's international status.[26] □

McClure distinguishes the linguistic politics of Leonard's work from those of his predecessors. This type of distinction, however, is contested by other critics who regard the working-class to be the direct inheritors of what can be identified as a distinctive Scottish identity. In contrast it is the aspirant middle-class Scot who has most dramatically lost his national identity. Critic Billy Kay argues: 'The working class continue speaking Scots, and if there is a slow erosion of the distinctive Scots vocabulary with every generation, it still remains very much the spoken language of the people.'[27] McClure's juxtaposition of the linguistic politics of the 1920s and more recent uses of vernacular is also contradicted by Roderick Watson. For Watson contemporary dialect writing draws directly upon MacDiarmid's fervent desire to defend minority language against the linguistic impingement of Standard English. For

Watson, both periods witness Scottish writers, albeit in different ways, involved in a related form of ideological resistance:

■ One of the main drivers of the modern Scottish Literary Renaissance was the need to establish cultural difference from what was perceived as the English tradition – to make room for one's own, so to speak. In this regard Hugh MacDiarmid's resistance to the hegemony of Standard English has been of immense importance to twentieth-century Scottish writing – even for those writers such as Tom Leonard and James Kelman who would disagree with his political nationalism. More than that, MacDiarmid's case was a seminal one in the development of all literatures in English, and his essay on 'English Ascendancy in British Literature', first published in Eliot's *The Criterion* in July 1931, is a key document in the early history of postcolonial studies. Nor would Kelman and Leonard be out of sympathy with the case it makes for difference, plurality and so-called 'marginal' utterance.[28] □

Leonard himself has something to say about the tradition he feels his work belongs to. In his essay on the American poet William Carlos Williams (1883–1963) he attempts to redefine the conventional terrain upon which the language debate in Scotland is conducted. In contrast to a distinction between Scots and English, one that would retrace a specifically nationalist politics, Leonard highlights the different registers that attend to one's place within the social hierarchy of modern Britain. For Leonard the regional accents of Britain can be readily distinguished between the middle/upper class (those whose went to private school) and the lower class (those that didn't):

■ The British are very sensitive about voice [...] And the answer lies as usual, not in the soil, but in the bankbook. There are basically two ways of speaking in Britain: one which lets the listener know that one paid for one's education, the other which lets the listener know that one didn't. Within these two categories there are wide variations, the line between the two is not always clear, and there are always loads of exceptions to any rule. But one can say that of the two categories, the latter – the 'free' education one – has much the wider variety. It is this very variety of regional working-class accents which the 'bought' education has promised to keep its pupils free from, and to provide them instead with a mode of pronunciation which ironically enough is called 'Received'. The 'Received Pronunciation' of Edinburgh will differ from that of Oxford (in its retention or elision of the 'r' in a word, for example) but the message of the medium is basically the same: this pronunciation is not received at all, but mummy and daddy paid for it: this pronunciation is important not in so much for what it is, but for what it isn't.[29] □

When it comes to the politics of language, this description would premise narratives of socio-economics over and above those of region or place.

On the one hand this perspective imbues Scottish dialect writing with a resonance beyond any local or nationalist context. On the other hand it can be accused of eliding important regional differences and offering merely a substitute simplified account of cultural identity. This type of reconfiguration might be regarded as merely replacing one reductive binary (Scots–English) with another (upper class-working class).

Earlier we saw both James Kelman and Cairns Craig employ the rhetoric of postcolonialism to describe the linguistic politics of Scottish writing. The critic Robert Crawford adopts a similar model in his reading of Tom Leonard's poetry. Crawford aligns the subversive energy of his work alongside that of Leeds poet Tony Harrison (born 1937) and the Northern Irish writer Seamus Heaney. Far from being embroiled in a set of local concerns, Scottish writing is seen to partake in a political and aesthetic discourse that is global in both scope and implication:

> ■ Leonard, like Harrison, is able to use non-standard forms as part of a gesture of solidarity with lower-class speakers of a provincial vernacular, as well as using these forms as a means of interrogating the established structures of linguistic and cultural power. Aware of linguists such as [Noam] Chomsky [born 1928] and [Edward] Sapir [1884–1939], his work in both English and Scots once again seeks to combine sophistication with an apparently barbarian inflection. It would be naïve to see this writing as limited in its concerns to comic or solely Glaswegian issues as it would to see Tony Harrison as simply a poet of Leeds. Leonard is aware that 'the criticism of "provincialism" is an international pattern', and, like Seamus Heaney, he is preoccupied with 'governance' – with issues of language and political control.[30] □

Scottish literature of this period can be increasingly seen in terms of wider theoretical debates concerning questions of authority and power. If the use of urban dialect writing flourished in the latter half of the twentieth-century, the same unfortunately cannot be said about writing in Gaelic. The forces of modernity and cosmopolitanism have continued to place an extreme amount of pressure on the Gaelic language community and it is to this subject that we now turn.

Gaelic

Any credible understanding of Scottish literature must take into account writing in Gaelic. There is a sense in which, similar to urban dialect, writing in Gaelic suffers from a form of double marginalisation, existing as part of a minority culture within the already marginalised field of Scottish literary studies. The overall number of Gaelic speakers has been in dramatic decline for almost two centuries. Bearing in mind Scotland's population of just over 5 million, the 1901 census recorded over 200,000 Gaelic speakers. By 2001 this number had fallen to 58,000 – from 4.5 per cent to 1.2 per cent of the total population.[31] One obvious and immediate impact of this decline has been a reduction in the size of any potential audience for Gaelic literature. Whilst there is some prose written in Gaelic, it is in poetry where the history and profile of Gaelic remains most visible. Even here though Gaelic writing is characterised by the story of emaciation and atrophy. In 1985 the Scottish Poetry Library estimated there were only 40 Gaelic poets living and writing in Scotland, whereas in 1900 there would have been hundreds.[32] In terms of geography today's Gaeltacht, or Gaelic speaking community, is centred in the north west of the country, primarily in the highlands and on the islands of Lewis, Skye and Uist. Gaelic faces the very real threat of language extinction. Unsurprisingly, this moribund possibility has preoccupied the work of most Gaelic writers at some point in their career.

Rather than talk of renaissance, whether of the 1920s or a more recent vintage, it is a story of gradual decline that remains one of the enduring motifs of twentieth-century Gaelic literature. In 'Shall Gaelic die?' the Lewis born poet Iain Crichton Smith (1928–98) declares: 'He who loses his language loses his world./The Highlander who loses his language loses his world.'[33] It is worth noting the similarity between Crichton Smith's statement and the sentiments of a writer like James Kelman quoted earlier ('language is your culture – if you lose your language you've lost your culture'). The sharp reduction in the sheer number of Gaelic speakers has had practical implications for the appreciation and dissemination of its literature. Gaelic does not receive the same amount of critical attention that Scottish literature in either English or Scots does. This issue foregrounds a rarely acknowledged, yet nevertheless fundamental, problem within the highly fashionable discipline of postcolonial studies. English speaking western critics rarely take into account writing in the indigenous language of postcolonialism's so-called Other cultures.

A growing trend in recent decades has been for Gaelic poets to publish bilingual versions of their work, that is editions with an English translation opposite the Gaelic. This strategy has increased the potential pool of readers, making it possible to study Gaelic poetry in translation with limited knowledge of the original language. Throughout the late twentieth-century, publishing opportunities for Gaelic poets have remained relatively scarce. Founded in 1952, the journal *Gairm*, or 'The Shout', was for four decades the most important outlet for new Gaelic writing. From the Gaelic for 'The Flood', *An Tuil: An Anthology of 20th Century Gaelic Verse* (1999) offers the most comprehensive collection of recent Gaelic poetry. In Chapter One we saw how Cairns Craig attempted to establish a sense of national continuity through the articulation of a distinctive Scottish literary tradition. The poet and critic Christopher Whyte, who himself learned Gaelic as an adult, argues that Gaelic poetry operates at an inevitable tangent to such nation-centred paradigms. Blind to the pull of the nation, Whyte maintains, Gaelic writing continues to operate by means of its own internal logic. Moreover Gaelic culture in fact predates the overt assertion of Scotland as a nation entity by several centuries. Such facts enable a welcome reprieve from what Whyte regards as the distorting influence of nationalism on the critical imagination in Scotland. He argues that when Gaelic poets did come into contact with other literary cultures, it was quite unlikely that those cultures would have been Scottish. Scottish Gaelic poets are much more likely to have been influenced by Irish Gaelic poetry. Or, if they did have experience with another literature in their formative years it was more than likely to have been English literature.

> ■ If one were to attempt an outline survey of Gaelic poetry and song written in Scotland over the past four centuries, there are real grounds for arguing that the significant intertext, rather than writing elsewhere in Scotland, would be writing in the Irish language of the same period. Where indeed does Gaelic poetry belong? [...] [M]any, perhaps a majority, of the poets dealt with in this study received their schooling and, in most cases, university education at a time when literature as a whole tended to be identified with English literature. Their acculturation, where books and examinations were concerned, took place against an English rather than a Scottish background.[34] □

The poet Iain Crichton Smith is an interesting figure in terms of the relationship between the *Gaeltacht* and the rest of Scotland. Smith admits to growing up on Lewis feeling estranged from any meaningful sense of Scottish national identity:

> ■ I had no feeling for Scotland at all as a country except through football. I didn't feel myself belonging to Scotland. I felt myself as belonging to Lewis. I had never been out of the islands in my whole life [...] I had hardly read any Scottish writers, not even MacDiarmid. Most of the writers I read were English ones. The island was in a way self-sufficient and there were even, strange to relate, many parts of the island I had never visited.[35] □

Ironically of course, due to its bilingual author, Whyte's *Modern Scottish Poetry* is one of the few critical monographs capable of considering Scottish poetry in all three of the nation's languages (Gaelic, Scots and English). In this book Gaelic writers including Iain Crichton Smith, Sorley MacLean (1911–96), Derick Thomson (born 1921) and Aonghas MacNeacail are examined alongside other Scottish poets such as Edwin Morgan, Norman MacCaig (1911–96) and Douglas Dunn (born 1942). As a result, and despite his own avowedly anti-national stance, Whyte's book presents us with one of the most inclusive accounts of Scottish poetry to date.

Derick Thomson's *Introduction to Gaelic Poetry* (1974) remains one of the most comprehensive English language texts about Gaelic poetry. Here he examines the changing contexts and themes of Gaelic writing, from the bardic poets of the early middle ages up to and including modern writers of the mid-twentieth century. Thomson outlines a wholesale transformation within Gaelic poetry of the last hundred years. Gaelic literature has altered fundamentally from a more traditional form of verse into poetry of a much more modern and modernist bent. One of the defining changes within the Gaeltacht during the twentieth-century has been the complete disappearance of the monolingual Gaelic speaker. Several factors have played a part in this narrative including the development of roads and transportation, the arrival of new technology like radio and television, and also the need for people to go to major cities for tertiary level education. By the end of the twentieth-century all Gaelic speakers are also English speakers. This has had a dramatic impact on the range of influences affecting Gaelic verse. We might attempt to describe more traditional Gaelic verse through a number of key characteristics. It existed primarily as part of an oral culture, as a poetry of celebration and participation. The poet's task was to produce an artefact which enabled the audience to participate in their culture. Much of the poetry was meant to be sung and as such, radical innovation was neither valued nor encouraged. Traditional Gaelic verse had to make an immediate impact. The skill lay in the expression of verbal wit and in the well-wrought, highly memorable phrase. In traditional poetry there was no place for the professional literary critic, or at least one that we might recognise today. There was also no meaningful distinction between the critic and the audience, they were one and the same, and a particular poem's success was measured in terms of the acceptance of its listeners. This above all played a determinate role in the poem's survival and dissemination. During the nineteenth and early twentieth-century a rapidly increasing contact between the Gaeltacht and the outside world saw this traditional style of poetry come under increasing pressure. The repertoire of successive generations of poets became increasingly stereotyped and limited in scope. In terms of intellectual content there was an overriding sense of familiarity, understandable for a culture confronting the slowly developing uncertainties associated with the onset of modernity. A lack of rhetorical power, a decline in inventiveness and an over-reliance on formulaic rhythms left much of the verse of this period stagnant and conservative. It is this gradual decay of Gaelic culture that the more modern poets can be seen to confront in the formal and thematic innovations of their own verse.

The writer most regularly identified with this sea-change in Gaelic poetry is Sorley MacLean. Published in 1943, MacLean's *Dàin do Eimhir, or 'Poems to Eimhir' is read as the decisive turning point in the evolution of modern Gaelic verse.* MacLean's journey, from the small island of Raasay off the east coast of Skye, to the University in Edinburgh, and then the battlefields of North Africa during World War II, is indicative of the range of influences and experiences he would draw into his poetry. Rather than existing as a hermetically sealed culture, through MacLean and others, modern Gaelic writing would increasingly incorporate more modernist poetics including those espoused by T. S. Eliot, the American born but Europe-based Ezra Pound (1885–1972) and the Irish poet W. B. Yeats (1865–1939). Whereas more traditional styles of Gaelic verse continued to endure, the globalisation of the twentieth-century exponentially multiplied the range of influences acting on the modern Gaelic poet. Derick Thomson points out that one of the most important developments has been the expansion of the Gaelic vocabulary, a necessary move if the language was to account for all the new experiences endemic to the modern world. He defines the break with the past as occurring on two fronts, one technical and the other thematic:

■ The chief markers of the non-traditional Gaelic verse of this century are perhaps of a technical nature, although this depends on the range of matters we class as technical. Clearly the choice and handling of rhyme, stanza form, and the usual metrical ornaments, are matters of a technical nature, and there has been a clear tendency to use these in a freer way, or to dispense at times with some of them.[36] □

Donald MacAulay's introduction to the anthology *Modern Scottish Gaelic Poems* (1975) identifies a similar tension between the forces of tradition and those of modernity in contemporary Gaelic verse. MacAulay's anthology features English translations of each of its poems and remains the most accessible and rich collection of post-MacLean verse. Rather than present a one-sided lambaste against the encroachment of English, MacAulay is candid about the limitations of traditional Gaelic writing. At the same time, he is particularly alert to the sense of loss that for many writers has come hand in hand with their more cosmopolitan existence.

■ Most of this poetry has been written by people who have been trans-planted out of their native communities into the ubiquitous outside world. Certainly this is true of the contributors to this anthology; they were all processed out in the course of their education, there being often no secondary school in their community, and certainly no university. Their move into the outside world and their contact with their contemporaries especially at their universities has given them a broader vision of life and a greater experience of exotic literary tastes – a new context in which to see their community and its art. At the same time it has created a con-viction in them that they have lost a great deal in exchange for what they have gained. They are strongly dependent emotionally on the communi-ties which were the source of their formative experience and, of course, of their language. But their outside experience has bred an intellectual independence. As Thomson clearly expresses it,

> The heart tied to a tethering post...
> and the mind free.
> I bought its freedom dearly.

They have become bi-cultural and it is this situation, a notoriously uneasy one, which creates the tension from which a great deal of their poetry derives.[37] □

At the beginning of the twenty-first century the future of Gaelic poetry remains uncertain. Some of these issues will be revisited in the conclu-sion to this Guide. If Gaelic writers continued to exist on the margins of Scottish literature, there is one group in particular who would dra-matically step in from the sidelines in the late twentieth-century. As we anticipated in our introduction, this is, of course, women writers.

CHAPTER THREE

Gender

The arrival of women's writing

One of the most significant developments within post-war literary studies in Scotland concerns the understanding, appreciation and visibility of writing by women. Martin Gray argues that in the wake of the 1960s any meaningful analysis of literature in general *must* consider the kind of questions raised by feminist studies:

> ■ Since the late 1960s feminist theories about literature and language, and feminist interpretations of texts have multiplied enormously. Feminist criticism is now a significant area of literary study and discussion, to the point of being a subject of study in itself. The changes in perspective involved in some feminist concepts have been revolutionary, and, as many have observed, the passion with which feminist points of view have been adopted has resembled a religious awakening, sometimes fundamentalist in its energy. Since the feminist revolution, no critic, even if unconvinced by feminist arguments, can write or speak without being to some extent conscious of the role that gender may have in the creation or production of literature or the reader's response to it.[1] □

In contrast to Gray's assertion, until very recently gender has, for the most part, remained a highly marginalised area within Scottish literary studies. Preoccupations with the cultural politics of nationalism have meant that until the 1990s, Scottish criticism showed little interest in the politics of emancipation being pursued by feminist scholars elsewhere. This seems to suggest an enduring and residual patriarchal bias at play in Scotland, one that could not readily be dislodged by the deconstructive energies of feminism that had gathered force in the 1960s. In an essay on this late blossoming relationship between Scottish literature and feminist theory Susanne Hagemann comments:

> ■ Gender is a comparatively recent issue in Scottish literary criticism. It is obviously true of all western cultures that women's writing and the theme of

gender in literature precede the advent of feminist criticism; but Scotland lags behind in another, more significant way. While gender rose to prominence in Anglo-American criticism in the late 1960s and early 1970s, in Scottish criticism this did not happen until the early 1990s. One of the main reasons, it has been argued, is the quest for Scottishness. The small-nation syndrome involved focusing on the quiddity [inherent nature or essence] of Scotland. The double marginalisation of writers who were both Scots and women tended to be overlooked, and the gendering of men's and women's texts long remained outside Scotticist paradigms.[2] □

Hagemann sets up a formal opposition between critical preoccupations with the nation and an interest in questions of gender. As we suggested earlier, there is a sense in which the politics of national identity have exerted a disproportionate influence on the critical imagination in Scotland. As Christopher Whyte argued, this gravitational pull towards cultural nationalism is charged with eclipsing a host of important themes, not least the emancipatory influence of feminism. When female writers were given a place at the table in the 1990s this issue about prioritising loyalties, toward one's sex or one's nation, remained an underlying theme for feminist critics of Scottish literature. In Chapter One of this Guide we saw Douglas Gifford argue that the vitality of contemporary writing signalled a renaissance within Scottish literature. In Chapter Two we saw Cairns Craig trace such exuberance to 'a liberation of the voice', first on the stage and then within the pages of Scotland's poetry and fiction. However, we might think about this recent rude health in a third and entirely different way. One might argue that much of the creative energy of this period was only tangentially related to questions of nationalism or language. Instead we might locate this exuberance within the long-overdue arrival and recognition of writing by Scotland's women.

Feminist theory can be usefully divided into two distinct strands. The first of these we might call socio-historical feminism. This is a discourse primarily interested in the re-examination of literary history, in reading against the grain, so to speak. Socio-historical feminism is particularly concerned with the recovery and re-constitution of women's writing. It seeks to contest the historic exclusion of this body of work from what it regards as patriarchal constructions of the canon. The second strand of feminist theory takes its inspiration from French deconstruction and the kind of psychoanalytic theory initially proposed by Sigmund Freud (1856–1939) and later taken up by the French psychiatrist Jacques Lacan (1901–81). This method seeks to explore the ways in which the subordination of women is interwoven within the very fabric of western culture, particularly in literary practice and the processes of writing and signification. It is in this area that critics like Hélène Cixous (born 1937), Julia Kristeva (born 1941) and Luce Irigaray (born 1930) have been most influential. Among other things this movement in feminist theory sought to articulate a practice of an *écriture féminine*, a mode of writing which deliberately resisted what was regarded as the masculine nature of conventional textual practice. During the 1990s it was first of these branches, a more socio-historically orientated feminism, which began to emerge in the study of Scottish literature. We have already seen Cairns Craig's attempts to challenge T. S. Eliot's dismissal of Scottish literature and in the process reconstruct an alternative Scottish literary tradition. Prior to this more recent reconstitution, the general perception was that the Scottish tradition was almost exclusively a male tradition. On this point we might consider that the canonical figures in Scottish literary history – Burns, Scott, Stevenson, MacDiarmid – have all been men. Furthermore, in many cases these writers' treatment of women, both literally and artistically, has often been highly suspect. Burns's healthy appetite for the opposite sex is well known. Hugh MacDiarmid's attitude was openly dismissive: 'Scottish women of any historical interest are curiously rare [...] our leading Scotswomen have been [...] almost entirely destitute of exceptional endowments of any sort.'[3] This perception, regardless of its truth value, is unequivocally refuted by contemporary Scottish literature and its abundance of writing by women. Kick-started in the 1970s by the poet and dramatist Liz Lochhead, by the end of the century there was no shortage of articulate, intelligent and highly sardonic female writers emerging from Scotland. An incomplete list would include the poets Kathleen Jamie, Jackie Kay, Angela McSeveney (born 1964) and Valerie Gillies (born 1948). A list of prose writers would feature Janice Galloway, A.L. Kennedy, Agnes Owens, Elspeth Davie (1919–95), Candia McWilliam (born 1955), Dilys Rose (born 1954), Anne Donovan (born 1966), Ali Smith (born 1962), Denise Mina (born 1966), Val McDermid (born 1955) and Louise Welsh (born 1965). This chapter seeks to chart the key theoretical debates that have arisen in response to this emergence of creative talent.

The 1980s and 1990s saw the publication of several anthologies that sought to recover the female voices that had been submerged within more traditional accounts of Scottish literary history. These included *The Other Voice: Scottish Women's Writing Since 1808* (1987), *An Anthology of Scottish Women Poets* (1991) and *Modern Scottish Women Poets* (2003). If the stage had been lit by the endeavours of creative writers in the seventies and eighties, the critical response was equally enthusiastic. During the 1990s a number of critical collections emerged that, for the first time, provided adequate space in which to discuss Scottish women's writing. These included Caroline Gonda's *Tea and Leg-Irons: New Feminist Readings from Scotland* (1992), Christopher Whyte's

Gendering the Nation (1995), Douglas Gifford and Dorothy McMillan's *A History of Scottish Women's Writing* (1997), Carol Anderson and Aileen Christianson's *Scottish Women's Fiction: 1920s to 1960s* (2000), and Alison Lumsden and Aileen Christianson's *Contemporary Scottish Women Writers* (2000). The majority of criticism featured in this chapter is drawn from these anthologies. This Guide itself might be read as part of the process of redress that continues to foreground the importance of women's writing in Scotland. Out of the eight writers whose work is featured at length herein, four are women! Having looked at the key themes surrounding Scottish women's writing this chapter will focus on the critical response to two female writers, Liz Lochhead and Janice Galloway. Emerging in the 1970s Lochhead's poetry and her subsequent writing for the stage are generally considered to have laid the foundations for a generation of female writers that would follow in her wake. Maintaining a sense of balance, this chapter will also examine the reactions to one of the most important pieces of women's fiction of this period, Janice Galloway's novel *The Trick is to Keep Breathing* (1989). Before beginning there is a necessary caveat: as with all the chapters in this Guide, Lochhead and Galloway's work has import and resonance far beyond merely the discussion of gender. This is especially relevant as often 'women's writing' can function as a reductive critical idiom, a label which delimits and distorts the significance of the female text. The critic Dorothy McMillan has highlighted the risk implicit in such gender-based critical discourse.

■ The advantages of greater exposure for the writers generated by a variety of ways of conceiving their work must always be balanced against the dangers of ghettoisation and of the production of totalising figures for language, style, belief and concern that may well blur what is special in individual writers, or what these writers have in common with figures who could never be anthologised with them according to the principles of sex or nation.[4] □

Despite the danger of ghettoising women's writing, McMillan justifies such a practice as a means of greatly expanding the critical space afforded to the discussion of this literature:

■ [T]he separation of women's writing from men's in anthologies has worried a number of poets of both sexes. Although I have begun by conceding the problem, I do not believe that this separation need be characterised as ghettoisation. In the 'Introduction' to *A History of Scottish Women's Writing* Douglas Gifford and I said that 'even if the only justification that can be offered for separatism is that it carves out more space to talk about women's writing, then that seems good enough to be going on with'; but I now feel that this is over-apologetic. I think rather that we should be even more pragmatic: all the evidence suggests that the focus on women's writing over the last 30-odd years has made a significant difference to the profile of women writers.[5] □

The work of both Lochhead and Galloway could easily have fallen under the rubric of other chapters in this Guide, for example those dealing with language, class or postmodernism. Chapter six is an attempt to explore the criticism of women's writing outwith any ostensible discussion of gender. Under the aegis of postmodernism it will consider critical responses to the work of two of Scotland's most prominent women writers, Muriel Spark and A.L. Kennedy.

Double marginalisation

In 1979 while interviewing the Canadian author Margaret Atwood (born 1939) for the literary magazine *Cencrastus* the critic William Findlay commented: 'there are and have been very few women writers in Scotland.'[6] The existence of such a blatant critical blind spot raises a number of important questions. Is it the case, as Findlay claims, that Scotland has simply not produced any female writers of distinction? Or, as others have maintained, is it that their work been systematically neglected by what is an inherently masculine and nation-centred critical discourse? Rather than denounce an inherent sexism on the part of the speaker, we might usefully locate this kind of comment within its own historical context. Findlay's assessment in part diagnoses the embryonic state of Scottish studies in the late seventies. It attests to one of a number of ellipses that existed within the discipline at this early stage of development. It is into these darkened rooms that the scholarship of the 1980s and 1990s would increasingly shine its light. Published in 1997, Douglas Gifford and Dorothy McMillan's weighty *History of Scottish Women's Writing* stands as an unequivocal rebuke to this type of historical ignorance. Containing 43 essays in total, the book explores the largely uncharted territory of Scottish women's writing from the sixteenth century to the present day. The quotation below is taken from Gifford and McMillan's introduction where they outline the key theory to have emerged from research into the history of Scottish women's writing: namely, that writing by Scotland's women has suffered from a form of double marginalisation. Just as male Scottish critics have largely ignored writing by women, international feminist scholars have also remained largely uninterested in their work. There is a sense of both an internal and an external neglect at work here. Gifford and MacMillan comment that to date Scottish women's writing has embodied only a 'vestigial presence in whatever larger stories are being told about either the national or the female canons [...] We can, however, claim with some confidence that what has in the past been perceived as the "Scottish Tradition in Literature" has been both male generated and male fixated, particularly on Burns, Scott, Stevenson and MacDiarmid.'[7] The dearth of female writers, or more accurately, their wholesale critical neglect, can be traced across the many surveys of Scottish literature written before the 1980s. In Chapter One of this Guide Peter Kravitz asserted that the arrival of Gray and Kelman rendered obsolete a number of the critical volumes which preceded them. There is a strong case for making similar claims about the arrival of contemporary women's writing in Scotland:

■ The relative absence of women from the official histories of Scottish writing is one thing. Perhaps more alarming and more in need of protest is the regular exclusion of Scottish women from general histories and anthologies of women's writing. Mrs Oliphant [1828–97], Susan Ferrier [1782–1854] and now some twentieth-century writers are recognised but it is taking far too long for many others to find their places. Recent feminist activity in Romantic studies has forced interest again in a number of late eighteenth- and early nineteenth-century Scottish woman poets, notably Joanna Baillie [1762–1851], but a huge number of women writers from Scotland still remain as ladies in waiting. For example, the influence of the Norton Anthologies on what gets taught in institutions of higher education is simply undeniable. The British publication of *The Norton Anthology of Literature by Women* was delayed by copyright problems but eventually appeared in 1996: nothing from Scottish literature, not even one story from Mrs Oliphant, finds a place.[8] □

The Norton Anthology of Literature by Women is over 2,500 pages long and contains the work of 176 different female writers. Born in Wallyford outside Edinburgh, Margaret Oliphant was a prolific Victorian writer who published 98 novels in her lifetime. Within the study of English Literature the rediscovery of women's writing has led to the enthronement of a select group of writers, the 'famous five' as they are colloquially referred to – Jane Austen, Charlotte Brontë (1816–55) and Emily Brontë (1818–48), George Eliot and Virginia Woolf. One of the results of this process has been the relative neglect of other female writers. Their work remains denied the institutional legitimation enjoyed by other female writers brought into this redefined, and ostensibly more equitable, version of the canon. Gifford and McMillan address this specific problem in response to the American feminist critic Elaine Showalter (bron 1941). In *Sister's Choice* (1991) Showalter asserts: 'English women's writing, until the past few decades, was racially homogeneous and regionally compact, with little ethnic, religious, or even class diversity.'[9] For Gifford and McMillan the history of Scottish women's writing cuts across and disrupts such easy generalisations. It maintains the relevance of both region and class, and prevents any simple story of sisterhood that would plaster over the cracks of history.

This idea of a double marginalisation is one of the recurring motifs within the criticism of Scottish women's writing. In her essay 'Canonical Double Cross: Scottish and Irish Women's Writing' Marilyn Reizbaum argues that this type of experience is not just a Scottish phenomenon. Like other critics she reads the Scottish situation as indicative of the more general, global treatment of woman's writing among peripheral cultures. She refers to 'a phenomenon of "double exclusion" suffered by women writing in marginalized cultures [...] where the struggle to assert a nationalist identity obscures or doubly marginalizes the assertion of gender.'[10] Reizbaum evokes affinities between the experiences of women writers in Scotland and those in Ireland. Her essay is particularly interested in how their work has been subordinated within a critical discourse that favours masculine ideologies like nationalism. The treatment of Scottish and Irish women's writing within their respective national canons is seen to mirror the experience of marginalised cultures around the world:

■ The feminist call in Scotland and Ireland for the reformulation of the canon of Scottish and Irish works parallels the challenge to the mainstream Anglo-American establishment presented by Scotland, Ireland, and other countries or cultures like them – former colonies who retain a marginalized standing in relation to the former colonizer. For example, while British anthologies often ignore Scottish and Irish authors, anthologies of Scottish and Irish writing typically treat women writers with the same disregard.[11] □

Again we notice the rhetoric of postcolonial theory being employed to describe the cultural terrain in Scotland. Nationalism is seen to act as a form of internal colonialism, subordinating and marginalising minority groups, in this case, women. The irony, of course, is that far from being a minority, women actually constitute 50 per cent of the population. Reizbaum's analysis of Scotland anticipates the work of the Indian postcolonial critic Gayatri Chakravorty Spivak (born 1942) and her seminal essay 'Can the Subaltern Speak?' (1995). Here Spivak examined the ways in which Indian independence merely reconfigured the networks of power which had been established under colonialism. For peasant women in India decolonisation did not entail a fundamental liberation. Instead it merely evinced the renewal and reconfiguration of pre-existing power structures as the native Indian elite, predominantly bourgeois and male, assumed the reins of power within the country. For Reizbaum this idea has come to define the way in which the study of minor cultures has subsequently been conducted: 'when a culture has been marginalized, its impulses toward national legitimization tend to dominate in all spheres and forms of cultural realisation.'[12]

The implication is that in places like Scotland women's interests have tended to run contrary to the perceived national interest. Novelist Janice Galloway articulates a similar view about the antagonism between nationalism and the politics of gender. She argues that historically the assertion of a female agenda in Scotland was at best regarded as a distraction and at worst an act of selfish disloyalty. Feminist concerns served only to deflect radical energy from the 'real' political struggle which in Scotland's case is, of course, the national one.

> ■ Scottish women have their own particular complications with writing and definition, complications which derive from the general problems of being a colonised nation. Then, that wee extra touch. Their sex. There is coping with that guilt of taking time off the concerns of national politics to get concerned with the sexual sort: that creeping fear it's somehow self-indulgent to be more concerned for one's womanness instead of one's Scottishness, one's working class heritage or whatever. Guilt here comes from the notion we're not backing up our menfolk and their 'real' concerns. Female concerns, like meal on the mother's plate, are extras after the man and the weans have been served.[13] □

For Galloway Scottish culture has in the past proffered little more than a set of clichéd and stereotypical representations of female identity. It is against such limited imaginative horizons that her own work strives to assert itself:

> ■ A particularly Scottish set of strangling caricatures make it hard to escape such guilt – from Maw Broon or one of the McIlvanney parade of miracle workers, silent sufferers and mystical creatures with tides and moons, brave nurturers all – they serve exactly the same message as the one served up from the general establishment's canon all these years. Nurture or be deviant and sorry. Pursue your own goals only if you acknowledge it as selfishness. (Non-nurturers are sex-starved old women or morally reprehensible – literal or metaphorical tarts.) So, on top of working out how to write (which is hard enough), on top of the need to reinvent the wheel, on top of finding time, there's the guilt, the guilt. Always the guilt.[14] □

From the Scottish comic series *The Broons,* mother of eight Maw Broon is tasked with running every aspect of the household and keeping Paw Broon in line. Galloway's comments echo those of Christopher Whyte regarding the debilitating effect of critical fixations on nationalism.

Whyte himself has also written extensively about the gender politics of Scottish literature. His work addresses not only literature by women, but also examines the kind of questions posed by gay and lesbian writing. The quotation below is taken from Whyte's introduction to the anthology *Gendering the Nation* (1995). Here he considers the antagonistic relationship between feminism, the politics of sexual minorities and their critical hegemony of cultural nationalism. Whyte asks whether or not in a country like Scotland it is more difficult to be a straight woman, or for that matter, a lesbian or a gay man.

■ 'Nationalism is always bad news for women.' When one of the participants at an academic day seminar I attended just over a year ago came out with this statement, I stopped to think. I wasn't just thinking if it was true. The tactical implications of the statement interested me [...] It would mean that cultures where nationalism was an acknowledged issue were by that very fact less tolerant of women (and therefore of other marginal groups, be they black, lesbian or gay). One could call them small cultures, minority cultures, nations without a state. [...] Anyone casting an eye over the canonical texts of twentieth-century Scottish literature would find much to support this statement. Scottish literature has succeeded, against all the odds, in emerging from under the shadows of English literature and establishing its own tentative canon. The texts in question are almost exclusively by male authors.[15] □

If there has been a shift in attitudes towards women's writing and the representation of female experience, for Whyte the same cannot be said about explorations of masculinity. Instead of a break he locates a sense of continuity between Scottish writing of the past and the present. Whyte maintains that the portrayal of working-class masculinity in the fiction of writers like William McIlvanney and James Kelman echoes the unsatisfactory models offered by Hugh MacDiarmid and Neil Gunn back in the 1920s. Whyte remains sceptical that there has been any real sense of liberation in terms of minority sexual politics within the pages of Scottish literature:

■ Much of contemporary Scottish writing has a narrow and drearily male focus, from the aggressive penis-centredness of MacDiarmid's *A Drunk Man* to Neil Gunn's men and women with their sharply differentiated roles, stereotypical behaviour and incredible prudishness about sex, from the tirelessness with which McIlvanney and Kelman go on exhuming outdated icons of maleness [...] Scottishness is about drink and football, interspersed with brief episodes of violence in a home where cold, wounded and rejecting wives and mothers have little comfort to offer. What, one wonders can the country described in these books offer women, children and men with minds of their own?[16] □

Simon Kovesi's study of James Kelman adamantly disagrees with locating the author's engagement with working-class masculinity within this type of misogynistic paradigm. For Kovesi *The Busconductor Hines* is a novel that deliberately questions many of the assumptions about masculinity.[17] Throughout the text Hines is seen to perform a number of historically female roles within the family. He shares child care responsibilities with his wife Sandra and he also cooks many of the family meals. At the same time as a white collar office worker Sandra is seen to be a more reliable breadwinner. Rather than merely regurgitate the same outmoded version of masculinity Kelman is specifically interested in the transformative nature of gender roles within post-industrial society. Berthold Schoene has also written at length about the issue of masculinity in contemporary Scottish literature in publications like *Writing Men* (2000) and *Posting the Male: Masculinities in Post-war and Contemporary British Literature* (2003).

The end of the twentieth century has witnessed a gradual acceptance of sexual minorities, although homophobia still exists as a problematically acceptable part of mainstream British culture. Contemporary Scottish literature has been sensitive to this changing climate. Edwin Morgan, an established poet since the 1960s, famously came out as a gay man as he celebrated his seventieth birthday in 1990. In retrospect, collections such as *The Second Life*, published in 1968, could be read in terms of Morgan's attempt to explore and express what was then a necessarily covert sexual identity. A degree of conservatism and an element of prudishness, part of the Calvinist hangover perhaps, can often be detected in Scottish attitudes toward sex and sexuality. Homosexuality, for example, was not legalised in Scotland until 1980, a full 13 years after the law had been changed in England. More recently, a number of gay and lesbian writers have sought to interrogate the issues pertaining to their sexuality in a more open and deliberate way. Notable examples include Jackie Kay and Ali Smith. Having said this, their writing and the treatment of such themes within Scottish literature still awaits the level of detailed critical scrutiny it undoubtedly deserves.

Returning to feminism, the competing prioritisation of gender and nation and their apparent antinomy, has been a primary focus for the critic Aileen Christianson. In contrast to Whyte, Christianson reads contemporary Scottish literature as having much to offer the purveyor of women's writing. The extract below is taken from her essay 'Gender and nation: Debatable lands and passable boundaries.' Christianson begins by defining nationalism in terms of its historical construction as an inherently masculine discourse. She endorses the sense of the double marginalisation outlined by Marilyn Reizbaum above. Christianson argues that writing by contemporary Scottish women offers a number of ways in which exclusionary and elliptical models of national identity may be revealed and ultimately reconfigured:

> ■ If nationalism is a post-rationalist or enlightenment substitute for religion, with fake-historical roots to legitimise it, as Benedict Anderson argues, then given the patriarchal, male centred nature of Christianity and most other world religions, and the oppressive nature of their relation to women, it is inevitable that the construction of the idea of the 'nation' should have been equally male-centred and patriarchal, manifesting itself in the traditions of warrior nations, warrior clan systems, with women as bearers of warriors or symbolic female figures of nationhood – the equivalent nationalistic muses to the traditionally female poetic muse.[18] □

Christianson argues that although Scotland did manage to maintain a distinct national identity in key cultural institutions, such as the Church and the law, the historic exclusion of women from full participation in either of these spheres has meant that, until very recently, such markers of Scottishness have continued to offer a partial and incomplete model of national culture:

> ■ If Scotland's sense of nationhood has a civic rather than an ethnic base, with our surviving national institutions such as the law and education, and the mixed ethnic origins of Scots, then it is not surprising that women may feel excluded from a full sense of being part of *this* imagined relation. Only in the last twenty-five years or less have women been able to participate fully in the civic institutions that constitute our nationness.[19] □

The emergence of female voices in the last 25 years marks a highly significant chapter in the history of Scottish literature. For Christianson this development mirrors the emergence of Scottish literature from the shadow of English Literature and its consolidation as a discrete object of critical interest. She quotes Janice Galloway who sees similar parallels in these coincidental moments of liberation:

> ■ [T]o reprioritise, to speak as though your norms are the ones that matter, is what's happening to Scottish writing as well recently. Scottish writers have started writing as though their language and national priorities signify, whereas for years we took on the fiction that they didn't. The Let's Imagine That We Matter thing is important. *What if I don't accept that I'm marginal, add-on territory* – it's the same root for me.[20] □

A similar tone of celebratory enunciation is present in the collection of essays, edited by Christianson and Alison Lumsden, *Contemporary*

Scottish Women Writers. This volume includes work on poetry, gothic writing and the short story, alongside individual studies of Kathleen Jamie, Liz Lochhead, Jackie Kay, Muriel Spark, Candia McWilliam, Agnes Owens, Janice Galloway and A.L. Kennedy. In the quotation below Lumsden and Christianson attempt to invert what has historically been a debilitating or unprofitable relationship between nation and gender. In contrast to the earlier critics, they suggest a new configuration in which nation and gender might be rearranged in a more symbiotic and meaningful opposition. They maintain that conceptions of a literary tradition premised on a predominantly masculine inheritance are no longer tenable in the context of contemporary Scottish writing:

■ The 1990s have seen the addition of many new Scottish women writing from a more confident assumption that being female and being Scottish are linked and culturally positive. The breadth of the work by contemporary women writers necessitates a redrawing of the literary map of Scotland. allowing for these writers a natural assumption of place in a culture previously more accessible to male Scottish writers. Women writers have become fully part of 'the bedrock' of this 'small / and multitudinous country'.[21] □

Post-war Scottish history, like that of many western countries, evinces a rapid transformation in the role, expectation and opportunity presented to women. For Lumsden and Christianson writing by and about women has played a key role in the vanguard of such 'alternative imaginings'. They maintain that it is the plural nature of identity that provides the key to understanding the relationship between gender and nationality in the twenty-first century.

■ [W]e must be wary of *assuming* that peripheralisation of nation can be straightforwardly equated with that of gender. Anderson argues that 'Communities are to be distinguished, not by their falsity / genuineness, but by the style in which they are imagined', but what is frequently interesting about the women writers discussed here is the way in which their work cuts across patriarchal constructions of Scotland to suggest alternative 'imaginings' or constructions of nationhood and their relationship to it than those offered by their male counterparts. Frequently, it is women writers within national cultures who seemingly disrupt homogeneity [...] Now that a greater degree of autonomy has been achieved in Scotland and what many would regard as the common political goal attained, what begins to emerge is a sense, or a reminder, of Scotland's own lack of homogeneity. Within its compact national boundaries there are significant geographical and cultural differences between Highland and Lowland Scotland, north-east, east and west, mainland and (diverse) islands.[22] □

For Lumsden and Christianson there is a sense in which our criticism of contemporary women's writing must avoid the kind of generalisation, the spurious quest for wholeness or completeness, which have characterised readings of Scottish literature in the past. We must remain open and alert to the possibility that the terms 'Scottish' and 'woman' can only be applied in the very loosest sense. Any attempt to construct a critical discourse from these terms must do so in full acknowledgement of the inevitable heterogeneity of its subject matter:

> ■ What perhaps is most notable about Scottish women writers today is their diversity; they write in a number of styles and genres and take as their subject-matter a wide variety of themes. Such a body of work means, similarly, that it is impossible to write critically of this work in only one way. There is 'no one version' either of women's writing in Scotland today or of critical response to it.[23] □

The heterogeneity of contemporary Scottish women's writing is played out across every literary genre. It is with this in mind that we turn our attention to the recent proliferation of writing by women in the field of poetry.

Poetry and gender

If Scottish literature has been a particularly masculine affair, then such inequalities are perhaps most visible in the field of poetry. An exclusively male lineage defines the evolution of the Scottish poetic tradition. The cast list of key players, from medieval Makars to mercurial Modernists is almost exclusively male – Henryson, Dunbar, Ferguson, Burns, MacDiarmid, Muir. This type of gender imbalance remained characteristic of the Scottish poetry scene for the first half of the twentieth century. One of its most clear illustrations is the painting by Alexander Moffat (born 1943) entitled 'Poet's Pub' (1980). The painting offers a snapshot of the bohemian literary life that characterised the Rose Street pubs of Edinburgh during the 1960s. It contains the ten most well known poets of the period: Hugh MacDiarmid, George MacKay Brown, Robert Garioch, Norman MacCaig, Sorley MacLean, Edwin Morgan, Iain Crichton Smith, Sydney Goodsir Smith, Alan Bold and John A. Tonge. Again what is most prevalent is the glaring absence of one thing: women. Prior to the 1970s, when Liz Lochhead burst onto the scene, the public profile of Scottish poetry was decidedly male. For the critic Joy Hendry such models are not an innocent reflection of an organic reality in which there simply weren't many female poets to speak of. Instead, Hendry argues that this model is symptomatic of a critical neglect whereby the work of female writers has been systematically downgraded to the status of mere song or verse:

■ The ratio of mentions, men to women, in critical tomes and anthologies is perhaps not the most definitive of literary yardsticks, but it can be revealing to discover in these volumes the degree to which the contribution of women in twentieth-century Scottish writing has been minimised and marginalised, particular in poetry [...] It is a widely held assumption in feminist thinking that in the male-dominated world, poetry as queen of the literary arts was clutched more lovingly to the male bosom. Like the role of the priest or mage, the role of the poet or bard was reserved for men, and women were kept at arms length, their poetic efforts, if any emerged, dismissed as either 'song' or 'verse'.[24] □

Hendry outlines her own version of the double marginalisation theory identified earlier: 'I invented the phrase the "double knot in the peeny" [peeny being the Scots word for pinafore] to describe the double disadvantage suffered by Scottish women writers in being firstly Scottish and secondly female.'[25] 'Peeny' is, of course, a highly appropriate metaphor; the double knot suggesting an added determination to secure women in their pinafores and hence confine them to a life of domestic drudgery. Hendry's argument that female poets have been much maligned by a patriarchal critical tradition finds support in Catherine Kerrigan's *Anthology of Scottish Women Poets* (1991). Kerrigan's book sought to re-discover the lost voices of Scotland's female poets. It features the work of over 100 female poets, in all three of Scotland's languages, dating from the eighteenth century to the present day. What is significant for Kerrigan is that differences generated by history, class or region are elided under a story of transgenerational sisterhood. It is this strategy which enables her to claim that there is a hidden, yet nonetheless coherent, tradition of Scottish women's poetry.

■ In the recovery of women's writing, the novel (for obvious reasons) has played a more important part than poetry. Yet, as I believe this anthology will show, it is in poetry that we find the most sustained tradition of women's writing. The work presented here, while rooted in a distinct geographical location, records an enormous range of poetry by women – ballads, working songs, political verse, love songs, satire, historical narratives, and much more. Dating back to at least the eighteenth century, this work crosses the boundaries of class, place and time to form an extraordinary continuum.[26] □

Other critics have disputed the validity of such gender-based narratives. In their introduction to *A History of Scottish Women's Writing* Douglas Gifford and Dorothy McMillan assert the limitations of exclusive female traditions. They make the sensible observation that women writers have often drawn positive inspiration from the work of their male contemporaries: 'A smooth story of sisterhood and continuity, subterranean or otherwise, may involve papering over the cracks, the ideological fissures between women writers. And also to recognise that women writers may often not have looked to "mothers" or "sisters" but rather to "fathers" and "brothers" as their literary forbears and present support.'[27]

Whether we maintain that Scottish female poets have been critically neglected, or that a significant body of women's writing simply did not exist, what cannot be denied is the sheer explosion of women's writing during the latter decades of the twentieth century. In comparison to Moffat's 'Poet's Pub', Donny O'Rourke's anthology *Dream State* features the work of 36 contemporary poets, one third of which are women. Scottish female poets have begun to enjoy an unprecedented degree of recognition both within and notably beyond Scotland. Glasgow-born Carol Ann Duffy won the Whitbread Poetry Award for her *Mean Time* (1993), while her more recent book *Rapture* received the T.S. Eliot Prize in 2006. Born in Renfrewshire Kathleen Jamie has enjoyed similar acclaim, winning the Somerset Maugham Award in 1994 and the Geoffrey Faber Memorial Prize in both 1996 and 2000. At the same time Jackie Kay's debut poetry collection, *The Adoption Papers* (1991), was awarded the Forward Poetry Prize. Ironically, the critical acclaim these female poets have received outside Scotland stands in direct contrast to the lack of international recognition garnered by their male antecedents such as MacDiarmid. The person traditionally credited with kicking the door down and opening the way for this generation came to prominence in Glasgow during the 1970s. Liz Lochhead's poetry combined a sharp eye and a quick tongue, and would mark an important change in direction for a generation of Scottish female writers that followed in her wake.

Liz Lochhead

Liz Lochhead is often regarded as a pioneer, an original frontier rider setting out across the badlands of a male dominated Scottish literature. Her debut collection *Memo for Spring* (1972) has been hailed as a decisive turning point in the evolution of women's writing in Scotland. In the introduction to *Modern Scottish Women Poets*

Dorothy McMillan comments: 'apart from [certain] exceptions we have to wait for Liz Lochhead for a modern craft that consistently comes close in its awareness of the new to the male writers. After her, generalisation is less easy.'[28] Lochhead's highly original voice set the tone for the confident iconoclasm which has come to characterise much contemporary writing by Scottish women. Margery Palmer McCulloch asserts: 'For the first time in Scottish poetry, readers were being confronted by poetry of high quality written about women's lives and women's perceptions of our human world, and written from the inside by a female poet using a modern idiom, in which metaphorical language and imagery was drawn from female experience.'[29] The poet Jackie Kay acknowledges her debt to Lochhead in the poem 'Kail and Callaloo' confessing: 'Liz was my teenage hero.'[30] Lochhead followed *Memo for Spring* with *Islands* (1978), *The Grimm Sisters* (1981), *Dreaming Frankenstein* (1984) and *Bagpipe Muzak* (1991). Performance and revue increasingly formed a major part of her repertoire, most notably in *True Confessions and New Clichés* (1985). Such developments indicated Lochhead's growing inclination toward the stage and dramaturgy. Throughout the 1980s she wrote several highly acclaimed plays – *Blood and Ice* (1982), *Dracula* (1989) and, most famously, *Mary Queen of Scots Got Her Head Chopped Off* (1989).

A key book in the critical interrogation of Lochhead's work is the collection edited by Robert Crawford entitled *Liz Lochhead's Voices* (1993). The volume features a number of critics examining various aspects of Lochhead's oeuvre. In his introduction Crawford identifies the male domain of Scottish literature that Lochhead entered in 1972 with the publication of *Memo for Spring*. If one looks at the poetry anthologies published just prior to this date, the preponderance of male writers is emphatic. Norman MacCaig and Alexander Scott's anthology *Contemporary Scottish Verse 1959–1969* (1970) contains 240 poems, of which only two are by women. Similarly Charles King's 1971 school text *Twelve Modern Scottish Poets* features only male poets. For Crawford, rather than denoting a cultural conspiracy, these anthologies reflect the relative absence of female voices from the Scottish poetry scene of the period.[31] The arrival of Lochhead, of course, would change all this. Crawford's own essay in the book looks to contextualise Lochhead's work in terms of the poetry scene she entered in the early seventies.

In an effort to illustrate the range and scope of Lochhead's art, the following section will juxtapose three different readings of her early poem 'Morning After.' In an essay entitled 'The Mirror and the Vamp' the critic Anne Varty focuses on the poem's specific implications for the politics of gender. The title of 'Morning After' evokes a number of important and interrelated themes. The title anticipates the female contraceptive pill which first became available in the 1970s and in more recent years has come to be known as the morning after pill. This technology was of monumental significance in female liberation, enabling women greater control over their bodies than ever before. For the first time women were able to engage in sexual activity free from the worry and social stigma attached to unwanted pregnancy. Lochhead's poem depicts the morning after a sexual encounter, with the two lovers at breakfast having spent the night together. They are both reading newspapers (*The Mirror* and *The Observer*) which function as metaphors for the unspoken sexual politics that underpin the scene. The female figure in the poem is equated with *The Mirror*. She is a secondary object, designed to reflect and flatter the masculine gaze. The male is aligned with *The Observer*, a broadsheet newspaper with connotations of intellectual gravitas and seriousness. There is also an implicit reference to the male gaze, a much vaunted area of feminist theory which describes the disempowering ways in which men objectify women. With reverberations of Aileen Christianson above, Varty aligns the sexual politics of the poem with questions of nationalism and Scotland's status as the weaker partner in the union with England. Varty comments:

■ The two newspapers named are both English; the allusion is therefore to the hierarchy of British politics. Syntactic elision of the verb 'to read' makes a metaphor of the relationship between reader and paper, so that the woman is not just associated with the tabloid, she actually is 'the mirror', a reflective role that is not so far from that of 'observer' as a first glance suggests. Despite the possible collapse of the distinction between 'mirror' and 'observer', conflicts between power and powerless, active and passive, man and woman, Scots and English, recurring polarities of Lochhead's work, operate here. And they anticipate her view that 'the English are like men – nonchalant and unquestioning about existing,' while 'Scotland is like a woman; the Scots know they are perceived from the outside'.[32] □

Whilst the cross-pollination of these themes becomes a leitmotif of Lochhead's later work, particularly *Mary Queen of Scots Got Her Head Chopped Off*, it is not as obvious in her early poetry. Lochhead herself has commented that in her early work she was not particularly interested in exploring issues related to the state of Scotland: 'until recently I have felt that my country was woman.'[33] The mapping of gender politics onto a larger narrative, one which reveals the power relationship between Scotland and England, echoes a familiar interpretive strategy which regards the 1707 Act of Union as a marriage of convenience, the Scots dowry being greater access to the opportunities of the British Empire. Varty goes on to describe Lochhead's willingness to disagree with rank-and-file feminist politics which is something the poet herself has commented on. For Lochhead an important aspect of her work is the degree to which it is willing to confront women and their occasional complicity in the dominant values of patriarchal society:

> ■ I'm very ambivalent about women: they're people with problems too. I get at them because I am one of them. I'm allowed to. Although I am a feminist, I don't want to give my writing back only to women, I don't want to become a feminist separatist, nor do I want to 'solve the world' solely for women because I find that position too bleak. I don't have a lot of faith in much of the male culture that's around in Scotland, but I think of its recent macho flowering as a last bastion, a mask. I don't like the splitting apart of the male and female that we have. What I would ideally like to do is give the male halves of themselves back to the women, and the female halves of themselves back to the men. We are divided within ourselves and the real task is the completion of selves.[34] □

Varty conceives Lochhead's poetry as interrupting some of the less self-aware, more dogmatic aspects of feminist theory. Throughout her work the poet exhorts that women are not to be exonerated as the innocent victims that many feminist writers would have us believe.

In direct contrast to Varty, Christopher Whyte argues that the feminist credentials of Lochhead's work are highly compromised. He suggests that the gender politics of her poetry are all too amenable to the mainstream, and hence masculine, discourse of Scottish criticism. Despite her artistic intentions Whyte claims Lochhead merely reproduces the kind of binary opposition (male-female, rational-emotional, strong-weak etc) that other feminist critics deliberately resist. Whyte's position is here informed by the work of Hélène Cixous and the concepts associated with *écriture féminine*.[35] He regards Lochhead's poetry as being constrained by the terms 'Scottish women's writing' and laments its reluctance to critique the reductive nature of such critical labels. Moreover, he maintains that Lochhead has been appropriated by nationalist critics in a dubious attempt to reconstitute Scottish literature, paying lip service to a more inclusive and heterogeneous body of writing.

> ■ Liz Lochhead's [poetry] in retrospect appears weakened by its commitment to a specific feminist agenda and the sometimes facile oppositions this implies.
>
> 'Morning After', from her 1972 collection *Memo for Spring*, exemplifies some of these problems, while at the same time highlighting aspects of Lochhead's style which were to become characteristic. The

female speaker has stayed over after a Saturday night of lovemaking and is now on tenterhooks, pretending to read a Sunday newspaper while in fact concentrating all her attention on the otherwise occupied male sitting next to her. She is in a victim position, begging wordlessly that he should focus on her rather than on the news, and the desultory attention he devotes to the pages of the colour section, reading them with 'too passing/an interest' becomes emblematic of his attitude to her. Lochhead makes no attempt to tip over the inherently unstable power relations in this situation, for it is the woman who both narrates and attributes meaning. The latter is done within well-worn stereotypes, with an adroit yet arch play on the newspapers' names [...] [T]he very nature of the search commits her to an ideology of gender oppositions which threatens to undermine any success she might achieve.[36] □

For Whyte, Lochhead's use of such oppositional thinking sees her employ the kind of conceptual framework which French feminist critics have sought to denounce. *Écriture féminine* was an attempt to delineate a much more fluid concept of writing. Hélène Cixous argued that a phallocentric and misogynist system of power was predicated on a form of oppositional thinking that contrasted male with female, rational with irrational, and so on. *Écriture feminine* advocated a way of writing that sought to eschew this mode of writing. It would be non-linear, cyclical and would literally embody the female. Whyte argues that Lochhead remained too amenable to traditional thinking about gender difference and as such 'risked becoming the kind of woman writer (and the very phrase is problematic) men are not afraid of, one who can all too easily be digested by and absorbed into the literary and academic establishment.'[37] In the end though, Whyte is somewhat understanding: 'Perhaps it was historically inevitable, even essential, that Lochhead should have sought to mark out a space with the ungrateful label "Scottish woman poet" attached to it, and then to inhabit that space.'[38]

Colin Nicholson would fundamentally disagree with Whyte's critique of Lochhead's feminist credentials. His reading of Lochhead focuses on her third collection of poems *The Grimm Sisters* which, as the pun in the title suggests, seeks to deconstruct the treatment of women within archetypal narrative including fairytale and myth. In doing so Lochhead can be seen to expose the patriarchal values embedded within such apparently innocent texts. In the quotation below Nicholson argues that Lochhead's later poetry is more complex, employing a range of strategies to satirise the misrepresentation of female identity. *The Grimm Sisters*, a pun on the German brothers Jacob Grimm (1785–1863) and Wilhelm Grimm (1786–1859), seeks to question fairytales and their preponderance of neglectful mothers, vindictive grannies and wicked step-sisters.

■ The original tales involve social, often marital or familial, relationships which are as observable, *mutatis mutandis* [the necessary changes having been made], elsewhere in Lochhead's writing. They propose stances and circumstances which Lochhead's satiric wit would always mould to her own intentions. Given the recurrence not only of wicked stepmothers and evil queens but also, in Hansel and Gretel, a mother who schemes for the deliberate abandonment of her own children, it is appropriate that 'The Mother' should turn archetypal account to disturbing contemporaniety, again incorporating elements from different tales, before concluding with comic incredulity [...] A constant concern in *The Grimm Sisters* is with a satiric subversion of the female stereotype, moulded according to priorities imposed from elsewhere, and interpreted according to dominant preferences. We watch Lochhead expropriating linguistic territory hitherto in male possession, as she satirises and parodies male assumptions about the social construction of reality.[39] □

This type of intertextuality was to become a regular trope within Lochhead's later work. Drawing heavily on the story of Mary Shelley (1797–1851), the title poem from the collection *Dreaming Frankenstein* explores the complex relationship between femininity and creativity, in both a biological and artistic sense. This technique also informs Lochhead's writing for the stage which became an increasing preoccupation during the 1980s. *Dracula* explores the bourgeoning and uncontrolled female sexuality that hovers in the margins of the original 1897 novel by Bram Stoker (1847–1912). The history of Mary Stuart (1542–87) and Elizabeth I (1533–1603; reigned 1558–1603) forms the basis of Lochhead's most successful play *Mary Queen of Scots Got Her Head Chopped Off*. In their essay 'Putting New Twists to Old Stories' Jen McDonald and Jennifer Harvie read this inter-textuality in terms of a specifically feminist preoccupation within Lochhead's work. In defamiliarising various historical and literary narratives one of Lochhead's goals is to expose how questions of gender remain crucial to the politics of popular culture and our understanding of the past.

■ Lochhead's plays do not simply repeat and thus reify 'official' versions of myths and legends or their subversions promulgated, and accepted, by popular culture. Rather, Lochhead's work reconfigures each story, both thematically and structurally, from a feminist standpoint [...] Lochhead's plays re-examine the myths, roles, and images, which historically have limited the signifying possibilities of 'women' – and hence the roles open to women.[40] □

In *Mary Queen of Scots* Lochhead makes extensive use of a dramatic technique known as *Vefremsdungseffekt,* or alienation effect. This theatrical practice is synonymous with the work of the German playwright Berthld Brecht (1898–1956). Made famous in plays such as *Mother Courage and Her Children* (1938–39), Brecht's aim was to prevent the audience from passively losing themselves in the performance on stage. Instead, the audience were encouraged to recognise that what they were watching was an artificially constructed piece of art. Their role was to assume the stance of critical observer, cognizant of and alert to the political and ethical implications of the production. This strategy allows us to locate Lochhead's drama within the kind of postmodern theoretical framework which will be addressed in Chapter Six of this Guide. McDonald and Harvie employ the term 'meta-textual' in describing the relationship between Lochhead's plays and the historical and fictional sources upon which they are based:

■ Metatextuality thus acts as one of several alienation devices evident in Lochhead's plays, each device estranging the audience from a complacent acceptance of the 'reality' presented in each play, and encouraging scepticism about any notion of reality as 'true', fixed, and therefore unchangeable. From *Blood and Ice*, to *Dracula*, to *Mary Queen of Scots Got Her Head Chopped Off*, elements which might contribute to audience alienation increase, so that the audience's fixity of perspective is likewise increasingly problematised. The plays' audiences are presented with increasingly unresolved and unresolvable texts, thus suggesting that the process of creating meaning may be more significant than the final stable product. Actively representing women rather than providing static representations, Lochhead's plays encourage fluid, adaptable understandings of 'women' and 'femininity', resisting appropriation into a stable and therefore potentially reductive model.[41] □

Such notions of fluidity challenge Whyte's criticism that Lochhead's work problematically neglects the feminist arguments concerning *écriture féminine* that were originally developed as part of French deconstructionism.

Besides addressing questions of gender, critics have sought to locate Lochhead's work in a variety of other contexts. This is part of a mindful approach to the dangers of ghettoising women's writing as primarily, or exclusively, interested in the politics of gender. Colin Nicholson argues:

■ Lochhead has made it her business to attend to the otherwise unremarkable circumstances and concerns that give definition to countless lives. Focusing upon the everyday, including the predictability of a hitherto constricting range of phrase and saying, she delivers cfrystalline expression in which the commonplace comes newly edged. As an apparently exhausted demotic finds invigoration, we look again at what might otherwise be passed by.[42] □

This concern with re-imagining the everyday and with a commitment to vernacular speech suggests that Lochhead had much in common with many of her west of Scotland *male* contemporaries such as Kelman, Gray, Leonard. There is a coherent reading of her work which situates its creative contours as following similar lines to these and other male writers. We are reminded of McMillan and Gifford's point, that brother and father figures are often as important to the female writer as those of a sister or mother.

Another writer influenced by the formal experimentation of her Scottish male contemporaries is Janice Galloway. Galloway confesses to falling in love with Alasdair Gray's *Lanark* when it first appeared in 1981. Whilst Lochhead's poetry has been accused of promulgating the kind of binary thinking which *écriture féminine* sought to denounce, Galloway's debut novel, *The Trick is to Keep Breathing* (1989), was more explicit in its attempts to represent the unstable and unhinged portrait of contemporary female experience. One of the most striking aspects of the novel is its use of textual experimentation to interrogate what it means to exist as a woman in our late capitalist consumer-driven culture. The novel diagnoses not only the ways in which women are sidelined by mainstream social values, but also how marginalisation is manifest in other spheres, not least in our attitudes toward issues of mental health.

Janice Galloway

If Lochhead's poetry announced the arrival of a female voice that was original and highly irreverent, Scottish fiction would soon harbour a similar set of energies in the work of Janice Galloway. Born in 1956 in Saltcoats, Ayrshire, Galloway made her literary debut in 1989 with *The Trick is to Keep Breathing*. Published by Peter Kravitz at Polygon after a recommendation by James Kelman, the story of the book's production embodies to a degree the sense of community that existed within Scottish writing during this period. It also reminds us of the importance of local publishing houses to the success of local writing during this period. *The Trick is to Keep Breathing* was shortlisted for both the Whitbread First Novel Award and the Irish Times International Fiction Prize. Its interest in mental health enabled it to qualify for and win the Mind Book of the Year award. Galloway followed this up with a collection of short stories *Blood* (1991), a second novel *Foreign Parts* (1994) and another collection of stories *Where You Find It* (1996). In 2002 she published *Clara*, a fictionalised account of the life of Clara Schumann (1819–96), wife of the famous Austrian composer Robert Schumann

(1810–56). The recovery and reinstatement of Clara's story, a composer and piano virtuoso in her own right, is symptomatic of the strong feminist vein that runs through Galloway's work. In the author's own words:

> ■ Simply for a woman to write as a woman, to be as honest about it as possible, is a statement; not falling into the conventions of assuming that guy stuff is 'real' stuff and we're a frill, a fuck or a boring bit that does housework or raises your kids round the edge. That stuff is not round the edge! It's the fucking middle of everything. Deliberately pointing up that otherness, where what passes for normal has no bearing on you or ignores you – that fascinates me.[43] □

In recognition of her growing stature the *Edinburgh Review* published a special edition devoted to Galloway's work in 2004. It contained 13 essays examining among other themes the author's interest in feminism, consumerism, alienation, and violence. *The Trick is to Keep Breathing* is arguably the most widely written about Galloway text and it is the critical reaction to this book that the remainder of this chapter is focused on. The novel centres on the experience of a middle-aged school teacher Joy Stone who, whilst on holiday with her lover, witnesses his accidental drowning. On returning home Joy suffers from depression, experiences acute mental breakdown and eventually finds herself in a psychiatric institution. In representing the reality of late-twentieth century female experience the text is highly experimental in regards to the novel as a literary form. Joy's narrative is interwoven with regular set pieces. These seek to parody various representations of female identity within popular culture. The often contradictory and pernicious messages provided by fashion magazines, with their problem pages, horoscopes and recipes, form a particular target within Galloway's fiction. The layout of the text is also highly unusual. Several scenes appear as dramatic scripts with the characters becoming actors in their own lives, merely reading out their lines. We are asked to what extent female identity is a performative exercise? In what way does contemporary culture coerce women to appear and to act in certain socially acceptable ways?

One of the earliest critical assessments of Galloway's work is Margery Metzstein's essay 'Of Myths and Men: Aspects of Gender in the Fiction of Janice Galloway'. We saw earlier in this chapter several critics outline the sense of double marginalisation pertaining to Scottish women's writing on account of both gender and nationality. For Metzstein the Scottishness of Galloway's work is incidental. In the extract below she begins by rejecting the critical appropriation of Galloway by those wishing to present a more diverse and well-rounded Scottish literature. Instead Metzstein's critique prioritises questions of gender. She locates

Galloway's work within a tradition of women's writing that includes writers like the English novelist Dorothy Richardson (1873–1957); Charlotte Brontë, author of *Jane Eyre* (1847); and Catherine Carswell, the Glasgow novelist and biographer of Robert Burns. For Metzstein this emphasis derives from Galloway's sustained interest in defamiliarising modern representations of female identity. Throughout the book Joy refuses to accept the various roles in which society would attempt to imprison her: wife, mistress, widow, and so on. For Metzstein these identities are all implied by a particularly masculine set of social values. That is, they depict a version of female identity that can only be validated in terms of how it refers to the figure of the male. Such models fundamentally enthrone the role of the male and render women as merely derivative, a society of second class citizens. *The Trick is to Keep Breathing* consistently cuts across and undermines these expectations about female identity and the role of women within contemporary society.

> ■ Although 'nurtured' in Scotland, Galloway's writing is important in the context of a wider history of women's writing, one which resists definition by malestream culture, and which has been edited out of the histories or canons of writing much as [Dorothy] Richardson suggests. If included at all, it has been subsumed into the language of 'universalism' or 'nationalism'. By focusing on gender issues, I hope to present a reading which recognises Galloway's 'tenacious talent', elucidates the importance in her writing of a feminist consciousness, and opens up the notion of Scottishness by questioning the concept of identity which it inevitably constructs and the applicability of this to women writers.[44] □

Metzstein picks up on the fact that Joy's disembodiment in the novel is a product of her relationship with her lover Michael. As his mistress, Joy is excluded from the official grieving that follows his tragic drowning on holiday in Spain. At both the funeral and memorial assembly at the school, where they were teachers, Joy is deliberately sidelined. Her presence is negated by the official authority figures overseeing these events, the minister and the headmaster. Metzstein comments: 'If she is not the mother-wife-daughter-sister, who is she? There is no legitimate name for her relation to Michael.'[45] Joy's assigned name 'mistress' is synonymous with the term 'prostitute', an implicitly degrading description and part of a pernicious move to objectify her in terms of her sexuality. For Metzstein Joy Stone can be read as belonging to a long line of literary heroines, characters who partake in a journey of self-definition and attempt to resist the coercive norms of female stereotype:

> ■ Thus Charlotte Brontë's Lucy Snowe, in *Villette*; Dorothy Richardson's Miriam Henderson, in *Pilgrimage*; or Catherine Carswell's Ellen Carstairs, in

The Camomile [1922], are all close relatives of Joy Stone, in that they risk cliché in their construction, yet are transmuted into figures who break the mould of masculinist discourse. All of the aforementioned characters start out as teachers: Snowe and Henderson are governesses, while Carstairs and Stone are music and drama teachers respectively. Each author, to a greater or lesser extent, uses this conventional figure and prises open the gap between the defined role and the woman who inhabits it.[46] □

Metstein's goal is to problematise the notion that women writers can be easily assimilated and appropriated under the aegis of national canonicity. Whilst posing as gender neutral, concepts such as 'Scottish writer' mask a set of predominantly masculine perspectives. These serve to distract and undermine the explicit critique of a misogynistic culture that forms the heart of Galloway's debut novel.

It is worth noting that Galloway herself questions the kind of elliptical model that is entailed within stories of literary sisterhood popular among feminist scholars: '[I]f you asked me to name writers that blow my socks off, a fair percentage would be Scots, a fair percentage would not be women, a fair percentage would not be prose writers. Where does that leave us?'[47] This kind of scepticism echoes the comments made by Douglas Gifford and Dorothy McMillan at the beginning of this chapter. They stressed the importance of brother/father figures as a point of influence upon the female creative consciousness. If the literary impulse does not follow a flag, as Marshall Walker reminded us, there is also a case for arguing that it cannot be cut up along gender lines in equally rigid ways. Gifford develops this specific point in his reading of Galloway's work. In the quotation below he aligns many of the themes and techniques of *The Trick is to Keep Breathing* with those employed by both her contemporaries, particularly James Kelman and Alasdair Gray:

■ Galloway works in the context of that astonishing revival of fiction in the West of Scotland which began with Alasdair Gray and James Kelman; indeed, her novel [*The Trick is to Keep Breathing*] exploits techniques which Kelman used in *The busconductor Hines* (1984) and Gray in *1982, Janine* (1984). The presentation of Hines's life in a long series of fragmented episodes separated from each other by a heading row of three small circles is adopted here to present Joy Stone's situation; and Gray's account of a disillusioned middle-class drunk coming to terms with traumatic memories through dialogues with his own inner voices is refashioned in young teacher Joy's negotiation with her traumatic memories.[48] □

In this context we might recall that Galloway herself has been particularly enthusiastic about the impact of books like *Lanark* on her literary imagination:

■ Alasdair Gray's was a voice that offered me something freeing. It wasn't distant or assumptive. It knew words, syntax, and places I also knew yet used them without any tang of apology: it took its own experience and culture as valid and central, not ancient or rural, tourist-trade quaint or rude-mechanical humorous. It spoke to the intellect directly and simply, didn't proscribe what I was meant to see or think, and was not afraid of fun or admissions of emotion [...] Even more, however, it was a voice that took for granted it wasn't the only voice. From its own experience of marginalization (and they are multiple), it knew the whole truth didn't belong to one sex either. In short, *it was a man's voice that knew that's all it was – a man's* [...] As a writer, Alasdair Gray's writing makes me feel braver. As a woman, it makes me feel acknowledged, spoken to.[49] □

This type of sentiment would seem to endorse certain of the assertions made in Chapter One of this Guide: the idea that contemporary Scottish literature constitutes a discrete body of writing, a contemporary renaissance even, where various writers co-exist in a cross-fertilising and mutually symbiotic relationship to one another. However, rather than simply appropriating the work of her male contemporaries, Galloway can be seen to borrow technique and apply it a number of highly original ways within her own work:

■ Galloway finds her own voice, however, with a more immediate sense of the absurd and a keener eye for banal detail than either Gray or Kelman. She opens her novel in something of the way of *Lanark*, with the reader struggling in media[s] res [in the middle of things], with the sense of something tragic having occurred. But where Gray uses fantasy in order to convey the breakdown of this central figure, Galloway presents a more immediate sense of horror, as Joy struggles to shut out memory and images of her drowned lover in a way that shockingly conveys unexpected tragedy.[50] □

Eschewing both explicitly feminist and overtly nationalist readings of the text, American critic Mary McGlynn focuses on Galloway's treatment of space in her novel. If *Lanark* sought to re-imagine Glasgow in all its intricate horror and delight, challenging its poor standing in our literary imagination, Galloway is also interested in this idea of an unreported and unrepresented world. In *The Trick is to Keep Breathing* it is the peripheral housing schemes on the outskirts of the city where Galloway locates her story. In 'Janice Galloway's Alienated Spaces' (2003) McGlynn picks up on this sense of space and reads it in terms of the mental isolation which Joy experiences in her life.

■ Joy's emotional retreats are represented physically, as her body wastes away. Moreover, her mental distance from others is reflected in her geographic distance. Throughout the novel, we hear about her difficulties with transportation and about how alienating the outskirts of Glasgow are. Edwin Morgan remarks in passing that *Trick* 'is not specifically a book about Glasgow, but the Glasgow background which it uses, a postwar estate on the outskirts, with a poor bus service and few car-owners, graffiti everywhere, slaters slithering in the porch, seems perfectly designed to be of least help to someone trying not to go mad' and indeed, the novel opens with a discussion of the shortcomings of Joy's house, moving within pages to the failed city planning that is responsible for her neighbourhood. In the constant interplay of internal and external throughout the text, body, home, housing estate, city, nation, and family are both setting for and cause of her drawn-out, viscerally painful, seemingly inescapable anxiety.[51] □

McGlynn's arguments can be seen to reverberate with the work of Scottish psychiatrist R. D. Laing (1927–89). Born in Glasgow, Laing came to prominence during the 1960s and remains a figurehead in what is known as the anti-psychiatry movement (although he himself rejected the label 'anti-psychiatrist'). Laing stressed the role of society, particularly the family, as a causal factor in patients repeated experience of mental illness, and in some cases madness. He saw psychopathology as rooted, not exclusively in the chemical functioning of the brain (the orthodox psychiatric view), but instead as intimately bound up with a patient's experience of their material world. Mental illness could be experienced as a transformative journey from which the patient could gain insights and learn how to better cope with existence. It is here that the similarities with an acid trip and Laing's subsequent popularity within 1960s counter-culture begin to become apparent. In terms of *The Trick is to Keep Breathing*, Laing's psychiatric model corresponds with Joy's experience of mental breakdown in the novel. Her illness becomes an opportunity for re-evaluation and a chance for her to develop coping strategies to counteract the pressures of existence. Laing's work on schizophrenia, articulated in *The Divided Self* (1960), has been taken up by a number of critics, most notably Gavin Miller in his book *R. D. Laing* (2004). In a move that parallels strategies of resistance offered by postcolonial critics like Homi Bhabha, there has been an attempt within Scottish Studies to reconfigure certain notions, such as the Caledonian Antisyzgy, transforming them from a disabling to an enabling diagnosis of the Scottish national psyche. The issue of cultural hybridity will be picked up in Chapter Five of this Guide.

Another trend within recent Scottish criticism has been to consider Janice Galloway and A.L. Kennedy as some kind of literary double act. The logic behind this seems reasonable enough; both are female and of similar age, they live in the Glasgow area and their work emerged at roughly the same point in time. Whereas Margery Metzstein had been openly hostile to considering Galloway's work in any kind of Scottish context, Aileen Christianson argues that both these writers share a preoccupation with challenging and rethinking the whole question of Scottish identity from a specifically female perspective:

■ They intertwine with these confident assumptions of being female and various in contemporary Scotland. The gaps in history where women were not, the lies about what women were, are refused by both, the notable silences are resisted and filled out. The cracks in the representation of women are duly and perfectly plastered over into a kind of accomplished completion. In their fiction, women are not covered over, disguised, or made invisible. Scottishness and femaleness may be problematised but they are also emphatically centralised.[52] □

Another point of contact between Galloway and many of her Scottish contemporaries concerns a concerted desire to experiment with their form of the novel. In her essay 'The Fictions of Janice Galloway: Weaving a Route Through Chaos' (1997) Glenda Norquay argues that it is this, the fragmented nature of the text, that provides the key to understanding the feminist politics of *The Trick is to Keep Breathing*. In the extract below she outlines how various patriarchal discourses compete in their attempts to define Joy. The novel reproduces and satirises such discursive practices, exposing and subverting the very power systems they disguise.

■ In *The Trick is to Keep Breathing* a whole set of institutional discourses – the languages of hospitals, of doctors, of health visitors – compete with the rhetoric of women's magazines, of romantic fiction, and of the consolatory clichés surrounding death offered by acquaintances and colleagues.
[...]
Galloway has developed a form of aesthetic experimentation that challenges established literary and linguistic conventions but represents more than textual subversion. Her writing offers a 'deconstruction' (in the sense of breaking down) of gendered subjectivities which takes into account the materiality of people's lives and has a definite political agenda. (In this enterprise her work might, I suspect, be linked to that of other Scottish writers such as James Kelman and A.L. Kennedy.) In her juxtaposition of discursive fragments, Galloway questions the authority of the word, and allows the silenced and that which is kept silent to be articulated.[53] □

Norquay reads Joy as an 'empty space' across which these and other contesting discourses clash in their efforts to label and define:

> ■ the text itself attempts a visual representation of this process, where space is emphasised – and the competing fragments from horoscopes, from diets, from woman's magazines, from the clichés of the health visitors trail across it, interspersed by empty – ooo – or moans. Language offers an illusion of order, space appears to represent chaos and yet for Joy to achieve control is to move into chaos.[54] □

The narrative upturn at the end of the novel begins with Joy reading her horoscope which instructs her to 'submit to chaos'. It is in admitting and accepting the inevitable absence of order, completion and control that Joy begins her journey toward some semblance of recovery. The key is to abandon the search for unerring stability, to reconcile oneself to the fact that all narratives are inevitably partial, insubstantial and incomplete. A particularly minimalist strategy, the trick, after all, is only that one keeps breathing.

Galloway, like Lochhead, is also interested in questioning women's participation, and complicity, in certain aspects of modern gender politics. In *Rewriting Scotland* (2002) Christie L. March homes in on the author's reluctance to be co-opted by dogmatic or militant brands of feminism. While *The Trick is to Keep Breathing* offers an unwavering exposé of the misogyny of consumer culture, it refuses unconditionally to exonerate its female characters.

> ■ [While] Galloway embraces alternative methods of reading and analysis that encompass women's writing, such as feminist analysis, she warily approaches the idea of herself as a feminist writer. The difficulty with such a label lies in the expectation it creates, she explains. The feminist publisher Women's Press told her 'one of my characters wasn't a strong enough role model for women'. The assumption that 'ideological reasons' should guide the writing, she argues, detracts from the real experiences she is trying to create in her fiction. 'My work is to ask, "What is it like to be an intelligent woman coping with the late twentieth century?" That's it', she declares. Such a narrative agenda requires failures as well as successes, weaknesses that often triumph over strengths in her characters.[55] □

Like Lochhead before her, Galloway is reluctant to allow a dogmatic feminist approach to skewer the signifying possibilities of her work. In this way too she has much in common with many of her male contemporaries in Scotland. For authors like Kelman, Gray and Leonard, art is not the straightforward endorsement of any one political creed. Instead it provides a crucible in which doctrines like nationalism, Marxism and feminism, and their impact on individual lives, are minutely examined and explored.

Writing from and about a specifically female perspective signalled a radical departure in the history of Scottish literature. A more enduring theme, pertinent for over two centuries in Scottish culture, has been class. As a country Scotland possesses a longstanding relationship with the history of the labour movement. The nineteenth century saw Scotland christened 'the workshop of the British Empire' with shipbuilding along the Clyde the focus for much of this activity. The first independent Labour Member of Parliament was the Scottish socialist Kier Hardie (1856–1915). In terms of literature, the experience of working-class communities, particularly in and around Glasgow, has been documented in a number of novels during the twentieth century. The sensationalist tabloid depiction of Glasgow's razor gangs of the 1930s was immortalised by Alexander McArthur (birth date unavailable) and H. Kingsley (birth date unavailable) Long in *No Mean City* (1957). More thoughtful representations of working class life have followed, most notably *The Dear Green Place* (1966) by Archie Hind (1928–2008) and *Mr Alfred M.A.* (1972) by George Friel (1910–75). However, it was in the 1980s that the representation of working class experience took on a level of artistic intensity that increasingly saw it spoken of in the same breath as work by James Joyce, Franz Kafka (1883–1924) and Samuel Beckett.

CHAPTER FOUR

Class

The reverberations of Thatcherism

If 1979 marked a specific turning point in terms of devolution and the much maligned fortunes of Scottish nationalism, it was highly significant in another context – class. Following the failure of the 1979 referendum the Scottish National Party tabled a motion of no confidence in Labour Government of James Callaghan (1912–2005; Prime Minister 1976–79) and forced a UK general election. The subsequent Conservative victory and the enthronement of Margaret Thatcher, Britain's first female Prime Minister, were to have dramatic consequences for Scotland, not least within its working-class communities. Thatcherism might usefully be thought of as both an historical moment and a set of specific ideological assumptions. Its politics were premised on the rolling back of the welfare state, the promotion of private enterprise and the sanctity of the free market. Instead of groups or classes, Thatcherism favoured a social perspective which elevated the individual as the primary unit of public life. Under the aegis of modernisation, successive British industries, the backbone of working-class labour for two centuries, were denationalised and in some cases simply discontinued. Aaron Kelly outlines the social and material transformations that defined the 1980s and their precise impact on the working-class communities within Scotland:

■ For the Scottish working class 1979 was a crucial year as it marked the failure of a referendum on devolution (that would eventually be achieved in 1999). Moreover, the lack of democratic control over their future was compounded by Margaret Thatcher's British general election victory and her government's vigorous assault upon the organised labour of Britain's industrial heartlands – a campaign that was never endorsed by the democratic majority in Scotland (or for that matter Wales or large areas of working-class England). Margaret Thatcher crystallised the ethos of her government and its neo-liberal economics with the proclamation: 'there is no such thing as society'. The Thatcher government privileged individualism, the market and the making of profit above all else and afforded the advantages of its social Darwinism to a limited few at the cost of dismantling the Welfare State and its macro-economic management, of nationalised and state-owned industries, the National Health Service, free education and welfare provision for all.[1] □

In decreeing 'there is no such thing as society' Thatcherism attempted to initiate a shift in the fundamental way in which people thought about themselves and their relationship to one another. Her policies were symptomatic of an attempt to reverse the critical consensus that had been enshrined in the post-war Welfare State. Under the leadership of Clement Attlee (1883–1967; Prime Minister 1945–51) the first ever majority Labour Government had set about compensating and buffering society from the worst excesses of free market capitalism. Thatcher wanted an end to the protectionist ethos of the nanny state which she regarded as leading to the near collapse of the British economy during the 1970s. In many ways Thatcherism was a reinvigoration of the economic principles first outlined in the Scottish Enlightenment by economist Adam Smith's *The Wealth of Nations* (1776). One of Smith's central premises was that the invisible hand of the free market must be allowed to influence individuals in their decision making. Furthermore, by pursuing their own selfish interests individuals were maximising efficiency whilst simultaneously serving the best interest of society as a whole. For students of literature, what is perhaps most significant about Thatcherism is its attempts to elide the language of class from the sphere of public debate. In his book *Class in Britain* (1998) historian David Cannadine (born 1950) traces how successive British Prime Ministers sought to emulate Thatcher in attempting to eliminate the language of class from the discourse of everyday life. John Major (born 1943; Conservative Prime Minister 1990–97) would assert his desire to transform Britain into a 'classless society' in the early 1990s.[2] Arguably though, Thatcher's greatest inheritor is not John Major, but Tony Blair (born 1953; Labour Prime Minster 1997–2007). During the 1990s, a re-branded New Labour Party sought to shed the baggage of its socialist past and recapture the centre ground of modern politics. Blair declared a determination to rid Labour of its 'Marxist intellectual analysis', with its 'false view of class' which was 'always out of kilter with the real world.'[3] Sociologist and New Labour ideologue Anthony Giddens (born 1938) neatly summed up this perspective when he wrote: 'we live in a world where there are no longer any alternatives to capitalism.'[4] The class element of Thatcherism, along with the lack of an electoral mandate north of the border, would be crucial factors in the revived fortunes of Scottish nationalism in the wake of the 1979 debacle. Scottish politics of this period saw questions of nationalism and class intertwined to the degree that they could not easily be untangled. Undoubtedly part of the success of Scottish devolution in 1997 grew from feelings that the British state was being run by and for the benefit of a wealthy elite based in the south-east of England. It will be interesting to watch whether or not a devolved Scottish parliament can offer working-class Scots any meaningful alternatives to the political and economic consensus embodied in the Thatcherite project of New Labour.

In terms of literature, the transformative nature of working-class experience during this period forms one of the most powerful currents within contemporary Scottish writing. In fact it is highly ironic that at the same time as Thatcher was attempting to discredit the language of class, Scottish writers were finding radical and innovative ways to redraw, redefine and re-assert its fundamental importance. In Chapter One we saw several critics assert that contemporary writing represented a new, and somehow more real, renaissance within Scottish literature. Again, we might view this recent rude health from an entirely different perspective. The vitality of contemporary Scottish literature could arguably be attributed to the emergence of a group of writers coming from, and seeking to write about, specifically working-class culture. Whilst previous Glasgow writers like George Friel and Archie Hind had penned a type of working-class realism, during the 1970s and 1980s a younger generation began to approach the subject from a number of daring angles. As we saw in his introduction to *The Scottish Novel Since the Seventies*, Gavin Wallace highlights the central importance of Alasdair Gray and James Kelman within just such a narrative: 'A movement of fictional innovation, led by the Glasgow writers Alasdair Gray and James Kelman, suddenly emerged, indebted to the parameters of working-class urban realism established in the preceding decades, but simultaneously transcending them.'[5] If Gray's *Lanark* has been critically hailed as a moment of *national* awakening, its particular focus on the city of Glasgow should not be overlooked. The history of the city is inevitably tied up and in some sense functions as a metonym (a part standing for a whole) for the story of working-class Scotland. An often quoted scene from *Lanark* emphasises the ideological importance of Glasgow to much of what the novel is trying to say. Looking out over the city the main character Thaw remarks to his friend McAlpin on Glasgow's relative absence from the pages of literary history:

■ 'Glasgow is a magnificent city', said McAlpin. 'Why do we hardly ever notice that?' 'Because nobody imagines living here', said Thaw. McAlpin lit a cigarette and said, 'If you want to explain that I'll certainly listen'.

'Then think of Florence, Paris, London, New York. Nobody visiting them for the first time is a stranger because he's already visited them in paintings, novels, history books and films. But if a city hasn't been used by an artist not even the inhabitants live there imaginatively [...] Imaginatively Glasgow exists as a music hall song and a few bad novels. That's all we've given to the world outside. It's all we've given to ourselves'.[6] □

The cultural invisibility of Glasgow can be read as exemplifying for the general exclusion of working-class narratives from the pages of literary fiction. The Kilmarnock-born writer William McIlvanney speaks of feeling like a literary orphan, growing up in a house filled with books most of which were completely devoid of the type of working-class culture he came from. McIlvanney's most famous novel *Docherty* (1975) is a depiction of a west of Scotland mining community at the dawn of the twentieth century. The author comments:

■ I wanted to write a book that that would create a kind of literary genealogy for the people I came from, the people whose memorials were parish registers. The most basic premise on which I was writing was that their lives were full of an immanent significance which, not being made explicit in literary form, was often regarded as not existing at all [...] *Docherty* is essentially an attempt to democratise traditional culture, to give working-class life the vote in the literature of heroism.[7] □

Whereas McIlvanney's novel seeks to re-visit and re-evaluate the origins of Scotland's working-class culture, James Kelman's work locates itself in the contemporary crisis facing a community that, in the 1980s, had the rug pulled from under them. It is worth noting though that Kelman describes his own early experience of literature in remarkably similar terms to McIlvanney:

■ When I started to write stories I was twenty-two and naturally enough I thought to use my own background and experience. I wanted to write as one of my own people, I wanted to write and remain a member of my community. That advice you get in the early days of writing, at any writers' workshop or writers' group, 'Write from your own experience!' Yes, that was what I set out to do, taking for granted that was how writers began. I soon discovered that this was easier said than done. In fact, as far as I could see, looking around me, it had never been done. If it had, I could never find it. There was nothing I saw anywhere. Whenever I did find somebody from my own sort of background in English literature, they were confined to the margins, kept in their place, stuck in the dialogue [...] They never rang true, they were never like anybody you ever met in real life.[8] □

Alongside McIlvanney, Kelman and Gray, the 1980s witnessed the emergence of a host of Scottish writers coming from and seeking to write about working-class experience. An incomplete list would include Tom Leonard, John Byrne, Tom McGrath, Liz Lochhead and

Agnes Owens. In the 1990s figures like A.L. Kennedy, Jeff Torrington, Janice Galloway and Irvine Welsh would also look to assert the validity of working-class culture as a suitable subject matter for serious fiction. So what explains this upsurge of working-class writing during these decades? In part it reflects the particular demographics of Scottish society. Few countries experienced the rigors of nineteenth-century industrialism with the same intensity that Scotland did. It seems only natural then that Scottish literature would eventually come to inter-rogate the experiences of this section of its population. The precise timing of this surfacing can be read as a direct consequence of the post-war welfare state, particularly the establishment of free second-ary education through the Butler Education Act (1944). As such many of the above writers were the first generation of their family to receive an extended formal education. It is worth noting that the profusion of working voices in this period was not limited to the pages of literary fiction. In Chapter Two we saw Tom Leonard create a highly sophis-ticated poetry from of the idiomatic speech of working-class Glasgow. Similar strategies inform the poetry of both Liz Lochhead and Edwin Morgan. Theatre was also a crucial vehicle in the artistic exploration of working-class identity. Echoing Carins Craig's comments regarding the liberation of the voice, Randall Stevenson argues that the origins of working-class fiction in the 1980s might be meaningfully traced to the proletarian leanings of Scottish theatre in the previous decade:

■ Glasgow's huge expansion after the industrial revolution left the city with problems more numerous and more extreme than experienced elsewhere, though with a sense of identity and community strengthened by the very pressures these problems created. Poverty, slums, squalor, crime, and the hard conditions imposed by heavy industry also shaped a working-class radicalism more determined than elsewhere [...] [I]t is the 1970s *themselves* which are often considered one of the best-ever periods of Scottish drama, whereas it is largely *since* 1979 – in a new renaissance led by Alasdair Gray and James Kelman that the Scottish novel once again developed as strongly as it did in MacDiarmid's day, in the 1920s and 1930s. What history refuses, it is sometimes supposed, culture and imagination provide.[9] □

Plays such as *The Sash* (1974) by Hector MacMillan (born 1929), *The Hard Man* by Tom McGrath and Jimmy Boyle (born 1944) and, per-haps most successfully, *The Slab Boys Trilogy* (1978) by John Byrne saw working-class life placed centre stage, both literally and figuratively.

This chapter presents the key debates that have arisen alongside the emergence of working-class writing during this period. These include the reassessments of traditional working-class fiction, and the ways in which new writing has sought to challenge pre-existing representations of working-class culture. The relationship between ideologies of class and nationalism are also important. We will also see that for some critics, the preponderance of working-class fiction exercises an excessive influence on our perceptions of Scottish literature. This can lead to mistaken assumptions that Scotland as a country is somehow 'prolier than thou'. Recent decades have seen working-class communities experience a process of radical, and often painful, transformation. The period since 1960 saw the traditional foundation of working-class culture, heavy industry, gradually disappear from the very fabric of Scottish life. The attempt to record this phenomenon will be considered alongside critical responses to the work of James Kelman. For over three decades Kelman's work has been at the vanguard of experimentalism within the Scottish novel. One of the underlying premises of his work is the belief that the experience of those jettisoned during the take-off of late capitalism constitutes a suitable subject matter for high art.

The Glasgow novel

One of the earliest pieces of criticism to diagnose a shift in the representation of working-class experience is Douglas Gifford's pamphlet *The Dear Green Place: the Novel in the West of Scotland* (1985). Gifford maps out a history of Glasgow fiction against which he looks to situate the work of contemporary writers like Kelman and Gray. Similar to Cairns Craig's articulation of a national literary tradition, Gifford locates Glasgow fiction within the broader context of twentieth century Scottish writing. His title evokes Archie Hind's novel *The Dear Green Place* and its ironic description of a modern industrial city. The juxtaposition of rural ideal with the reality of urban experience forms the central axis of Hind's landmark novel. Gifford's essay begins with a similar comparison. He argues that writing about Glasgow disrupts the artistic and political preoccupations of the 1920s renaissance. Renaissance writers envisioned the Scottish past through a specifically rural set of mythological signifiers. Scotland's past functioned as a lost arcadia, a place to be resurrected and re-imagined as a foil to the pressures of modernity. Just as the Reformation had conspired to sever modern Scotland culturally from its medieval roots, the industrial revolution had compounded the problem, forcing people off the land and into the squalor of urban slums. Gifford argues that the rural bias within Scottish literature of the 1920s is rendered problematic by the reality of modern Glasgow. In his book of travel writing *Scottish Journey* (1935) the poet Edwin Muir foregrounds the way in which

Glasgow not only disrupts certain narratives of nationalism, but also, at the same time, embodies a kind of universal experience, one familiar to citizens of other industrial cities across Europe.

> ■ [A]t the same time Glasgow is not a typically Scottish town; the worst of many evils with which it festers were not born of the soil on which it stands or of the people who live in it – a mixed population of Lowlanders, Highlanders and Irish – but of Industrialism; and in writing about I shall be writing about a particular area of modern civilization which is independent of national boundaries, and can be found in England, Germany, Poland, Czecho-slovakia and most other countries as well as on the banks of the Clyde. This No Man's Land of civilization comprises in Scotland an area which, although not very large in extent, is very densely populated. In one way it may be said that this area is modern Scotland, since it is the most active and vital part of Scotland as well as the most populous [...] But from another point of view one may say that it is not Scotland at all, or not Scotland in particular, since it is merely one of the expressions of Industrialism, and Industrialism operates by laws which do not recognize nationality.[10] □

Muir's perception of Glasgow is deeply affected by his childhood. Born and raised on the Hebredian island of Orkney, his family moved to Glasgow in 1901 when Edwin was 14. This geographical wrench was for Muir the equivalent of time travelling. He describes an Orkney largely unchanged since the eighteenth century and the radical disjunction he experienced on arriving in the dark heart of industrial modernity: 'I was really born in 1737 [...] then in 1751 I set out from Orkney for Glasgow. When I arrived I found that it was not 1751 but 1901, and that a hundred and fifty years had been burned up in my two days journey.'[11] This seismic shift is manifest in Muir's poetry through recurring themes like expulsion, estrangement and ideas of a lost Edenic landscape. Glasgow's role as a catalyst in this realisation permits us to locate Muir's work alongside that of other modernist writers such as T. S. Eliot or the Irish poet W. B. Yeats. In his poem 'The Stolen Child' Yeats would invite us to escape with a faery hand in hand, from a world more full of weeping than we can ever understand. The notion that humanity had somehow lost its way forms one of the characteristic responses to the experience of modernity in this period.

So, throughout the twentieth century Glasgow is a place that is often seen as problematic, sometimes overtly hostile, to the nourishment of the creative imagination. The fumes of industrialism pollute the air as this barren landscape crowds in on the aesthetic sensibility of the artist. Material poverty is regarded as the bedfellow to a deep spiritual malaise. As Douglas Gifford argues, prior to the emergence of Gray, Kelman and others, the Glasgow novel is devoid of any 'green places of the mind', a space in which the artistic imagination might flourish and grow.

■ When Archie Hind called his famous novel of 1966 *The Dear Green Place* he exploited an image, a name, a loving memory which, although not exactly clear to those who came across it, set off echoes and associations [...] Glasgow as the most beautiful little orchard town in Europe – was it Defoe who said that? Glasgow as *Gles Chu* – was that the Gaelic for "the dear green place"? [...] Hind explicitly meant his image to work in terms of the immediate surroundings of his protagonist, Mat Craig; and this is proven by the closing four lines of 'childish jingle' which run through his mind as he ponders *Gles Chu*'s coat of arms [...]

This is the tree that never grew,
This is the bird that never flew,
This is the fish that never swam,
This is the bell that never rang.[12] □

Reverberating with Eliot's lament of London in *The Waste Land*, the place that had 'undone so many', Hind's novel regards the industrial city as a stifling and debilitating landscape:

■ [In the Glasgow novel] images of growth and sense of place are effectively struck down, frosted, faded, blacked out. Vision is lost. [...] [T]he novel will present a sensitive protagonist struggling to articulate his reactions to his environment; in ways, firstly, in which he has been encouraged at university, at art school, or even within the books he's read and the company he's kept. Gradually he will realise that he cannot accept these ways – or it will be borne in violently upon him. A failure of language or communication will take place. He will turn in upon himself in increasing solipsism, rejecting his art, his friends, and tormenting himself with the destruction of anything he has achieved in art and relationships. Alienation or nervous breakdown, mocked by a sense of total loss of 'green places of the mind', will often be the end; or a sense of bewilderment about future evolution.[13] □

In the 1960s the poetry of Edwin Morgan sought to challenge negative perceptions of Glasgow as a barren waste land, a place inimical to the artistic impulse. In the post-war period the city underwent a radical facelift as many of its slums were knocked down and their citizens relocated to modern housing schemes, such as Drumchapel and Castlemilk, on the periphery of the city. This process, specifically the levelling of the Gorbals, forms one of the central themes of the novel *Swing Hammer Swing* (1992) by Jeff Torrington. The idea that Glasgow might provide a place in which a sophisticated art might flourish finds one of its most significant origins in Morgan's poetry. Inspired by the possibilities of technology and the optimism of the sixties, Morgan asked whether it was possible for a city like Glasgow to be born again, to have an opportunity to live what the title of his 1968 collection called a 'Second Life'. Of course, the problems engendered by the nature of these housing schemes have begun to emerge in more recent years: cheap mass produced housing; districts with few amenities; people isolated from one another and the rest of the city. As we will see, these themes underpin the treatment of working-class experience for contemporary writers like James Kelman, and the Edinburgh-based Irvine Welsh. For Morgan though, writing in the 1960s, there remained a spirit of hope. As the architecture of Glasgow reached for the sky, in the process emulating cities like New York, there was a momentary feeling that after years at the coal face of industrialism, the city was at last being allowed to wash itself off and join the party.

So Glasgow presents itself as an anomalous and deeply problematic issue for the Scottish writer. It is a place where narratives of class can be seen to interrupt the rhetoric of nationalism. For Cairns Craig there is no such antinomy, as one of the defining features of Scotland's literary tradition has been its enduring Leftism. Craig maintains that whilst renaissance writers of the 1920s would turn away from urban space and foreground a mythic rural landscape, their writing was nevertheless characterised by a sense of folk allegiance and a preoccupation with proletarian politics.

■ The most striking fact about the major literary contributions of twentieth century Scotland is that they originate from and are focused around the experiences of working people – not necessarily working-class people, in the sense of an urban proletariat, but working people in the sense of those who sell their labour for their week-to-week survival. However much the Scottish renaissance movement of the 1920s was imbued with the spirit of European modernism – often seen as the product of a high bourgeois culture – the major Scottish writers were all from lower class backgrounds and – whether it is the peasants of Muir's Orkney, the fishermen of Gunn's Sutherland, the industrial workers of Grassic Gibbon's Duncairn in *Grey Granite*, or the mill workers of MacDiarmid's 'The Seamless Garment' – made the experiences of the 'folk' the basis of their art.[14] □

Whether we regard Glasgow writing as a composite part of the national story, or as a body of work which constitutes a fault line within this meta-narrative, what cannot be denied is the quantity and quality of the literature coming from the city in recent decades. Since the 1980s the list of writers that have sought to write about Glasgow has continued to grow. This profusion has seen an ironic shift in certain critical perceptions. If before there was not enough West of Scotland fiction, for some critics there is now a surfeit of proletarian prose. The poet Douglas Dunn is highly critical of what he reads as an aesthetic distortion created by writing from the west of Scotland. For Dunn the preoccupation of these novels with working-class experience runs the risk of limiting the relevance of contemporary Scottish writing. The problem comes from reading working-class fiction as a metonym for Scottish literature as a whole. Whilst praising the artistic technique of writers like Kelman, Dunn is wary of the potential for such work to drown out the voices of other Scottish writers.

> ■ Kelman's achievement can be admired, but it is hard to see how it can be exemplary for Scottish fiction as a whole. Even if it is to be admitted to be a perennial dimension of Scottish writing that its innovative, self-renewing desires and tussles often take the form of vernacular upsurges, it can be a source of anxiety that their consequence can be to exclude other writers (and readers) from the contemporary picture. There is an atmosphere of 'political correctness' which encourages social narrowing in favour of a working-class, left wing, vernacular authorship. More than a hint of perverse cultural censorship can be detected in the critical favouritism of the day; and as it is one which denies the full identity of the country, it can be considered serious.[15] □

Dunn highlights a number of well-known Scottish writers who remain highly marginalized within a critical discourse that is much more amenable to certain forms of left wing, anti-establishment politics. One such writer is William Boyd (born 1952). Having attended the exclusive Scottish boarding school at Gordonstoun, which counts Prince Charles (born 1948) among its former pupils, Boyd went on to study at Glasgow University and then Oxford. Although he has published 11 novels since 1981 and won a host of literary prizes, he remains conspicuously absent from the majority of critical anthologies devoted to contemporary Scottish writing. One writer about whom the above statement cannot be made is James Kelman. 'The crown prince of the Scottish avant-garde', as Alasdair Gray called him, Kelman has been a constant presence for over almost four decades. His work takes a microscope to lives of many people who remain otherwise excluded from the pages of literary fiction. As we shall see, Kelman's unremitting and unapologetic approach to his art has won him condemnation and adulation in equally impassioned terms. For some he is a literary savage, whilst for others he is the Kafka of the Clyde.

James Kelman

Since the late 1970s Kelman's writing has attracted controversy and acclaim in almost equal measure. His first collection of short stories *An*

Old Pub Near the Angel was published by a small American company, Puckerbrush Press, in 1973. Since then Kelman's output has been substantial. He has published six novels: *The Busconductor Hines* (1984), *A Chancer* (1985), *A Disaffection* (1989), *How Late It Was, How Late* (1994), *Translated Accounts* (2002), and *You Have to be Careful in the Land of the Free* (2004). He has also produced six short story collections and written several plays for radio and stage. In 1989 he joined such luminaries as E. M. Forster (1879–1970), Aldous Huxley (1894–1963) and Graham Greene (1904–91) when he won the world's oldest literary prize, the James Tait Black, for his novel *A Disaffection*. 1994 would see Kelman become the first Scottish writer to win the Booker Prize. For certain critics Kelman's work signals an affront to the very institution of literature and culture; for others it belongs alongside the work of iconic figures like Joyce, Beckett and Kafka. This latter critical strategy, appropriating the reputations of literary heavyweights to bring gravitas to new writers, can in some instances be highly reductive. It is a strategy that often has more to do with marketing than critical considerations. In Kelman's case, however, such comparisons have been argued at length by a number of well-informed critics. In Chapter One we addressed the tension between reading Scottish literature within a national as opposed to a more international context. Similar debates characterise the responses to Kelman's work. For Ellen-Raïssa Jackson and Willy Maley there is a false dichotomy at work here: 'Often compared with a whole host of major European literary figures – Beckett, Joyce, Kafka, Émile Zola [1840–1902] – [Kelman] also belongs firmly within a radical Scottish tradition, and is keenly aware of, and arguably part of, new literatures in English.'[16] The allusion to 'new literatures in English' recalls the question of postcolonialism within Scottish criticism which will be addressed in Chapter Five of this Guide. Maley and Jackson's comments are taken from the introduction to a 2001 special issue of the *Edinburgh Review* devoted to Kelman's work. The journal contains eight essays, under the broad aegis of 'commitment', which examine Kelman's work from a number of angles. The themes of place, gender, philosophy, class and nationalism all figure prominently and provide a useful starting point from which to approach Kelman's fiction. In the discussion of women's writing in the previous chapter of this Guide we alluded to the dangers of pigeon-holing writers through confining them within certain critical paradigms. Jackson and Maley highlight a similar process at work in the critical interpretation of Kelman's fiction. Whilst the issue of class remains vital, it must not be mistaken as the sole signifying possibility at play here:

■ James Kelman is a 'Scottish writer', 'a working class writer', 'a political writer', 'a dialect writer', 'a Glasgow writer', 'an angry writer', 'an experimental writer', 'a writer in the tradition of Kafka', 'a writer following Beckett', 'a post-modernist writer' [...] Some of [these terms] like 'working class writer' are deeply problematic, in the way they seem to liberate the author from the usual constraints, while actually operating to stifle him by narrowing down our horizons of expectation.[17] □

The Booker prize is a useful crucible in which to consider the political implications of Kelman's work and particularly his treatment of class. The prize is awarded annually to the best novel, written in English, from a citizen of the British Commonwealth. Administered from London, the former heart of the British Empire, the award implicitly provokes a number of questions related to postcolonialism and the cultural legacy of imperialism. The exclusion of non-English writing from the award is highly provocative, prohibiting as it does writing in a number of indigenous languages including Gaelic (Scotland and Ireland), Urdu (India) and Maori (New Zealand). Under the guise of inclusiveness, the award can be seen to re-enact some of the worst practices of cultural imperialism. These issues bubbled to the surface in the controversy surrounding Kelman's success in the 1994 Booker for his novel *How Late It Was, How Late*. Written primarily in urban dialect, the novel begins with an unemployed Glasgow man, Sammy Samuels, suffering a beating at the hands of the police. As a result of the assault Sammy temporarily loses his eyesight. The remainder of the book follows his attempts to navigate the labyrinthine systems of power that constitute life on the socio-economic margins of contemporary Glasgow. Considering subsequent objections about the book's language, it is highly ironic that Sammy's blindness deliberately foregrounds the whole issue of speech and the different ways various characters talk in the novel. At the time one of the Booker judges, Rabbi Julia Neuberger (born 1950), resigned in protest over the decision to award Kelman the prize. Neuberger objected to the novel on the grounds of its use of 'broad Glaswegian dialect', the fact that it was 'littered with F-words' and that it was 'too inaccessible, and simply too dull.'[18] Kelman received his award amongst the great and the good of the publishing industry at the Guildhall in London. In his acceptance speech he delivered a vitriolic attack on what he regarded as the inherent elitism of contemporary literary culture. In another highly ironic moment Channel 4, who televised the event, cut from Kelman's condemnation and went to a commercial break just as the author was getting into his stride. The silencing and censorship of the artist, whether premeditated or not, has rarely been so enticingly acted out before the public gaze. Kelman's speech, a section of which is printed below, echoes both Robert Crawford and Cairns Craig's use of postcolonial theory as a way of explicating the politics of contemporary Scottish writing. Kelman goes one step further, however, claiming that the exclusion and inferiorisation of vernacular writing is simply racism by another name. The author claims his work belonged to 'a literature of decolonization' and aligns his own fiction with that of the British-based Jamaican poet Linton Kwesi Johnson (born 1954), the Nigerian writer Chinua Achebe (1930), and the Kenyan writer and academic Ngũgĩ wa Thiong'o (born 1930). His alliance with these writers suggests there exists a new cultural context, one in which contemporary Scottish literature has yet to be fully explored. In Chapter One we examined the discussion of tradition as an important term in Cairns Craig's reading of Scottish literature. Kelman's speech sought to redefine exactly which traditions we might wish to think about Scottish writing as partaking in.

■ There is a literary tradition to which I hope my own work belongs, I see it as part of a much wider process - or movement - toward decolonisation and self -determination: it is a tradition that assumes two things: 1) the validity of indigenous culture; and 2) the right to defend in the face of attack. It is a tradition premised on a rejection of the cultural values of imperial or colonial authority, offering a defence against cultural assimilation, in particular an imposed assimilation [...] The second tradition to which my work belongs is the existential tradition.[19] □

The existential tradition includes figures such as Algerian novelist Albert Camus (1913–60), French philosopher and novelist Jean-Paul Sartre (1905–80), and the Russian novelist Fyodor Dostoevsky (1821–81). Existentialism as a philosophical movement is traditionally traced back to the nineteenth-century Danish thinker Søren Kierkegaard (1813–55). It postulates the absence of a transcendental force, such as God, as a governing influence over man's life. As a result the individual is entirely free to choose how to live. Existentialism is grounded in a belief that there is no overriding purpose to human existence. It maintains that finding a way to counter this sense of nothingness is the task we are all confronted with. In a reversal of the famous dictum 'Cogito ergo sum' (I think therefore I am), originally articulated by French philosopher Rene Descartes (1596–1650), existentialism offers us 'I am, therefore I think'. The nature of our own existence becomes the determinant factor governing how we mediate our experience of the world. In Kelman's work this philosophy compels us to examine the reality of life on the socio-economic margins of contemporary society. Kelman offers us a kind of working-class existentialism. He is concerned with representing a specific reality as experienced by certain marginalised individuals – the bus conductor Hines, the disaffected school teacher Patrick Doyle, and the blinded Sammy Samuels. His fiction addresses the ways in which the individual attempts to cope when confronted by an impoverished material environment. As such, Kelman's work signals a paradigm shift in the traditional representation of working-class experience. It is not the working class as a collective community that concerns the author. Rather it the disempowered and isolated individual, struggling to find meaning in an otherwise absurd universe that holds his attention. Kelman's work can be seen to diagnose the sense of loss that accompanied the death of heavy industry and the rise of neo-liberal economics in the late twentieth century. Unlike in previous generations, the working class no longer experience themselves as part of a community. They no longer experience the type of mass labour, such as working in a shipyard alongside 3,000 other men, which in the past rendered everyday life meaningful. Instead the working class face the uncertainties of the post-industrial economy as a group of isolated individuals, increasingly estranged and cut off from one another.

Kelman's acceptance speech at the Booker Prize provoked a considerable reaction from certain sections of the mainstream media. Writing in *The Times* the columnist Simon Jenkins (born 1943) was particularly outspoken in his criticism, decrying that the award of the Booker Prize to Kelman was an act of 'literary vandalism'. We might remember in passing that vandalism is a term normally used to designate an attack on private property, an observation which perhaps tells us something about Jenkins's own literary value system. Like Neuberger, in lambasting the award, Jenkins would also focus on the issue of language. He distinguished Kelman's work from what he regarded as the more acceptable versions of literary Scots: 'His language is not Older Scottish, or Scots English, or Lallans, or any dialect of Burns's "Guid Scots Tongue". *The Guardian* called it "the authentic voice of Glasgow", a libel on that city. I would call the language merely Glaswegian Alcoholic With Remarkably Few Borrowings.'[20] For Jenkins the Glasgow speech of *How Late It Was, How Late* bears little resemblance to the good Scots of MacDiarmid or Burns. Kelman's award received similarly negative coverage elsewhere in the press. For Alan Clarke (1935–90) in the *Mail on Sunday*, the novel was 'a humiliating insult to Scottish culture [...] Compiled? Scripted? I am trying to avoid the word "written" – by a Glaswegian [...] it seems unfair on real authors to call him an "author".'[21] For Gerald Warner in *The Sunday Times*, what Kelman calls his culture, 'in reality [...] is not properly a "culture", but the primeval vortex of underdevelopment that precedes culture.'[22] Denis Canavan (born 1942), at the time Labour M.P. for Falkirk West, described the book as a contrived and essentially unrealistic portrait of the Scottish working class: 'I think he goes over the top with the f-word. Nobody in Scotland or anywhere else uses so many.'[23] For Stuart Wavell the novel was a '4,000-expletive blot on the national character.'[24] While Kathleen Monroe of the Saltire Society lamented: 'It's an unfortunate portrayal of Scotland. I am afraid we are our own worst enemy sometimes.'[25] Several of these comments echo McClure's earlier point regarding the friction between the discourse of Scottish nationalism and the more overtly radical politics embedded in urban dialect writing.

It is important to note that the response to Kelman's novel was not entirely negative. If fact, the vitriol of the above reactions was more than matched by the heady praise of a number of other critics. Several letters in the press recommended the verisimilitude of the novel's language: 'I did think that with so many expletives it had to be stretching belief for him to say that he was recording the authentic voice of the working class of Scotland. But then on Saturday afternoon I was at Tynecastle in Edinburgh for the visit of Celtic, and lo and behold, I was wrong in thinking as I did, and Mr Kelman was (and is) right.'[26] One of the more pernicious tendencies within the Booker debate was to reduce Kelman's language to a mere question of swearing. In his essay 'Swearing Blind: Kelman and the Curse of the Working Classes' (1996) Willy Maley defended the artistic subtlety that underpinned even this aspect of the author's work:

■ Swearing is the public phatic communion of the factory, the barracks, the pub, the street 'phatic' is a form of language used for general social interaction rather than to convey specific meaning]. A sign of violent and impoverished masculinity, disenfranchised youth and socialised labour [...] The very idea of 'bad language' is of course linked to a particular elitist theory of art [...] Kelman's use of Scots is tightly meshed with his use of swearing, and this allows his detractors to fasten upon the latter when the chief objection is to the former [...] The swearing is integral to Kelman's power as a writer. It is neither a vulgar and superfluous supplement nor an offensive coating, concealing shortcomings in narrative dialogue, or characterisation.[27] □

The ferocity of the debate surrounding Kelman's Booker illustrates the degree to which language remains a highly charged issue. Moreover, it casts aspersions on claims by successive British Prime Ministers who would seek to make redundant the discourse and politics of class. Contemporary Scottish writing foregrounds the fact that, despite the loss of traditional industries and the rhetoric of multi-cultural pluralism, Britain is still a society in which the politics of class continue to provoke a reaction.

Cairns Craig has written about the ways in which Kelman's work, both in content and form, marks a series of radical departure within the history of working class fiction. He considers Kelman's writing within a tradition of working-class writing that includes *The Ragged Trousered Philanthropists* (1914) by Robert Tressell (1870–1911), *Saturday Night and Sunday Morning* (1958) by the Nottingham writer Alan Sillitoe (born 1928), and the film *Kes* (1969) directed by Ken Loach (born 1936). What differentiates Kelman's fiction is its specific relocation of working-class culture. Following the decline of heavy industry, working-class experience is no longer to be found in its traditional sites such as the factory floor or the coal mine.

> ■ Kelman's novels are located quite differently from the traditional narratives of working-class life [...] [His] novelty in this context is that it is not the skilled, the potentially politically active working class, who are the location of his fiction; it is those who are marginalised from traditional working-class values, who do not believe in the possibility of communal political action, who do not believe in the viability of a personal escape from their conditions. Kelman's depiction is not of a working-class *community* so much as of a working-class world which has become atomised, fragmented, and in which individuals are isolated from one another – a world in which political hope has been severed and only economic deprivation remains. It is a working class, in other words, without a possible salvation through the political or economic transformation of history.[28] □

In the absence of employment in the 1980s, Kelman's fiction evinces the transposition of working-class experience from the shipyard dock and the factory floor to the dole queue, the snooker hall and the dog track. Ironically, for the working class it is no longer work, but rather the lack of it, which defines their existence:

> ■ Kelman's novels, then, take place not in the traditional sites of the working-class struggle for power (the trades unions, the educational system as liberator), nor in the traditional sites of working-class escape from work and exploitation (sport, domestic solidarity), but along the margins of that traditional working-class life. And they do so because that traditional life has been decimated: founded as it was on heavy industry, on the idea of a mass society whose masses could be brought into solidarity, it has been wiped out by the destruction of the traditional Scottish industries.[29] □

Following the crisis within traditional forms of working-class politics, Kelman's protagonists resist identification as spokespersons for their class. Instead they embody a more isolated and alienated existence. In this sense they have become doubly marginalized, sidelined within capitalist society but also from any sense of solidarity within a wider working-class community. Craig maintains that Kelman's working-class existentialism is crucial to understanding his depiction of these lives:

> ■ Kelman's central characters are symbols of the collapse of working-class life into a dispirited and isolated endurance: there is no hope of transformation; there is no sustenance in community. In Kelman's fiction, there is a brutal awareness that the Scottish working class, who saw themselves as the carrier of historical change [...] are now the leftovers of a world which has no need of them; their choices are limited to acceptance of the atomisation of social improvement, or submission to becoming fodder for the only industry they have left – the poverty industry. There is no way out that is not a denial of a possible solidarity; there is no solidarity that can be activated to change the world. There is only anger and nostalgia.[30] □

Craig also examines the technical ways in which Kelman's work attempts to challenge traditional depictions of working-class experience, particularly through its use of language. As outlined in Chapter Two, Kelman is not merely interested in the authentic representation of working-class speech. Rather, his work functions to undermine the inherent power structures of conventional narrative form. A key target for Kelman is the elitist value system embedded within traditional realist fiction, and specifically its use of third person narrative. This formal structure sets up a power relation between the working-class speech of the characters on the one hand and the Standard English of the narrator on the other. The omniscient narrative voice becomes an authoritative force within the text. It assumes the role of interpreter, and becomes the purveyor of ultimate meaning, presiding over the working-class lives that populate the text. Kelman's use of free indirect discourse is designed to resist such forms of narrative arrest – hence the pun in Craig's title on 'Resisting Arrest'. Kelman does not cede control of the narrative to an omniscient Standard English narrator. Instead, his narrative oscillates between an objective description of the world and the direct transcription of his characters' subjective experience. As such we are given access to the inner life of these characters and the daily psychological humiliations suffered by those on the socio-economic margins of contemporary society. Craig comments:

> ■ Kelman might be said to be fulfilling Virginia Woolf's assertion that the novel ought to examine 'an ordinary mind on an ordinary day', exploring the 'myriad impressions', the 'incessant shower of innumerable atoms' that 'shape themselves into the life of Monday or Tuesday' [...] Kelman's narratives are not concerned with progression along a temporal trajectory of events; they are concerned with an unchangeable context into which

human beings are thrown and from which there is no escape. They are concerned fundamentally, therefore, not with the progress implied by a narrative sequence but with repetition – repetition as the systematisation and dehumanisation to which working-class people, above all others, are subjected.[31] □

Kelman's working-class realism is tactical rather than essential. His purpose is to undermine and expose the elitism inherent in certain forms of writing, a formal structure which would denigrate and demean working-class experience in the very act of representing it. Ultimately for Craig, this conclusion suggests that Kelman's work might be better thought of in terms of a European existential tradition, rather than one that is identifiably British and working class:

■ It is by this re-envisaging of the nature of working-class life and the realism which is required to represent it that Kelman's fiction has transcended all the paradigms of previous writing about the working classes. Kelman's working-class realism is tactical rather than essential, for what is essential is that the working-class characters, and especially the marginalised working-class characters who are his protagonists, are the sites not of a social – a class – conflict, but of an existential awareness from which most human beings are insulated by their society. The alienation of the working class becomes the context not for the exploration of social issues and possible political improvement, but for the exploration of humanity's existential condition. Kelman's tormented characters become heroic because of their continuous and restless need to confront the fact of being absurdly and gratuitously thrown into an existence which makes no sense and has no place for them. It is this that justifies the connection of Kelman's fiction not with the work of the British working-class writers of the 1950s and 1960s, but with the continental traditions of Kafka, Camus and Beckett.[32] □

Kelman himself has written about several of these themes in his two essay collections *Some Recent Attacks* (1992) and *'AND THE JUDGES SAID...'* (2003). These volumes contain criticism on a number of topics including censorship, radical politics and the role of art. In 'The Importance of Glasgow to My Work' Kelman grounds his own literary praxis in a set of assumptions about the artistic validity of working-class culture: 'Born and bred in Govan and Drumchapel, inner city tenement to the housing scheme homeland on the outer reaches of the city [...] The stories I wanted to write would derive from my own background, my own socio-cultural experience.'[33] At the same time the author seeks to resists attempts to label his work and encase it within certain restrictive critical paradigms. He denies any sense that his fiction is parochial or concerned in a narrow or exclusive way with depicting working-class Glasgow:

■ 'Glaswegian' is a late 20th century construct. Apart from direct experience I have access to other experiences, foreign experience, I have access to all the areas of human endeavour, right back from the annals of ancient history; in that sense Socrates or Agamemnon is just as much a part of my socio-cultural background as the old guy who stands in the local pub telling me of the reality of war as experienced by his grandfather in the Crimea War.[34] □

In Chapter Two we saw how renaissance writers of the 1920s used the question of language as a conduit to thinking about the politics of national identity. For Kelman the use of dialect goes beyond any set of specifically Scottish concerns. He maintains:

■ There is nothing about the language as used by folk in and around Glasgow or London or Ramsgate or Liverpool or Belfast or Swansea that makes it generally distinct from any other city in the sense that it is a language composed of all sorts of particular influences, the usual industrial or post industrial situation where different cultures have intermingled for a great number of years.[35] □

In this sense Kelman's aesthetic politics resemble those of the poet Tom Leonard. We might recall Leonard's comment that there are basically two ways of speaking in Britain, one which lets the listener know that one paid for one's education, the other which lets the listener know that one didn't. It also reverberates with Edwin Muir's comments about Glasgow as an anomalous space, a place that is simultaneously the most Scottish part of the country whilst somehow not being Scotland at all. Critics such as Simon Baker have argued that the class politics of Kelman's work resonate far beyond any local or exclusively Scottish context: 'Implicit in this is the rejection of a Scottish or nationalist mode of address, and a concentration on the dynamics of post-imperial de-industrialising urban life as it is lived in all the decaying, abandoned cities in towns of the English commonwealth.'[36]

If Kelman's radicalism includes a critique of certain formal literary techniques, he is equally scathing about the role played by literature within capitalist society. He regards both the educational establishment and its treatment of literature as predicated on the kind of cultural elitism his work deliberately seeks to resist:

■ [At university] I felt uneasy when a writer I didn't think deserved to be called an artist was being described as 'good', and often 'major', by the academics. Even the fact that you were given such writers at university meant they were *assumed* to be 'good'. The lecturers and university authorities hold the power: they can say something is good without having to prove it.[37] □

As the provocative title of her essay – ' "Middle-Class Wankers" and Working-Class Texts: The Critics and James Kelman' (2002) – suggests, Mary McGlynn is interested in the tension between Kelman's fiction and what the author regards as the bourgeois values of the critical establishment. McGlynn reads the controversy surrounding the 1994 Booker Prize as symptomatic of the disjuncture between Kelman's politics and the predominantly middle-class values of literary criticism. She quotes Kelman: 'Ninety per cent of the literature in Great Britain concerns people who never have to worry about money at all. We always seem to be watching or reading about emotional crises among folk who live in a world of great fortune both in matters of money and luck.'[38] McGlynn's essay is indicative of a popular strategy by which Kelman is read alongside the work of other authors like Samuel Beckett, Franz Kafka or Albert Camus: 'Kelman rejects the tastes and norms of the British metropole he is "supposed" to please. He writes instead for a local audience, his prose showing as well a studied application of both the techniques and ideas of continental European modernism.'[39] In McGlynn's case the point of reference is the Irish modernist James Joyce. Such tactics are not merely an exercise in prestige by association. They encourage us to read Scottish literature beyond any sense of an immuring national tradition. McGlynn uses Joyce to explain the subversive intent underpinning Kelman's use of free indirect discourse. As intimated above, Kelman is highly alert to the ways in which traditional realism functions as a repository for a host of elitist values: '[T]he standard third party one, the one that most people don't think of as a 'voice' at all – except maybe the voice of God – and they take for granted that it is unbiased and objective. But it's no such thing. Getting rid of that standard third party narrative voice is getting rid of a whole value system.'[40] Through looking at Joyce, McGlynn argues that the peripatetic nature of Kelman's work, the jumping between public and private worlds, deliberately seeks to challenges a host of normative literary values.

■ Joyce was another metropolitan colonial writer who sought to destabilize the reader's experience, in part, like Kelman, through his disinclination to use quotation marks. As Richard Ellman notes, Joyce, 'was eager to preserve one typographical feature of the manuscript, the use of dashes instead of quotation marks, on the grounds that the latter "are most unsightly and give the impression of unreality," in short, are "an eyesore" '. Joyce's calls for realism here resemble Kelman's; neither seeks an established realism so much as a way beyond it. As with Kelman, in Joyce the lack of quotation marks works simultaneously to liberate historically underrepresented modes of expression (whether dialects, inappropriate thoughts, or fragments of advertisements) and to suggest that the notion of the individual is flawed, that we are all, in fact, collections of voices and phrases. As André Topia points out about *Ulysses*, 'This disappearance of quotation marks is crucial. [...] Nothing permits us to know apriori if a sentence "belongs" to Bloom or not'. Indeed, the idea of 'ownership' of sentences, even phrases or words, is what is being explicitly interrogated.[41] □

For McGlynn there is a direct connection between these Joycean techniques and the aesthetic politics of Kelman's writing:

■ Kelman regularly eliminates all speech tags in extended dialogues, making it extraordinarily challenging to keep track of who is speaking. Together, these practices leave the reader unmoored, far removed from a comfortable reading position of narrative knowingness. The effect is again to render us as blind as readers as Sammy is in his world (both he and we are used to far more cues than we are given), as well as to render all voices and moments potentially equal. But the most important aspect of these stylistic choices is the way they work against plot or development of story: the flatness of the narrative gives a static, redundant feel, preparing us stylistically for the denial of narrative satisfaction at the novel's end.[42] □

Whilst Kelman's writing looks self-consciously to interrogate ideologies such as class and nationalism, critics have often sought to appropriate his work as an endorsement of such politics. McGlynn argues that critical readings of Kelman's work often attempt to re-inscribe the very positions that the texts themselves seek to problematise. Dietmar Böhnke's book, *Kelman Writes Back: Literary Politics in the Work of a Scottish Writer* (1999), the only full-length study of the author's work to date, is one such case in point. The title is a pun on the seminal work of postcolonial theory *The Empire Writes Back* (1989), which we will address in Chapter Five of this Guide. In working out this model Böhnke follows the example of early postcolonial critics and assumes the nation as the inevitable unit of decolonisation: 'Terms such as "nation", "national literature", "nationality", "national identity", "nationalism" and "internationalism" are key concepts in the continuing debate about the state of English-language literature after the decline of the Empire.'[43] Böhnke is forced to argue that the textual strategies in Kelman's work evince a specifically nationalist politics. Kelman becomes 'the chronicler of the nation' with his use of dialect encouraging Böhnke to read him as inheriting the cultural nationalist agenda of MacDairmid and the 1920s renaissance:

■ If the issues of national identity, nationalism and internationalism are not to be found overtly with James Kelman, how then can we try to detect them in his work? First, by turning to the past, to tradition – to this concept so important for the nation and for nationalism. It will be attempted to sketch the Scottish literary tradition of this century, in which James Kelman is working, and find influences that could be of importance to his writing. Second, by having a closer look at his work and attitudes and how Scottish national identity and nationalism express themselves there. It will emerge that he can be seen as a 'chronicler of the nation' rather than a theoretical nationalist.[44] ☐

In contrast for Laurence Nicoll such nationalist readings evince a critical reductionism within the secondary literature devoted to Kelman's work. In two separate essays, 'This Is Not A Nationalist Position: James Kelman's Existential Voice' (2000) and 'Gogol's Overcoat: Kelman Resartus' (2001) Nicoll argues against reading Kelman through the critical lens afforded by questions of nation and nationalism.[45] In the extract below he begins with the author's Booker speech and the suggestion that his work belongs to two contexts: a writing of de-colonisation and an existential literary tradition. Nicoll claims that critics have misread the former whilst completely ignoring the latter of these two perspectives: 'This problem can be simply described as an inability to think outwith a critical taxonomy the parameters of which are set by the concepts of "nation" and "nationalism".'[46] The key to understanding the anti-authoritarianism of Kelman lies in his existentialism. Nicoll reminds us that existential philosophy is grounded in the everyday experience of the individual and as such, affords theoretical primacy to direct experience rather than any abstract concept such as the nation.

■ A cursory reading [of Kelman's Booker speech] would want to maintain that here Kelman is locating himself within a national struggle, that 'indig-inous' signals that the referent of the noun 'culture' is *Scottish* culture; Scottish culture is struggling against its principal protagonist and this is (have you guessed yet) English culture. Fine, simple enough, but wrong. Part of the difficulty can be expressed as a logical fallacy, 'affirming the consequent', which goes something like this: cultural nationalists oppose cultural colonisation, therefore James Kelman is a cultural nationalist. But those tempted to read Kelman as a prose analogue to MacDiarmid have to circumvent a further and rather more pressing problem.[47] ☐

Nicoll quotes Kelman himself who has written about the problem-atic nature of nationalism and its residually inauthentic description of everyday experience:

■ we have to be clear what we don't mean [...] we don't mean some kind of 'pure, native-born Scottish person' or some mystical 'national culture.'

> Neither of these entities has ever existed in the past and cannot conceivably exist in the future. [...] entities like 'Scotsman,' 'German,' 'Indian' or 'American'; 'Scottish culture,' 'Jamaican culture,' are material absurdities. They aren't particular things in the world. There are no material bodies that correspond to them.[48] □

Nicoll asserts that nationalist readings fail to contend with the second tradition, the existential, to which Kelman argues his work belongs. This in part is due to the loose and vague number of ways in which existential philosophy has been applied within literary criticism. Nicoll attempts to rescue the existential from such woolly thinking by focusing on its primary assumption about what constitutes the proper subject of philosophical analysis. Rather than abstract concepts such as nation or class, existential philosophy begins its interrogation from our experience of 'being-in-the-world'. Again he quotes Kelman to clarify this position: 'I think the most ordinary person's life is fairly dramatic; all you've got to do is follow some people around and look at their existence for 24 hours.'[49] Nicoll argues:

> ■ Both literary and philosophical existentialism begin from the everyday, from the analysis of an ordinary individual in an individual set of ordinary circumstances. What is being argued by both Kelman and philosophical existentialists is that issues of great philosophical importance do not simply take place in paneled studies or seminar rooms but in cafés, in streets, in parks, at dog tracks and in snooker halls. These ordinary circumstances produce enough of philosophical and literary interest without the need either to move into the abstract or to import complex plotting.[50] □

One of the most astute attempts to navigate a path between the national and international in Kelman's work is Allan McMunnigall and Gerard Carruthers' essay 'Locating Kelman: Glasgow, Scotland and the Commitment to Place'. McMunnigall and Carruthers suggest an affinity between Kelman's use of dialect and its role in Lewis Grassic Gibbon's trilogy of novels *A Scots Quair* (1932–34). In this context we might recall Gibbon's own commitment to questions of poverty and deprivation over the posturing of nationalism:

> ■ There is nothing in culture or art that is worth the life and elementary happiness of one of those thousands who rot in the Glasgow slums. [...] If it came (as it may come) to some fantastical choice between a free and independent Scotland, a centre of culture, a bright flame of artistic and scientific achievement, and providing elementary decencies of food and shelter [...] I would welcome the English in suzerainty over Scotland til the end of time.[51] □

McMunnigall and Carruthers read Kelman and Gibbon in terms of a shared aspiration to provide a voice to those communities that have been silenced within mainstream literary discourse. Importantly, this does not commit Kelman to the kind of dogmatic nationalism often associated with the 1920s renaissance:

■ Lewis Grassic Gibbon re-energised the traditional Scottish literary focus of the small rural community through a modernist aesthetic in which this community is allowed its own voice. A pertinent analogy can be drawn with Kelman. Gibbon wrote about a place paralysed by the collapse of labour-intensive agricultural work practices in the early decades of the twentieth century, and Kelman writes of a late twentieth-century city-based workforce likewise muted and marginalised by the force of structural unemployment.[52] □

McMunnigall and Carruthers also attempt to situate Kelman's work within what remains a widely unacknowledged and understudied history of radical politics in Scotland. To this end they evoke the author's praise for James Hogg, author of *The Private Memoirs and Confessions of a Justified Sinner* (1824). Hogg's status as an outsider figure – he worked as a shepherd in the Scottish borders for most of his life – meant that in his own time his work was also patronised, in a pejorative sense, by certain sections of the literary establishment. Moreover, Kelman's play about the Radical War of 1820, *Hardie and Baird* (1978), demonstrates the author's own interest in recovering the hidden narratives of Scottish history.

■ Kelman has perhaps more cautiously participated in a similar project of reclaiming 'lost' Scottish history in his radio (and later theatre) play, *Hardie and Baird* (broadcast in 1978, staged in 1990 and published in 1991). Kelman's most historical work deals with an 'episode of suppressed radical history', during the 1820s when the two weavers were hanged for treason after organising armed insurrection in protest over economic conditions in their industry. In choosing these two politically and metaphysically literate protagonists, Kelman pays tribute to the long tradition not only of leftist activism in Scottish culture, but the ethic of accessible education embodied in eighteenth-century Common Sense philosophy.[53] □

The link between philosophy and everyday experience, highlighted in Nicoll's existential reading, coheres with what McMunnigall and Carruthers identify as the Scottish tradition of the Democratic Intellect. This philosophical movement espoused a universal, common sense approach to philosophical questions. At the same time it deliberately sought to resist the enthronement of experts and elites as the purveyors of moral authority:

■ Kelman acknowledges this outlook, as interpreted by George Davie, most powerfully argued in *The Democratic Intellect* (1961), as 'a generalist philosophy resisting mental specialisation which resists an atomised culture of 'experts' who take exclusive possession of a very disparate range of knowledge and expertise. Such specialisation is resisted in Common Sense philosophy's prioritising of the innate 'power of judgement and critical evaluation'. In this emphasising of a centrally important philosophical faculty (practically institutionalised in Scotland in the traditional 'ordinary' degree and the school curriculum of widely spread higher grade certification), what is opposed is the dominant British or English arrangement of specialised activity.[54] □

We saw Douglas Dunn earlier argue that the predominance of Glasgow fiction during the 1980s risked skewering perception as to the scope and range of Scottish writing. There is another sense in which these working-class narratives have had a distorting influence. As well as eclipsing less proletarian fiction, there is a risk that Glasgow can be seen as taking ownership over the rights of narratives of poverty and despair. Were cities like Edinburgh, Dundee and Aberdeen not also party to some of the adverse effects of Thatcherism? The book that single-handedly destroyed this misperception was Irvine Welsh's *Trainspotting*. Set in the Edinburgh district of Leith, Welsh's depiction of the capital's heroin scene blew apart any preconceived notion that class was merely a Glaswegian issue. Welsh himself admits to being heavily influenced by Kelman in the 1980s: 'Kelman was like Year Zero.'[55] The critic Robert A. Morace notes that Welsh's Edinburgh-based novel did much to redress the imbalance implied by west coast representation of working-class culture. The novel undermined a host of ideas about Edinburgh as a living embodiment of the Scottish Tourist Board and its tartan-shortbread image of the country:

■ Kelman's Glasgow, despite having been designated 'European City of Culture', seemed to have a literary lock on urban blight and doomed vernacular. Welsh's 'Edinburgh dirty realism' provides an alternative style and vision, one that derives from the culture of disaffected youth rather than the working class solidarity that Welsh maintains was, as a viable political position, destroyed in the eighties.[56] □

Whilst similarities exist between both authors' work, there are also significant differences. Drew Milne warns against any easy conflation, highlighting Welsh's commercial popularity, his vivid depiction of sex and drugs, and his easy crossover to more mainstream forms such as the cinema: 'Kelman's work has affinities with the modernist dissidence of Franz Kafka, Samuel Beckett and Albert Camus, whereas Welsh offers something more like a populist postmodern blend of William Burroughs [1914–97] and Quentin Tarantino [born

1963].'[57] Just as Welsh brought anger and resentment to bear on representations of Edinburgh, a number of writers would take heed and begin to examine how social exclusion was manifest in other Scottish locales. Notable examples include Alan Warner's novels set in a fictional version of Oban – *Morvern Callar* (1995), *These Demented Lands* (1997), and *The Sopranos* (1998). Kevin MacNeil's scathing critique of the Island of Lewis, *The Stornoway Way* (2005), is another case in point. Both Kelman and Welsh were crucial in breaking the mould for this subsequent generation of writers.

If Glasgow is synonymous with the history of class in Scotland it is implicated in another equally important narrative – empire. The street names (Jamaica Street, the Kingston Bridge) disclose the story of the city's emergence as a trading port that prospered under the British Empire in the eighteenth century. For Christopher Whyte this coincidence renders Glasgow somewhat of an anomalous space when it comes to discussing questions of national identity. A city of empire, Glasgow's meteoric rise coincided with a period of history after 1707, when Scotland had ceased to function as an independent nation state.

■ [Glasgow's] relation to the rest of Scotland is problematical. As an industrial metropolis it came into being at a time when Scotland had for more than a century ceased to be an autonomous political or cultural unit. This means that Glasgow has never experienced an independent or organically functioning Scotland. It is the child not of the nation, but of empire, which alone can explain the savagery of its expansion and decline. This makes Scotland an inappropriate context for understanding Glasgow, and the distrust is often mutual.[58] □

Kelman invokes the discourse of decolonisation as a way of describing what he regards as the social, economic and cultural marginalisation of working-class Scots. Similarly, writers from the Gaeltacht have been keen to employ postcolonial discourse as a way of theorising the historic subordination of Gaelic culture. However, there is another sense in which Scotland was a willing participant, and a significant beneficiary, from the very excesses of imperialism which contemporary historiography is so quick to decry. It is this tension that the following chapter seeks to chart.

CHAPTER FIVE

Postcolonialism

Scotland the colonised, Scotland the coloniser

Since the 1980s postcolonial theory has become one of the most fashionable fields of inquiry within the academic study of English literature. Broadly speaking, postcolonialism is canonically associated with the work of writers and critics like Frantz Fanon (1925–61), Edward Said (1935–2003) and Ngũgĩ wa Thiong'o. It has its origins in the post-World War II struggles for independence within various countries living under colonial rule. The use of the prefix *post* in postcolonial is important. It implies that the activities of decolonisation continue to endure long after the occupying power leaves and national independence is secured. Underpinning postcolonial theory is the view that colonialism was not only a military, economic and political form of subordination; it was also a cultural one. In the past native populations were actively encouraged to adopt the language and culture of the incumbent colonial power in place of their indigenous customs and speech. Part of the process of colonisation lay in denying native peoples a sense of meaningful cultural identity and persuading them, often with force, to imitate and aspire toward the culture of the coloniser. John McLeod defines the basic terrain of the cultural discourse that has arisen in response to this realisation: '[Theories of postcolonialism] explore the ways that representations and modes of perception are used as fundamental weapons of colonial power to keep colonised peoples subservient to colonial rule.'[1] Postcolonial critics explore how culture functioned as both a weapon of colonial oppression, and a means by which native peoples sought to resist imperial hegemony.

In recent years the language of postcolonialism has been appropriated by a number of Scottish writers in an attempt to frame the aesthetic politics of their work. As we saw, James Kelman asserts his place within 'a literature of decolonisation', one that includes writers like Jamaican-born, English-based poet Linton Kwesi Johnson and Nigerian authors Wole Soyinka (born 1934) and Chinua Achebe.

Janice Galloway has also used a similar context to describe the political undercurrents of recent Scottish writing:

■ It's hardly contentious to say that a significant number of Scottish novels are more notable for their preoccupation for what is *not* said than what *is*; with the struggle to find a 'voice'. This, of course, has much to do with my country's history as a colonised nation, our lack of real political clout, marginalization and neglect by successive Westminster governments who can afford to be smug even when they acknowledge their cultural ignorance if all territories north of Manchester.[2] □

One of the other areas where postcolonial theory has been consistently applied to Scottish culture concerns the historic treatment of the Gaeltacht. Since the sixteenth century successive Scottish and British governments pursued a variety of policies designed to subdue the 'barbaric' Gaels of the Highlands and bring them under the influence of 'civilised' authority. In Chapter Two we saw the Gaelic poet Iain Crichton Smith defend the validity of Gaelic as both a language and a culture. The most infamous example of postcolonial rhetoric in recent years is unarguably in Irvine Welsh's novel *Trainspotting*. The book's anti-hero Mark Renton pours vitriol on the state of modern Scotland and its pathetic status as a victim of English imperialism: 'Fuckin failures in a country ay failures. It's nae good blamin it oan the English fir colonising us. Ah don't hate the English. They're just wankers. We are colonised by wankers. We can't even pick a decent, vibrant, healthy culture to be colonised by.'[3] The ideological implications of this kind of rhetoric will be examined in the discussion of Welsh's work below.

Whilst several contemporary writers make use of this type of language, others have remained highly sceptical regarding the whole enterprise of Scottish postcolonialism. For the novelist and commentator Andrew O'Hagan (born 1968) Scotland's historic complicity in the British imperial adventure renders any such assertion highly problematic:

■ [Scotland] has always wanted a little bit of what England has; its commercial and ideological roots go down quite far with England's; their entanglement is of a kind that might raise a laugh in the breast of those who know enough history to know that – unlike, say, Éire – Scotland, far from being a colonised country, has been a bitter harvester, in its own right, of other people's freedom.[4] □

In a similar vein the Irish commentator Fintan O'Toole (born 1958) argues that Scotland's success during the nineteenth century is inextricably linked with the ill-gotten gains of imperialism: 'The nineteenth-century rise of Scotland occurred in [...] the supreme

British century – in the era of Queen Victoria (1819–1901; reigned 1837–1901) and David Livingstone (1813–73), of industry and empire. [As a result] it is impossible for Scotland to cast itself as an oppressed and colonised nation and at the same time to locate its golden age in a time when it was most profoundly at one with the supposed aggressor. It needs a different story.'⁵ The reluctance of both O'Hagan and O'Toole to entertain a Scottish postcolonialism finds its roots in the history of the British Empire. We might recall that the immediate aftermath of the Union of the Crowns (1603) saw Scottish landowners at the forefront of one of the earliest imperial projects, the plantation of Ulster. Almost a century later the Act of Union (1707), when the Scottish parliament voted itself out of existence, occurred as a direct consequence of Scotland's failure to establish its own colonial outpost at Darien, on the isthmus of Panama. For most of the seventeenth century the English parliament had deemed Scotland a 'foreign' nation and legally excluded it from engaging in direct enterprise with the colonies. A successful colony at Darien would have halved the sailing time between Europe and Asia, and provided Scotland with a considerable foothold in the ever burgeoning field of colonial trade. As is well known the Darien project ended in complete disaster. Inhospitable terrain, a shortage of provisions and an outbreak of fever, along with military defeat by rival Spanish forces, left the Scottish nation almost bankrupt. As a result, when talk of union arose in the subsequent decade the landed and mercantile classes of Scotland, 1,500 of which had invested heavily in Darien, were particularly receptive to the notion of a British state. Darien has an important symbolism, reminding us that the 300 year hiatus in Scottish self-government was a direct result of the nation's desire to reap the rewards of the British imperial adventure.

Access to the ever-burgeoning markets of the British Empire was to have a dramatic effect on Scotland for the next three centuries. Nowhere was this transformation more dramatically illustrated than the growth of Glasgow. By the 1770s the city was importing more tobacco from the Americas than all other UK ports put together. Glasgow's continued expansion during the nineteenth century was primarily due to shipbuilding, an industry born out of the demand for servicing a British Empire upon which the sun never set. Moreover, throughout the eighteenth and nineteenth centuries ambitious Scots found ample outlet for their energies in the machinery of Empire. Particular aspects of colonial administration were made up of significant numbers of Scots including the army, the medical profession and the civil service. One of the areas where Scots played a disproportionately high role was in the sugar plantations of the Caribbean. Between 1750 and 1800 between 12,000 and 20,000 Scots are estimated to have emigrated to the West Indies. The islands of Dominica, St Vincent, Grenada and Tobago were all settled by Scotsmen. By the 1790s the sugar islands had become the Clyde's premier partners for overseas trade.[6] The unspoken story underpinning this imperial enterprise forms one of the most shameful episodes in British history. It is of course slavery. A largely unexamined chapter in Scottish history, the ownership of slaves in the Caribbean plantations forms the central theme of the novel *Joseph Knight* (2004) by James Robertson (born 1958). The book is based on the true story of Joseph Knight, a slave brought back from Jamaica to Scotland in 1769 by his master and plantation owner John Wedderburn. On hearing of a case in England questioning the legality of slavery Knight demanded wages from his owner and upon being refused these ran away. He was arrested and tried with the case eventually reaching the Court of Session in Edinburgh in 1777. Here the court pronounced slavery to be against the law in Scotland and subsequently freed Knight. This verdict predated the official abolition of the slave trade in Britain (1807) by some 30 years. Robertson's book confronts a number of issues concerning Scotland's involvement in one of the most notorious chapters of the British imperial story. Much of Robertson's novel is set in 1802 with Joseph Knight an invisible figure, one that haunts the memory of an elderly John Wedderburn. The text offers a comparison with contemporary perceptions of slavery, whereby they are seen to function as something of a repressed memory within Scottish historical conscience. Wedderburn's flashbacks to his time in the Caribbean reveal a brutal world, one that cannot be fully understood by way of statistical and historical accounts of the plantations. Whilst John Wedderburn is restrained in his treatment of his slaves, his brother James forces several female slaves to share his bed, in the process fathering several illegitimate children. Their youngest brother Sandy comments on the trouble he has writing to his mother and sister back in Scotland. There is so much that happens on the plantation that is simply beyond the pale and cannot be disclosed to those back home. Having established himself in Jamaica Wedderburn buys Joseph Knight when he is a boy of 12 and trains him up for domestic service. He dresses Knight in European clothes, teaches him English and gives him some basic education. We are reminded of the grand narrative of imperialism, whereby European colonialism marketed itself as an attempt to 'civilise' and 'improve' the so-called savage races it encountered around the world. When Wedderburn returns to Scotland with Knight the slave functions as both a souvenir and status symbol for the returning planter. Robertson's book overlays the story of the plantations with that of the Scottish Enlightenment, when figures like David Hume and Adam Smith were in the process of shaping the evolution of European civilisation. In doing so *Joseph Knight* explicitly foregrounds the relationship between the cruelties of Empire and the age of improvement which coincided with it.

Robertson's novel resurrects a host of issues which problematise any straightforward claims that Scotland's history is that of a colonised nation. In *Scotland's Empire 1600–1815* (2003) T.M. Devine argues that the story of modern Scotland cannot be disentangled from the wider narratives of British imperialism. For Devine it is no coincidence that 1707 announced the beginning of what would become known as 'the British imperial age':

■ So intense was the Scottish engagement with empire that it affected almost every nook and cranny of Scottish life: industrialization, intellectual activity, politics, identity, education, popular culture, consumerism, labour markets, demographic trends, Highland social development and much else. In a word, empire was fundamental to the moulding of the modern Scottish nation. The discussion, therefore, needs to maintain a continuous dialogue between domestic Scottish issues and those generated at the global peripheries.[7] □

It is the enduring contradiction, between Scotland the colonised and Scotland the coloniser, which preoccupies the discussion of post-colonial theory in recent Scottish criticism.

Despite the assertions of Welsh, Kelman and others, several international commentators have shown a reluctance to include Scotland within the wider canon of postcolonial literatures. The most famous example of this appeared in *The Empire Writes Back* (1989), one of the first texts to offer a theory and practice of postcolonial literature. Its authors Bill Ashcroft, Gareth Griffiths and Helen Tiffin argued against the inclusion of white European nations within what they defined as a canon of postcolonial cultures:

■ While it is possible to argue that these societies [Ireland, Scotland and Wales] were the first victims of English expansion, their subsequent complicity in the British imperial enterprise makes it difficult for colonized peoples outside Britain to accept their identity as post-colonial.[8] □

As we have seen in the case of Scotland, such reluctance seems well grounded. Whilst events such as the Highland Clearances resemble the experience of native peoples elsewhere, many Scots were among the most enthusiastic participants in the British imperial adventure. If Scotland cannot unashamedly don the badge of colonial victimhood, there is a case that it ought not to be ejected from the discussion altogether. Our analysis of this critical terrain begins with Craig Beveridge and Ronald Turnbull's *The Eclipse of Scottish Culture* (1989). This was the first critical attempt to deploy postcolonial theory at length in the examination of Scottish culture. Beveridge and Turnbull appropriate the concept of 'inferiorisation', made famous by Frantz Fanon, as a way of diagnosing the historical neglect of Scottish culture and what they regard as the enduring crisis of confidence within the national psyche. They argue for the recovery and reconstitution of Scottish Studies outwith predominantly Anglo-centric systems of cultural value. Robert Crawford and Cairns Craig have both been influenced by the challenge laid down by Beveridge and Turnbull. In *Devolving English Literature* Crawford refers to the 'barbarian' aesthetics of contemporary Scottish writing, whereas in *Out of History* (1996) Craig maintains 'it is by the colour of our vowels' that Scots have become déclassé within the British cultural context. Berthold Schoenes's essay 'A Passage to Scotland' marks a significant intervention in the Scottish postcolonial debate and is also considered in due course. Rather than seek to assert the wholesale exclusion or inclusion of Scotland from the postcolonial debate, Schoene focuses on questions of local difference. He asks how, and in what ways, did various groups within Scotland experience the kind of narratives associated with the colonial encounter? Schoene's work represents a move towards a more subtle and nuanced form of analysis and, as such, is symptomatic of the secondary debates that have arisen within postcolonial studies during the 1990s. He is also alert to questions of internal colonialism and the exploitation suffered by many Scots at the hands of their own native elites. This class element is reminiscent of the issues addressed by Gayatri Chakravorty Spivak and the Subaltern Studies group in India. As we saw in Chapter Two, Edwin Muir famously diagnosed the predicament of Scottish writers in terms of a fractured cultural identity. Postcolonial theory, particularly the work of Indian scholars like Homi Bhabha, has tried to reconfigure this notion of hybridity. The concern has been with transforming this idea, remoulding and repackaging it, turning it from a disabling to an enabling cultural condition. Hybridity becomes part of a strategy of resistance by which the colonised native can undermine and expose the contingency of imperial cultural authority. In Scotland the work of the Russian Formalist Mikhail Bakhtin (1895–1975) has been used in a similar vein and this will also be examined.

The inferiorisation of Scottish culture

Craig Beveridge and Ronald Turnbull's *The Eclipse of Scottish Culture* represents the first real encounter between Scottish criticism and postcolonial theory. Beveridge and Turnbull employ Frantz Fanon's concept of 'inferiorisation' to re-examine the dominant paradigms of Scottish historiography. Inferiorisation was a term initially coined by Fanon in his seminal study *Black Skin, White Masks* (1952). Born and raised on the Caribbean island of Martinique, Fanon became a professional psychiatrist who worked in both Paris and Algeria during the 1950s. Coinciding with Algeria's war of independence (1954–62), Fanon witnessed both the direct and indirect ways in which colonial administrations attempted to exercise control over their native populations. It became clear to Fanon that culture played a vital role within this matrix of domination. The culture of the settler colony was depicted as infinitely superior and more advanced than that of the flawed and uncivilised natives. Hence, native culture was 'inferiorised'. As a result of this hierarchy of values, the organisation and subordination of the local population was imbued with a veneer of moral legitimacy. Domination and exploitation were able to masquerade as a form of social improvement. As Beveridge and Turnbull explain:

> ■ In the long term, constant disparagement of the local culture creates self-doubt, saps the native's self-respect and so weakens resistance to foreign rule. The strategy of inferiorisation is fully successful when the native internalises the estimation of local culture which is propagated by the coloniser, acknowledging the superiority of metropolitan ways. The imperial refrain, which upholds the coloniser as the representative of civilisation, progress and universal human values, is then taken up by the *évolués*, those natives who try to escape from their backwardness by desperate identification with the culture of the metropolis.[9] □

Beveridge and Turnbull take this model from Fanon and apply it to the dominant paradigms of Scottish history. The period around the Act of Union in 1707, when Scotland formally joined the British state, provides a locus for their argument. Pre-union Scotland is portrayed as a dark, uncivilised country, awaiting the enlightenment of incorporation within the British state. Beveridge and Turnbull offer a list of values which they argue have come to characterise the ways in which historians generally regard this era:

Scotland	dark	England	enlightened
	backward		advanced
	fanatical		reasonable
	violent		decent
	barbaric		civilised
	illiberal		tolerant
	parochial		cosmopolitan
	uncouth		refined
	intemperate		moderate
	savage		mild

unruly	orderly
severe	kind
harsh	gentle
primitive	sophisticated[10]

Where this story of inferiorisation has been most prevalent has been in the ways in which the history of pre-Union Scotland has been read by generations of historians. For Fanon colonial ideology could be seen to function retrospectively; it looks backward and systematically seeks to devalue pre-colonial history. The underlying purpose of this strategy is to justify the present, to convince colonised peoples that they are in fact better off under occupation than they were before their occupiers arrived. Beveridge and Turnbull argue:

■ Orthodox opinion about Scotland's condition prior to the Union – prior, that is, to the 'opening up' to English influence – has faithfully reflected Fanon's account of the imperial distortion of pre-colonial history. Darkness reigned. To quote Hugh Trevor-Roper [...]: 'At the end of the seventeenth century, Scotland was a by-word for irredeemable poverty, social backwardness, political faction. The universities were the unreformed seminaries of a fanatical clergy.' Scotland was, indeed, 'the rudest of all the European nations'.[11] □

The above lists of oppositional values are symptomatic of much early postcolonial theory. The use of binary opposition as a way of framing the colonial encounter is one which a number of critics would increasingly come to question. There is an implicit assumption that we can talk about nations as homogenous units in which every section of the population experienced colonialism in roughly similar ways. This is simply not the case. In Scotland the landed gentry, the middle classes (doctors, civil servants and military officers), the Highland peasant and the Glasgow labourer all had radically different experiences of Empire. The German critic Berthold Schoene picks up on the reductive tendency within these early attempts to locate Scotland within a postcolonial framework. In contrast to implicit assertions of national homogeneity, of Scotland's wholesale exploitation under English influence, Schoene highlights the varied and uneven nature of Scottish experience within the grand narratives of Empire. He maintains that a postcolonial critique of Scottish culture requires a more subtle engagement than the kind of Manichean dualism offered by Beveridge and Turnbull:

■ The idea of a uniform Scottish identity is an illusion: Glaswegians are as different from the people of Edinburgh as Shetlanders or Orcadians are from Highlanders and insular Scotland as a whole is from Scotland's cosmopolitan centres. Significantly, in the writings of authors from the Western and Northern Isles, and most notably in the work of George Mackay Brown, mainland Scotland itself has been likened to an imperial power, with anglicised clan chiefs or lairds, resident in Edinburgh and London, as the main perpetrators of economic and cultural erosion, imposing on the original rural communities a new additional class of doctors, teachers, factors and ministers and thus introducing to them British-orientated views and ways of life that inferiorise their own communal heritage.[12] □

Again there is the use of Fanon's term 'inferiorisation'. This time, though, it functions to introduce the idea of an internal colonialism, one acting within Scottish society rather than being imposed from without. This more nuanced approach to questions of power cuts across the simplistic binaries of coloniser and colonised. It reminds us that for both the rural peasantry and industrial proletariat in Scotland, exploitation did not always wear the cloak of English military uniform. Scottish elites were often the most enthusiastic prosecutors of British state policy abroad and the harvesters of other people's freedom within their own country. One of the more unexamined aspects of the Clearances is the degree to which fellow Scots benefited financially from the commercial transformation of the highlands and the enforced migration of its indigenous population.

Schoene's essay 'A passage to Scotland: Scottish literature and the British postcolonial question' is one of the most detailed engagements with the issue of Scottish postcolonialism to date. The essay begins by highlighting one of the flaws within *The Empire Writes Back* and its attempt to form a canon of postcolonial cultures. Where *The Empire Writes Back* attempted a generic model of postcolonial discourse, Schoene argues that such a project is fundamentally flawed: 'Ashcroft, Griffiths and Tiffin appear to deny the nature of English imperialism as a gradually evolving phenomenon which has influenced different nations in different ways [...] the postcolonial experience of Indians is different from that of Australian aborigines, Africans or Canadians.'[13] The fact that different countries experienced colonialism in a variety of forms and with various levels of intensity forces us to reconsider our analysis and reconstruct a more sophisticated theory of postcolonialism. It is certain that the Australian aboriginal peoples had a dramatically different experience of colonialism to the Maoris in nearby New Zealand. This was partly due to the fact that the latter lived a more settled, tribal existence and had significant experience of both commerce and war-making. At the same time, Scotland remains different from these colonies in another significant way. Unlike most other countries within the postcolonial canon, Scotland was not invaded and forcibly occupied by England. Instead its parliament voted itself out of existence. Moreover, whereas places like India secured their independence from Britain during the twentieth century Scotland remains constitutionally and politically bound up with the British state. It continues to be strongly influenced by its numerically and financially superior neighbour south of the border. These important differences persist. However, for Schoene there are several similarities between aspects of Scottish history and the experience of colonised people's elsewhere.

■ [A]lthough the Scottish people have never been threatened by any large scale attempts at ethnic extirpation comparable to the traumatic experiences of the colonised peoples of the New and Third Worlds, their history of colonial oppression has been more brutal and incisive than the mere cultural marginalisation deplored and inveighed against by contemporary white Canadians, Australians and New Zealanders. At the end of our twentieth century the Gaelic-speaking population of the Scottish Highlands and Islands is still struggling for cultural survival. The communal memory of the Clearances of the late eighteenth and early nineteenth centuries constitutes an elementary part of the Scottish cultural heritage and national self-image. Comparable in impact and significance only to Irish memories of the Great Famine [1846–51], it will always weigh much heavier on the Scottish psyche than the occasional taunt of a backwater origin or comic provincial accent.[14] □

Schoene highlights in particular the suffering of Gaelic Scots during the Highland Clearances. Between the mid-eighteenth and the end of the nineteenth century tens of thousands of Gaels were forcibly evicted from their highland farms following the realisation, born out of the industrial revolution, that sheep were more profitable than people. As a result for Schoene:

■ it does not seem plausible that postcolonial theory and criticism – so far exclusively reserved for the new literatures in English that have originated in the non-European colonies of the former British Empire – could not or should not be applied productively to the study of marginalised or, rather, categorically affiliated and subsequently de-emphasised, literatures of the British Isles themselves.[15] □

Beginning with the fourteenth-century Makars and ending in the present day, Schoene examines the historical evolution of Scottish literature from a postcolonial perspective:

■ In Scotland, loss and lack of statehood have functioned as a strong stimulus and incentive for national self-expression, confirming that identity is strongest when threatened by annihilation. Nothing is more apt to challenge and invigorate native traditions than sudden historical change and the necessity to fight for cultural survival. In this respect, Scottish writers since the early eighteenth and perhaps even the early seventeenth centuries are likely to have much in common with contemporary writers from the formerly colonised and now independent Commonwealth countries.[16] □

Where this type of postcolonial analysis runs dry, for Schoene at least, is when it comes to contemporary Scottish writing. The lack of a clearly defined national project means that contemporary literature in Scotland ceases to benefit from being placed under the postcolonial lens in the same way as, say, writing from the 1920s renaissance:

■ In late twentieth-century Scottish literature the patriotic pathos of the rural myth-makers has been replaced by the cosmopolitan realism of a new avant-garde. Whereas the search for an all-embracing national identity used to be the predominant creative impulse, the emphasis is now on the differences between various individual and group identities. The main issue is not any more the status of the Scottish nation as a minority within the United Kingdom but rather the status of minority communities within Scottish society; not essential Scottishness but rather the differences and the similarities between different kinds and ways of Scottishness.[17] □

In this context we might usefully ask if narratives of decolonisation must always be read in the context of a nationalist resistance. Does the fact that writers like Kelman remain highly critical of cultural nationalism inevitably exclude them from the issues which postcolonial theory confronts? Schoene's aim is to liberate Scottish literature from what he regards as the intellectual straitjacket of cultural nationalism:

■ The aim of contemporary Scottish literature is to emphasise individuality and intracommunal difference rather than to construct dubious all-in-one myths of a nationalist quality. While retaining its own characteristic timbre and twist it has become truly cosmopolitan. After looking first at its navel, then at its underbelly, it has now set our to explore the whole of its anatomy, fetching skeletal national stereotypes from the closet to bring them under close literary scrutiny. Contemporary Scottish writers are not interested in the portrayal of English-Scottish tensions or yet another vain autopsy of the scar tissue of English imperialism. Fully aware of the unsatisfactory nature of their political situation yet nonetheless secure in their identity, contemporary Scottish authors have started to look at Scotland as a country, nation and society of great diversity and potential, not one-sidedly as a shut-up victim of imperial anglicisation.[18] □

A residual question for us is whether or not, in the twenty-first century, imperialism must inevitably take the form of one state dominating another? In our own time globalisation and the emergence of multi-national capitalism means that the exploitation of various populations around the world can seldom be traced to a single and easily defined source. This does not mean that the cultural politics explored by postcolonial theory have ceased to be of critical interest. We might usefully recall that the original purpose of colonialism in places like Africa and India was to increase the efficiency with which European powers could economically exploit these places. The underlying narrative of colonialism was always an economic one. In the words of Ngũgĩ: 'The real aim of colonialism was to control people's wealth — what they produced, how they produced it, and how it was distributed.'[19] Bearing this in mind we might begin to question the validity of a prefix like *post-* when it comes to postcolonial theory. There is an implicit assumption that the power relationships under scrutiny have vanished and are merely an object of historical interest. The imperial power may have officially left. Independence may have been achieved. However, the enduring cultural and economic subordination of many former colonies suggests that a term like *neo-colonialism* is perhaps more appropriate when it comes to examining the power relations which operate within the contemporary world.

One of the more original aspects of Schoene's work is its willingness to acknowledge the uneven nature of colonial experience within Scotland. He argues that postcolonial theory provides a way of deconstructing the politics of national identity. One of the most urgent targets for this type of practice is the whole notion of tartanry and its ubiquitous presence within popular/global perceptions of Scottish identity. Schoene scrutinises the problematic nature of tartan, beginning with the notion that modern Scottish identity is born out of a certain sense of dualism. The post-union Scot is seen to embody two identities. He is a chameleon-like figure and is able simultaneously to occupy notions of Scottishness and Britishness with ease. This idea puts a particular postcolonial twist on Gregory Smith's notion of the intrinsic doubleness of the Scottish character, the renowned 'Caledonian Antisyzygy.' Schoene applies postcolonial theory to the iconography of Scottish national identity, particularly the enthronement of the tartan kilt as the national costume in the early nineteenth century:

■ The question in need of addressing is how the culture of the Scottish Highlanders – once despised by the anglicised Lowland Scots as incorrigible barbarians and submitted to a systematic destruction of their indigenous ways of life by dint of decrees prohibiting, amongst other things, the use of the Gaelic language and the wearing of the kilt – could eventually become the main signifier of pure, uncontaminated Scottishness.[20] □

Schoene locates the adoption of the kilt as a national costume within Scotland of the early nineteenth century. In doing so he situates this event in the period of Romanticism within Scottish literature, the apotheosis of which remains the Waverley novels of Sir Walter Scott. It is highly ironic that in a period when Gaelic communities (the traditional wearers of the tartan plaid) were being systematically cleared off their lands, lowland Scots were busy appropriating the kilt as a sign of their cultural difference from England. In a similar fashion to the church, the law and the education system, the kilt enabled Scotland to maintain a distinct sense of cultural difference, whilst at the same time reaping the political and economic benefits of being British. Schoene quotes historian John Prebble in illustrating the irony of this situation:

> ■ while the rest of Scotland was permitting the expulsion of its Highland people it was also forming that romantic attachment to kilt and tartan that scarcely compensates for the disappearance of a race to whom such things were once a commonplace reality. The chiefs remain, in Edinburgh and London, but the people are gone.[21] □

An important aspect of this historical process is the degree to which it was other lowland Scots who benefited from the eviction and enforced emigration of the Gael during the clearances. Schoene comments:

> ■ While the Clearances may ultimately have been instigated by England, eager to expand its sphere of influence even to the most remote regions of the British Isles, most of the immediate agents or perpetrators of the evictions were anglicised Lowlanders [...] Hence, the Lowlanders' historical complicity in English imperialism, as well as their ensuing contemporary postcolonial predicament, conspicuously reflects that of the white settler colonies of Canada, Australia and New Zealand, who now likewise find themselves in a double-bind situation of being at once erstwhile coloniser and contemporary (post-)colonised.[22] □

A postcolonial rereading of Scotland's history reveals longstanding tensions that inevitably interrupt simplistic accounts of Scottish victimhood and English villainy.

Scotland's uneven experience of colonialism reminds us of recent arguments put forward under the aegis of Subaltern Studies. Centered on the work of Ranjit Guha and Gayatri Chakravorty Spivak in India, Subaltern Studies offers a Marxist slant on the issues raised by postcolonial theory. Its primary interest is in the ways in which mechanisms of colonial power continue to function long after individual nations have secured their independence. Subaltern Studies argues that in the wake of colonialism, rather than democratic emancipation, the reigns of power are assumed by a small native elite. These elites are bourgeois in character and, for the most part, rule in the narrow interests of their class. For the majority of the population independence signals not real liberation, but merely a reconfiguration within their experience of domination. In the Scottish context the role of native elites in the administration and execution of British state policy remains to be fully explored. A key essay in the Subaltern Studies debate is Spivak's 'Can the Subaltern Speak?' which examines the marginalisation of peasant women in India following the country's secession from the British Empire in 1947. H. Gustav Klaus argues that for Kelman and others it is through such narratives of class-based disenfranchisement that Scottish experience most resembles that of erstwhile former colonies:

> ■ This focus on the working class and the concomitant attack on middle-class values, singular as it may appear in the 1980s in an all-British context, is by no means a Scottish peculiarity, but widespread in what goes under the name of 'New Literatures in English', resulting as it does from the association of the native ruling elite with the colonisers.[23] □

Another critic to have ventured into the field of Scottish postcolonialism is Michael Gardiner. Gardiner is interested in what he calls 'Scotland's double-determination', its dual status as both victim and perpetrator within the wider narratives imperialism. Like Schoene, he argues that we still need to assess Scotland's historic complicity within the British imperial adventure: 'Accounts of Scotland's role in British colonialism are still pointedly absent, a need implied here in the idea of "Scottish postcoloniality". Such accounts cannot however involve analysis of a Scottish colonial state ideology, since Scotland has never been a colonising *nation-state*. Scotland, as such, has had no foreign policy since 1707 (and there is no path as yet to bringing it within the competence of the Scottish parliament), yet an over-identification with a new British union on the part of professional and public Scots in the century and a half following the Act of Union put them at the forefront of British colonialism.'[24] Gardiner argues that there are two key areas where Scottish experience significantly overlaps that of other former colonies. The first of these is in terms of language. As such Gardiner's work can be seen to echo both Craig's notion of the colour of [Scottish] vowels and Crawford's analysis of the 'barbarian' tongue and its role in the history of Scottish literature.

> ■ Scottish children, especially in Lowland Scotland, where English occupies more or less the whole linguistic horizon, are unusual in growing up diglossic (speaking two substantially discrete dialects), educated away from

a native dialect which corresponds with remarkable accuracy to the shape of the Scottish nation. Indeed, the semi-volitional coherence of a 'national dialect' in this case is a major reason for stressing the specificity of that nation at all. As is now recognised, the nation *restated* as a level of cultural and linguistic restructuring of the social was paradigmatically described in Frantz Fanon's *Black Skin, White Masks*, one of *the* founding works of 'post-colonial theory'.[25] □

The second point of meaningful overlap between Scottish experience and that of colonised peoples elsewhere relates to an enduring pre-occupation with questions of identity:

■ A historical splitting of local, civic context (Scotland), and statehood (the UK), has left devolving Scotland with the need to ask questions of self-determination – or determination of the self – not only on the level of identity, but also to that of contingent and contradictory *identifications* working simultaneously within the person.[26] □

For Gardiner the macro-politics of statehood manifest themselves at a micro-political level. The dislocated and unstable state finds its corollary in the uncertainties that characterise the existence of so many of the characters that populate contemporary writing.

This kind of identity crisis resonates with theories of cultural hybridity espoused by the postcolonial critic Homi Bhabha. Bhabha argues that the colonial subject emerges as a form of hybrid, living in the interstices of two cultures – Indian and British, or in this case, Scottish and British. As we saw Fanon argue earlier, this state of cultural hybridity served to undermine and inferiorise the native. Regardless of how much he might eventually come to resemble his colonial master there is a residual sense in which the native is a deformed and imperfect copy. Bhabha attempts to reverse the political implications of this kind of cultural hybridity. He argues that it becomes a method by which the native is able to resist and undermine the cultural hegemony of the colonial power. In such a context the search for authentic origins, the recovery of a pure identity (Scottish-ness, Indian-ness etc) is no longer the most crucial matter. For Bhabha the hybridity of the postcolonial native exposes the ultimate contingency of imperial culture. The hybrid is seen to be the superior category. It includes cultures of immigration and diaspora which, in our globalised world, are a more valid index of cultural vitality. In Scotland, such ideas offer a way of re-thinking the identity crisis outlined by Edwin Muir. Instead of signifying an inherent anomaly or a specifically Scottish fault line, the 'predicament of the Scottish writer' can be read as symptomatic of a more general postcolonial experience. The Scottish writer is enriched and enabled by his ability to switch between different cultures. For Scottish critics Michael Bakhtin's study of the form of the novel has been particularly useful in attempting to re-theorise Scotland as a sight of cultural hybridity. For Bakhtin the novel, whilst written in a single language, is in fact constructed from a number of different sociolects. These may be identified as belonging to different generations, particular professions or certain social classes. It is out of the interanimation of these various linguistic codes that many of the novel's most significant effects are achieved. This model has been employed by Scottish critics in order to assert the existence of a national voice that is inclusive, heterogeneous and polyphonic. Cairns Craig writes:

> ■ Challenging critical traditions that identify cultures with national territories, Bhabha applauds that 'range of contemporary critical theories' which 'suggest that it is from those who have suffered the sentence of history – subjugation, domination, diaspora, displacement – that we learn our most enduring lessons for living and thinking'. Those who live in the interstices between cultures are the models for the modern culture-critic, since 'it is from this hybrid location of cultural value – the transnational as the translational – that the postcolonial intellectual attempts to elaborate a historical and literary project'. Bakhtin's linguistic hybridity becomes the foundation of a cultural hybridity which overturns the univocal cultures typical of traditional national formations.[27] □

During the 1990s the celebration of Bakhtin became Scottish criticism's version of Bhabha's cultural hybridity. It allowed critics to interrogate the linguistic variety of writing produced in Scotland whilst at the same time asserting that this constituted a discrete object of interest, namely 'Scottish Literature'. Rather than be unmoored by the lack of a homogenous language, Scottish literature can be seen to be enlivened and enriched by the diversity and eclecticism of its voices. In 1994 Robert Crawford set up the literary journal *Scotlands*, which ran for five volumes, as a focal point for the debates that arose out of this realisation. For Crawford: 'a nation whose culture is under pressure often clings to traditional notions of itself, since change seems to threaten the dissolution of identity. [Bakhtin provides a conception of] identity not as fixed, closed, and unchanging, but as formed and reformed through dialogue'.[28] The critic Alastair Renfrew, however, has argued that Scottish literature's affair with the Russian theorist is a somewhat misguided adventure. Instead of marking a radical departure from traditional nationalist paradigms, he claims Bakhtin has been misappropriated within Scottish criticism. For Renfrew the critical deployment of Bakhtin's ideas signals an attempt to lend theoretical credibility to the familiar nationalist rhetoric that he regards as having consistently dominated the interpretation of Scottish literature.[29]

If critics in the 1990s were increasingly interested in the theoretical potential of postcolonialism, a similar pattern was discernible in the pages of Scottish fiction. The scene from Irvine Welsh's *Trainspotting* (Scots as the lowest of the low...the scum of the earth...colonised by wankers), later immortalised by Ewan MacGregor in the film version of the novel, is undoubtedly the most iconic example of this. Welsh's second novel, *Marabou Stork Nightmares* (1995), would see this kind of rhetoric taken even further. When the Strangs, a working-class family from the Edinburgh, emigrate to South Africa, a number of comparisons are suggested between the experience of Scottish scheme dwellers and black South Africans under apartheid.

Irvine Welsh

Since its original publication in 1993, Irvine Welsh's debut novel *Trainspotting* has assumed a somewhat iconic status, not only in Scottish literature but also in the wider field of late-twentieth-century fiction. Compared with other recent Scottish writing the book's international profile is unrivalled, a process aided and abetted by Danny Boyle's 1995 film of the novel, which we will also consider below. In one sense *Trainspotting* comes out of the formal experimentation and the political anger of earlier Scottish fiction. Welsh himself comments:

> ■ this is a fucking great writer [William McIlvanney] using his own voice, and it's like James Kelman, to me, is doing that but taking it one stage further. And Alasdair Gray's taking it off in another direction. So it's always been there for me and I feel really lucky living at this time cause I've got McIlvanney, Kelman, Gray and Janice Galloway.[30] □

In another sense though, *Trainspotting* marks a radical departure within the Scottish literary imagination. Kelman and Gray's fiction focused on a working class community in the process of abandonment under the politics of Thatcherism in the 1980s. In contrast, Welsh homes in on the next generation, the disaffected offspring of the protagonists that Kelman and Gray write about. In writing about the junkies, the casuals (football hooligans) and the psychotic hardmen of Leith, Welsh considers a generation of people that has never really worked. They came of age in the wake of Britain's industrial decline and as such constitute an underclass as estranged from the politics of the Left as they are from each other. Welsh is the godfather of what has become known as the 'Repetitive Beat Generation', to quote the title of Steve Redhead's book. This new cohort that emerged in the 1990s and includes such writers as Irish novelist Roddy Doyle (born 1958) and Alan Warner. These authors take the everyday pop culture of drugs, music and football and make it the stuff of literary fiction.[31] *Trainspotting* is arguably the first volley of an all-out attack on what constitutes a suitable subject matter for serious art. British style magazine *The Face* dubbed Welsh the poet laureate of the chemical generation. The critic Willy Maley picks up on this importance sense of cultural crossover within *Trainspotting*:

■ Welsh's influences, or effluences, range across contemporary film, music and television rather than resting on the canon. He excels at that potent blend of excremental and existential, 'keech' and Kierkegaard, that is all the rage in new Scottish writing, a social surrealism that takes its cue from cinema and dance as much as literature.[32] □

Trainspotting was the most commercially successful Scottish novel of the 1990s. It also brought literature to a new audience as books would increasingly become available in places like record shops. Such circumstances underpin Robert Morace's comment that, 'Irvine Welsh is not a "writer" in sense that, say, Martin Amis [born 1949] is. Rather, Welsh is a cultural phenomenon of sociological as well as aesthetic significance.[33] Indeed, much of the secondary material devoted to *Trainspotting* examines the novel as a cultural artefact in the widest possible sense. Never one to miss a marketing opportunity, the 1990s would see a number of publishers release new titles under the auspices of 'the new *Trainspotting*'. Within Scotland a number of writers have applied the iconoclastic energy of *Trainspotting* to various locales with equally devastating effect. Alan Warner's novel *Morvern Caller* (1995) depicts a fictionalised Oban every bit as dysfunctional as the Edinburgh of Welsh's fiction. Similarly, Kevin MacNeil (birth date unavailable) deconstructs Gaelic culture in *The Stornoway Way* (2005), a tale of alcoholism and despair set on the Hebridian island of Lewis. The jacket of MacNeil's book is adorned with the following quote from *The Scotsman*: 'The best Scottish book since *Trainspotting*.'[34]

Aaron Kelly's book *Irvine Welsh* (2005) offers the most detailed and extensively researched analysis of the author's work to date. Kelly's primary project is to locate Welsh's work against the backdrop of Thatcherism, specifically its material and psychological effects on the working-class community of Leith, the geographic muse for almost all of Welsh's fiction. The heroin subculture of *Trainspotting* is read as a symptom of a more general social malaise. The self-destructive junkies are symptomatic of a working-class community consigned to the scrap heap of history, discarded under Thatcherite claims that there is no such thing as society. *Trainspotting* can be read as challenging traditional literary approaches to the representation of drug culture. Novels that are relevant here include *Junkie* (1953) and *Naked Lunch* (1959) by the American Beat writer William Burroughs, and *Cain's Book* (1961) by the Scottish exile Alexander Trocchi Kelly quotes Welsh himself regarding this shift in the depiction of heroin: 'The junkie in Trocchi and Burroughs' fiction was by and large a culturally middle-class figure – a member of the intelligentsia, a rebel who saw society as not having done anything for them, so they're into this drug that's their own, a symbol of rebellion.'[35] In contrast the heroin scene that arose in the 1980s had its most devastating effects on the peripheral housing schemes and working-class communites of Scotland. It involved a group of people who would not traditionally have been involved in this type of scene. These were people who, unlike say Trocchi's junkie, were not deliberately setting themselves up in a self-consciously affected pose of social opposition. Welsh's work does not represent the junkie as an isolated individual, purposely cutting himself off from the rest of society. In *Trainspotting* he is a product of his environment. Heroin addiction is explored as a reaction to the misery and despair engendered by late capitalist society and its acute pressure on those living on the economic margins of Scottish society. Kelly also considers *Trainspotting*'s deliberate use of postcolonial rhetoric in its portrait of a decaying modern Scotland. He starts with Renton's vitriolic outburst with which we began this chapter, foregrounding the process by which Renton attempts to align Scots with other marginalized groups. In doing so Renton is seen to make explicit use of the language of racism, sexism and homophobia. Kelly posits this hatred of Scotland as an example of the inferiorisation that Frantz Fanon identified within the psychology of colonial oppression:

■ Renton's loathing of Scotland and its baseness notably echoes the title of one of postcolonial literature's foundational texts – Frantz Fanon's *The Wretched of the Earth* [1961]. Fanon maintains that in the power dynamics of the colonial relationship: 'Every effort is made to bring the colonised person to admit the inferiority of his culture which has been transformed into instinctive patterns of behaviour, to recognise the unreality of his nation.' Renton's outburst is entirely in keeping with Fanon's diagnosis since it not only locates the Scottish as inferior but also castigates Scotland's failure to be a coherent nation.[36] □

For critics like Martin Brüggernmeier and Horst Drescher, Renton's vitriolic outburst symbolises a call for a new cultural independence for Scotland, one which could restore the nation's self-pride and overturn this kind of inferiorised self-loathing.[37] In this context it is worth noting that as addicts the main characters in *Trainspotting* are dependents, or in other words, they lack independence. Ironically they are dependent on something which will actually destroy them; it will eventually erase their identity completely. This type of destructive process echoes the power relations of colonialism. The native's lack of freedom conspires slowly to eradicate his sense of himself as possessing a distinct identity. Moreover, the native can be seen to partake in a system of political and cultural domination, one which he has very little agency to resist.

If Renton's self-loathing is conducive to a reading of postcolonial inferiorisation, there is another sense in which *Trainspotting* dissolves the ideological primacy of the nation within postcolonial theory. The binary opposition of coloniser and coloniser, British metropole and Scottish margin, as distinct and homogenous entities is rendered problematic within Welsh's text. Kelly quotes the Irish critic Colin Graham:

> ■ An essential component of postcolonial criticism has been its evolution as an ethical criticism. In that it is diagnostic of a political and historical situation, postcolonialism makes the crucial identification of who is the coloniser and who is the colonised – it also morally evaluates this colonial relationship as one of fundamental inequality [...] But to allow the nation to monopolise the postcolonial field is to withhold [...] a more radical interrogation by the difficult ethics of the colonial encounter.[38] □

Mentioned earlier, the Subaltern Studies Group in India derived its name from the work of Italian Marxist Antonio Gramsci (1891–1932) and his description of oppressed and marginalised groups as subalterns:

> ■ The term subaltern incorporates class analysis but also expands upon it to investigate how class intersects with other disempowerments related to gender, sexuality, race, colonialism and so on [...] Hence, the nation does not have to be the ethical *telos* or ultimate aim of decolonisation, nor should an analysis of colonialism as process be necessarily conducted in national terms.[39] □

As such the junkies and misfits which populate Welsh's texts do not merely symbolise an inferiorised Scotland. They also evoke a group whose emancipation is not guaranteed by the discourses of nationalism and the politics of devolution, so prevalent within contemporary Scottish criticism. The fragmented and episodic nature of the narrative in *Trainspotting* reverberates with Gramsci's perception of the kind of history written about such groups: 'The history of the subaltern is necessarily fragmented and episodic [and is] continually interrupted by the activity of the ruling groups.'[40] Moreover, despite Renton's identification of Scots as 'the lowest of the low' the novel evinces a number of examples whereby certain people continue to profit from Scotland's incorporation with the British state. Renton's brother Billy, for example, is a soldier serving on the streets of Northern Ireland. We are reminded of the history of imperialism and the outlet provided for generations of Scots enforcing Britain's military interests abroad. Homi Bhabha's theory of 'colonial mimicry' is also pertinent to a postcolonial reading of Welsh's novel. Bhaba describes the way in which the native imitates the discourse and identity of the coloniser as part of an ideology of resistance. This performance exposes the contingency of the imperial claims to a morally legitimate exercise of authority: 'mimicry is at once resemblance and menace [...] what emerges between mimesis and mimicry is a writing, a mode of representation, that marginalizes the monumentality of history, quite simply mocks its power to be a model, that power which supposedly makes it imitable.'[41] Within *Trainspotting* Sick Boy's penchant for impersonating James Bond is one such example of this type of mimicry. Created by the Scottish writer Ian Fleming (1908–1964), Bond is the archetypal hero of Empire, the loyal Scot, ruthless and highly efficient, in the service of British interests abroad. The other scene where Bhabha's mimicry is evident is one mentioned in Chapter Two of this Guide, the scene where Renton and Spud are in court facing charges of shoplifting. It is Renton's ability to code shift, to mimic the official discourse of the court that generates the leniency of the judge who only gives him a suspended sentence: Thank you, your honour. I'm only too well aware of the disappointment I've been to my family and friends and that I am now wasting court time [...] I'm no longer indulging in self-deception. With god's help, I'll beat this disease.'[42]

Beyond postcolonialism, *Trainspotting* engages with several of the themes featured elsewhere in this Guide. The novel is a tapestry in which questions of gender, nationalism and class intertwine creating a complex and intricate weave. As intimated above, the book offers a highly original representation of drugs through locating the consumption of heroin within the more general narratives of late capitalist consumer culture. The rise of consumerism during the twentieth century coincides with the decline of other social bonds, particularly class, which has its origins in the nineteenth-century peoples' relationship to the modes of industrial production. The ideological heart of contemporary consumerism is choice. Advertising promises us that in the material world of the late twentieth century the individual can have anything he or she chooses. In *Trainspotting* there is a deliberate attempt to invoke such narratives of choice in a playful and highly subversive way. Renton offers a famous tirade against the highly unsatisfactory choices that modern consumer society presents us with:

■ Choose life. Choose mortgage payments; choose washing machines; choose cars; choose sitting oan a couch watching mind-numbing and spirit-crushing game shows, stuffing fuckin junk food intae yir mooth. Choose rotting away, pishing and shiteing yersel in a home, a total fuckin embarrassment tae the selfish, fucked-up brats ye've produced. Choose life.

Well, ah choose no tae choose life.[43] □

Heroin addiction is cited as the negation of this type of empty and ultimately unsatisfactory choice. As Kelly argues: 'Consuming heroin [...] provides a telling metaphor for the loss of identity in late capitalist consciousness and the putative pleasures and freedoms of consumer society. It affirms that consumer pleasure is a deeply alienated enjoyment.'[44] The specious nature of the kind of freedoms on offer in consumer society is addressed by the critic Alex Callinicos. The freedom of consumer culture comes wrapped in the possibility of transcending existing categories of political identification including nation, class and gender: 'one listens to reggae, watches a western, wears Paris perfume in Tokyo and "retro" clothes in Hong Kong.'[45] However, for Callinicos these choices are highly circumscribed, being that they are only really choices for those wealthy individuals who can afford to make them. He asks: 'To whom then is this particular combination of experience available? What particular political subject does the idea of a postmodern epoch help constitute?'[46] This highly compromised form of choice throws into relief Renton's decision at the end of the book to steal the money from the drug deal and move to Amsterdam, thereby rejecting the world of heroin and ironically choosing to 'choose life'. For the majority of the text, *Trainspotting*'s peripatetic structure mimics the deadening logic of addiction with its terminal cycle of highs and lows, its periods of scoring and those of kicking the habit. Whilst seeming to reject literary conventions concerning plot and teleology, the denouement of the story sees *Trainspotting* suddenly adopt the form of the bourgeois novel. The final chapter is related in a third person, Standard English narrative. Our hero, Renton, has learned from his past and finishes the book a reformed character, ready to start life over from a new perspective. Ironically, it is the stolen money from the drug deal and the abandonment of social belonging that ultimately enables this freedom. Do these actions represent an antidote to the dominant values of Thatcherism and the vacuous freedoms of consumer society? Or are they instead the fulfilment of the free market ideology, its destruction of traditional social bonds and the primacy it affords to the individual in the pursuit of their own selfish ends? Whilst Renton's flight to Amsterdam is highly suggestive, the moral ambiguity at the end of the novel has encouraged several critics to question Welsh's own credentials as a writer on the Left of the political spectrum. In 'The Bourgeois Values of Irvine Welsh' Elspeth Finlay accuses Welsh of a degree of 'literary slumming'.[47] She argues that the success of

Trainspotting derives from allowing middle-class readers to wallow in other people's misery before returning to the safety and comfort of their own insulated lives. It is highly ironic that the prolific commercial success of *Trainspotting* transformed it into the very kind of cultural commodity upon which consumerism thrives.

The international profile enjoyed by *Trainspotting* was in no small part helped by the media attention created by Danny Boyle's highly successful film version of the book. The novel was adapted for the screen by John Hodge (born 1964) and featured a cast of up and coming actors including Ewan MacGregor (born 1971) as Renton, Robert Carlyle (born 1961) as Begbie and Jonny Lee Miller (born 1974) as Sick Boy. Both Welsh and Hodge made cameo appearances in the film, the author playing dodgy drug dealer Mikey Forrester, with the screenwriter as one of the security guards that chases our junkies down Edinburgh's Princes Street in the movie's opening sequence. The film's popularity spawned a sequence of imitators as a number of directors made film versions of recent Scottish novels. As mentioned earlier in this chapter Alan Warner's *Morvern Callar* and Alexander Trocchi's *Young Adam* stand as prime examples of this trend. The film *Trainspotting* catapulted Welsh to the attention of a global audience giving his work an unprecedented level of media exposure. However, such results were not without their cost. For several critics, including Aaron Kelly, the film version of the novel succeeded in entirely erasing the scathing political critique ubiquitous in Welsh's original:

■ To screen is not only to display but also to vet and to conceal. Much as Danny Boyle's 1995 film version of *Trainspotting* makes visually stunning use of Welsh's grotesque realism, it in many ways jettisons important aspects of the novel's political force. John Hodge's screen play occludes issues of de-industrialisation, class tensions, racism, sectarianism, domestic violence, sexism or homophobia, precisely due to the film's need to reach an international youth culture market.[48] □

Kelly accuses the film of replacing the novel's existential musings on *life* with an exploitative and highly circumspect focus on *lifestyle*. The class content which pervades Welsh's original is displaced by the self-aware poses of youth culture. This substitution serves further to illustrate the novel's own critique of the political transition ushered in under Thatcherism. The language of class, it would seem, has been banished from contemporary cinema and replaced by an easily digested, market-friendly depiction of popular culture. Much of the filming for *Trainspotting* actually took place in Glasgow and, as such, ironically undermines the novel's original challenge to west coast domination of narratives of poverty and despair. The film itself makes much use of the fragmented and highly episodic style of Welsh's book. Stylistically *Trainspotting* marked something of a departure in terms of traditional filmic representation of working-class life, grounded as they are in conventions of social realism. If traditional social realism operated on the principle of 'making visible' the working class, the film version of *Trainspotting* enacts at a stylistic level the very politics the book sought to redress.[49] Much of it resembles an MTV video with its blend of visual surrealism and thumping soundtrack. In the film Renton moves to London during the 1980s and sets himself up in the lucrative property business. This journey symbolises an ideological trajectory which sees him embrace the dominant values of Thatcher's vision for contemporary society: 'There was no such thing as society, and even if there was I most certainly had nothing to do with it. For the first time in my adult life I was almost content.'[50] There is no equivalent of such explicit political posturing in the original novel. Where Welsh's text climaxes with a degree of moral ambiguity, the film leaves us in no doubt as to which side of the political fence Renton comes down on. Ironically this move to London to work in the property business is one which Irvine Welsh himself made during the 1980s.

Novelist and commentator Will Self, himself a former heroin addict, was highly critical of the film's exploitative use of heroin as just another lifestyle choice for the 1990s generation of overindulged youth. He argued that few of the film's viewers would emerge from the cinema compelled to debate the whys are wherefores of intravenous drug use. For Self, Welsh is a 'drug voyeur' rather than someone who had done serious time incarcerated in the world of real addiction:

■ The great virtue of *Trainspotting*, the book, is that it avoids the acts of closure involved in linear narrative. The 'story', such that it is, is rather a torch of awareness, passed from one character's internal monologue to the next. But the film is utterly linear: bloke is on smack, has horrible time, gets off, goes to London, his mates catch up with him, they go back to Scotland, do a smack deal, go back to London, fall out over the proceeds, and the hero heads off with the swag into the wild blue yonder.[51] □

For Self the image of Renton at the end of the film, disappearing over the horizon with his bag of ill-gotten loot, is symptomatic of the author as he 'breaks for the border with his profits from this meretricious adaptation of an important book.'[52]

The novel's critique of consumer culture and the commodification of everyday life is ironically highlighted in the successful re-release and repackaging of the book that accompanied the film. Reprints of the novel featured a shivering Ewan MacGregor following his surreal swimming episode in a public toilet with the strap-line 'Choose life'. What had begun as an acerbic comment on the vacuous nature of consumerism had itself been metamorphosised into an advertising slogan. Moreover, to mark the tenth anniversary of the film a DVD box set was marketed with the following publicity line: 'Choose the 2 disc Definitive Edition, pumped full of extras; Choose the best British film of the decade. Choose *Trainspotting*.' *Trainspotting* as a product can be seen to partake in the very meaningless processes of cultural production which the novel sought deliberately to jettison. If the novel was part of a criticism of the enduring inequality of post-industrial society, the film version was all too easily assimilated within the rhetoric of multiculturalism espoused by New Labour during the 1990s. Under the guise of 'Cool Britannia', the spin doctors of New Labour presented Britain with a guitar playing Prime Minister, an outlaw, an outsider, a rebel with a cause. Tony Blair courted rock and roll stars at Downing Street, most famously Noel Gallagher (born 1967) of Manchester band Oasis, and had himself been part of a 1970s punk band called Ugly Rumours. This type of media manipulation was used to draw attention away from the fact that the leader of the Labour Party, that bastion of working-class values, had himself attended one of the most exclusive private schools in Britain, Fettes College in Edinburgh. The 1990s saw the discourse of multicultural pluralism invoked by successive politicians in an attempt to further erase the language of class, and notions of inequality, from our perception of modern Britain. Ironically, at a moment when the Celtic margins were attempting to disassociate themselves from ideas of Britishness, the metropolitan centre was attempting to rebrand British identity for the twenty-first century. Here is Mark Leonard of the political think tank *Demos*:

> ■ Britain is a hybrid nation – always mixing diverse elements together into something new [...] Britain is also the world's capital of ways of living, the home of happily co-existing subcultures – from punks and ravers to freemasons and gentlemen's clubs. Britain is the least pure of European countries, more mongrel and better prepared for a world that is continually generating new hybrid forms.[53] □

The erasure of social inequality and its replacement by the rhetoric of diversity can be read in terms of a more general move toward depoliticisation, one that is highly characteristic of late capitalist consumer culture.

To return briefly to the issue of postcolonialism, Welsh's second novel *Marabou Stork Nightmares* (1995) makes even more deliberate use of such language in its description of the underclass he writes about. The novel centres on the experience of the Strang family. Living in Muirhouse, a peripheral housing scheme on the outskirts of Edinburgh, the family attempts to escape their circumstances by emigrating to South Africa when apartheid is still in place. Here, the racial tension between blacks and whites offers a framework in which the novel reconfigures the class politics of contemporary Scotland. The quotation below is taken from Ellen-Raïssa Jackson and Willy Maley's essay 'Birds of a Feather?: A Postcolonial Reading of Irvine Welsh's *Marabou Stork Nightmares*.' Jackson and Maley highlight the 'suspicious ease' with which Welsh attempts to jump across the racial divide that separates black South Africans from impoverished white Edinburgers. The novel's narrator Roy Strang tells us:

> ■ Edinburgh to me represented serfdom. I realised that it was exactly the same situation as Johannesburg; the only difference was that the Kaffirs were white and called schemies or draftpaks. Back in Edinburgh, we would be Kaffirs; condemned to live out our lives in townships like Muirhouse or So-Wester-Hailes-To or Niddrie, self-contained camps with fuck all in them, miles fae the toon. Brought in tae dae the crap jobs that nae other cunt wanted tae dae, then hassled by the polis if we hung around at night in groups. Edinburgh had the same politics as Johannesburg; it had the same politics as any city.[54] □

The attempt to align questions of class with those of race bears remarkable resemblance to James Kelman's Booker statement and its explicit conflation of the two. For Jackson and Maley this passage is symptomatic of Scotland's uncertain orientation within the wider postcolonial debate: 'In this passage, social differentiation within Edinburgh is collapsed into racial differentiation in Johannesburg. We are urged to recognise "the same politics"':

> ■ A comparison implies parity, but Welsh's colonial comparison works by equating inequalities, racial and social. Has this statement moved on from the self-loathing of Renton or is it a re-capitulation of a similar sentiment? Welsh claims a solidarity with Black South Africans through the naming of townships/new towns. The pun on Soweto and Wester Hailes develops the central point - that the 'only difference' is linguistic: 'the Kaffirs were white and called schemies or draftpaks'. To some extent this passage demonstrates the ambiguity of Scotland's colonial status and the role of Scots in administering the British Empire.[55] □

Aaron Kelly picks up on the slippery nature of this type of ideological maneouvre. He describes the Strangs' emigration as underpinned by a 'geographics of empowerment', whereby the right racial identity enables the Scot in South Africa to enjoy certain privileges regardless of social class. Rather than experience any meaningful affiliation with black South Africans, the Strangs attempt to take advantage of the structural discrimination of apartheid. Roy's move to South Africa is informed by the imperial adventure stories such as those of Scottish writer John Buchan (1875–1940). Kelly quotes Buchan's own vision of the British Empire as a beneficent force for good around the world:

■ I dreamed of a worldwide brotherhood with the background of a common race and creed, consecrated in the service of peace; Britain enriching the rest out of her culture and traditions, and the spirit of Dominions like a strong wind freshening the stiffness of the old lands. I saw in the Empire a means of giving the congested masses at home open country instead of a blind alley.[56] □

For Kelly *Marabou Stork Nightmares* reveals an attempt to bolster its working-class credentials through the dubious appropriation of the suffering of others.

■ This elision of difference between Scotland's housing schemes and the townships of apartheid [...] is highly problematic, especially given that the novel tasks itself with undermining the assumptions of colonialism. There is a marked danger here of a perverse residual imperialism whereby an oppressed group in the Western world – in a seeming moment of solidarity – actually colonises and appropriates the suffering of others in order to bolster its own subaltern credentials.[57] □

The questions provoked by postcolonial theory necessitate a comparison of Scottish literature with writing from other places. In the process of internationalising the debate we introduced a number of key critical terms – globalisation, multicultural pluralism, late capitalism. These are drawn in a large part from the final critical context in which we will consider Scottish literature, that of postmodernism. Alongside the postcolonial no other theoretical term has been so regularly employed as a way of dissecting contemporary culture as the postmodern. Almost all of the authors considered so far in this Guide have at some stage been placed under the microscope of postmodern theory. The question remains, is the rise of postmodernism in Scottish studies part of a cogent and meaningful critical turn? Or is it simply an attempt to appropriate a highly fashionable critical discourse in order to bolster the credentials of contemporary Scottish writing?

CHAPTER SIX

Postmodernism

The problem with postmodernism

Postmodernism is one of the most widespread terms within our contemporary critical vocabulary. In the last two decades it has penetrated almost every field of the humanities. Literature, cultural studies, sociology, philosophy and politics all bear the marks of its theoretical wrangling. A trawl of the catalogue of any university library will reveal hundreds of titles that feature the term 'postmodern', the majority of which were published after 1990. Despite this incontestable modishness, attempts to understand and apply the term remain highly varied. The critic Simon Malpas explains:

> ■ [D]efining the postmodern can seem an intractable problem. But things are even more difficult than this. Few critics agree about what exactly it is that they are dealing with. There is little consensus among its numerous supporters and detractors about what the postmodern might be, which aspects of culture, thought and society it relates to, and how it might or might not provide ways to comprehend the contemporary world. Rather than too little evidence, there is too much that has been brought to bear on the discussion, debate and frequently furious arguments that have attempted to determine what exactly postmodernism and postmodernity are about.[1] □

Malpas's own book, *The Postmodern* (2005), provides an excellent primer for someone approaching the concept for the first time. Whilst acknowledging the problems of definition, a useful preliminary exercise is to differentiate between two terms: 'postmodernism' and 'postmodernity'. Broadly speaking, postmodernism refers to a particular style of artistic representation, one that is premised on techniques including pastiche, irony, self-referentiality and inter-textuality.[2] Postmodernity on the other hand, has primarily been used to signal a particular epoch.[3] The first is an aesthetic concept, whereas the latter is a historical one, attempting to define a specific era.[4] No sooner have we performed this act of differentiation, than we find the two terms inevitably collapsing back in on one another. For the critic Fredric Jameson (born 1934), postmodernism refers to a specific form of 'cultural dominant', one that has arisen in the context of a particular epoch. Instead of 'postmodernity', where the prefix 'post-' risks implying a complete break with the past, Jameson defines this new age as the era of 'late capitalism'. The relevance of this to questions of class, and the socio-economic changes charted in the discussion of *Trainspotting* in the previous chapter of this Guide, emerge from Jameson's full description of late capitalism:

> ■ Its features include the new international division of labour, a vertiginous new dynamic in international banking and the stock exchanges (including the enormous Second and Third World debt), new forms of media interrelationship (very much including transportation systems such as containerization), computers and automation, the flight of production to advanced Third World areas, along with the more familiar social consequences, including the crisis of traditional labour, the emergence of yuppies, and gentrification on a now global scale.[5] □

For us it is the interaction between postmodern theory and contemporary Scottish literature that is of acute interest. The work of almost all the writers featured in this Guide has at some stage fallen under the gaze of postmodern critical theory. Here is Mary McGlynn on James Kelman: 'His reshaping of the genre involves an embrace of incompletion and fragments, textual experimentation, pastiche, anti-novel, non-story – the territory of the postmodern.'[6] Alasdair Gray's *Lanark* is consistently interpreted by way of the formal techniques synonymous with postmodern fiction. Gray himself, however, is wary of attempts to codify his work in this way: 'Postmodernism is a school of criticism that is trying to pretend it is a school of literature.'[7] Similarly Kelman has claimed: 'terms like "postmodernism" [...] just show an ignorance of a broader tradition and a lack of wide learning.'[8] An attempt to address this overt scepticism on the part of certain authors is also included in the discussion that follows. Having looked at responses to both Kelman and Gray earlier in this Guide, the current chapter will feature reactions to the work of two other writers often identified under the rubric of postmodern theory: Muriel Spark and A. L. Kennedy. Before arriving at this point we will consider three more general interrogations of Scottish postmodernism in essays by Randall Stevenson, Cairns Craig and Eleanor Bell. Each of these critics examines postmodern thinking about Scottish literature from a different perspective. For Randall Stevenson postmodernism encourages us to reconstruct Scottish fiction within a number of important international contexts. These include the artistic inheritance of modernism and the philosophical crisis confronting the ideological inheritance of the Enlightenment, particularly concerning ideas of progress and civilisation. Such ideas were rendered highly problematic within the Western psyche following such events as the battle of the Somme (1916), the Nazi holocaust, and the bombing of Hiroshima at the end of World War II. Stevenson argues that Scotland's place at the heart of the Enlightenment, and the industrial revolution which followed, makes it particularly important to the philosophical implications of postmodern theory. Moreover, he attempts to re-situate contemporary Scottish writing within a much broader cultural trajectory. Yes, contemporary fiction *does* build on national traditions handed down from the likes of Robert Louis Stevenson and Lewis Grassic Gibbon. However, it is equally indebted to the work of non-Scottish writers including James Joyce, Samuel Beckett and Virginia Woolf. For Cairns Craig Scottish literature has always possessed the kind of motifs that would in recent years fall under the umbrella term postmodernism. Stretching back to the eighteenth and nineteenth centuries, and the work of James MacPherson (1736–96), Sir Walter Scott and James Hogg, issues of epistemological uncertainty and ontological doubt have been at the heart of the Scottish literary imagination. As such Scottish literature takes on a privileged status. It was in fact postmodern 200 years before the rest of the world had woken up to what the term itself meant. In contrast to Craig, Eleanor Bell argues that the language of postmodernism offers a reprieve from more overtly nationalist interpretations of Scottish literature. Bell links postmodern aesthetics with the idea that we live in a 'postnational' era, a concept which she borrows from the Irish philosopher Richard Kearney. She argues that a postmodern Scottish literature offers a more sophisticated and satisfactory way of mapping the nature of identity in the modern world, a place where cultural boundaries are more porous than ever before.

Stevenson: modernism and modernity

In his essay 'A Postmodern Scotland?' Randall Stevenson addresses the reluctance of Scottish criticism to engage with the kind of questions provoked by postmodern theory:

■ Concepts of postmodernism and postmodernity have been discussed thoroughly, even excessively, in recent decades and critics working outwith Scotland have regularly applied them to Scottish writing. Yet in criticism and literary history recently produced within Scotland, 'postmodern' is a term conspicuous by its absence, or the scarcity of its use [...] [I]t would be improvident of Scottish critics to consider postmodern thinking so suspect as to be condemned out of hand, or remote enough from the Scottish scene to be eliminated from their enquiries almost before these have begun.[9] □

Acknowledging the labyrinthine nature of much of the discourse that trades under the name 'postmodern' Stevenson outlines two distinct strands that offer a navigable route through an uneven and often difficult terrain. One of these focuses on the literary and artistic consequences of modernism. This way of framing postmodernism is indebted to critics like Ihab Hassan (born 1925) and Brian McHale, the latter of whom argues for a sense of consequentiality. By this McHale means that 'post-modernism follows *from* modernism [...] more than it follows *after* modernism.'[10] The second pathway which Stevenson suggests echoes the work of Thomas Docherty who argues that to invoke the postmodern is to address a whole trajectory of philosophical thought that has its origins in the Enlightenment, and that was thrown into acute crisis by certain historical events of the first half of the twentieth century. Let us begin with the first of these strands which locates postmodernism as an after-effect, a continuation and a consequence of the artistic innovations of modernism during the early twentieth century. Stevenson focuses on Alasdair Gray's *Lanark*, aligning its formal and thematic concerns with those of modernist writers like Virginia Woolf, James Joyce and D.H. Lawrence:

■ Gray's portrait of the artist as a young Glaswegian in *Lanark* (1981) – which includes regular discussion of painting, as well as examples of Gray's own graphic art – shares clearly in a tradition of interest of art and artist-figures established by modernism and widely influential on later, postmodernist writing. As Gray's 'Index of Plagarisms' sometimes confirms, this tradition can be retraced through the work of Joyce Cary (1888–1957)to modernist novels such as Virginia Woolf's *To the Lighthouse* (1927), or *Tarr* (1918) by Wyndham Lewis (1882–1957), as well as those of James Joyce. Artist figures in these novels were often used self-consciously, as in Gray's work, to discuss author's interests, or to provide figural analogues for the fiction in which they appear. Lily Briscoe's painting in *To the Lighthouse*, for example, coincides with the tripartite structure of Woolf's novel itself: 'a line there, in the centre' establishes 'unity of the whole' for both painting and fiction, allowing satisfactory, concurrent completion of the vision of each.[11] □

Stevenson traces a number of central preoccupations in the work of modernist fiction and the aesthetic legacy for a writer like Alasdair Gray. These include an interest in the role of art and artist figures in general; a focus on questions of language; and a degree of narrative self-reflexivity. Another widespread theme within modernist writing was industrialisation, or rather a reaction against some of its more pernicious effects on human psychology. These objections manifested themselves in a retreat from linear narrative and notions of objectivity, and in moves towards more private subjective accounts of the world.

For modernist writers, objective 'time on the clock' was increasingly replaced by subjective accounts premising 'time in the mind':

> ■ Ezra Pound's determination to 'make it new', or Woolf's to write 'Modern Fiction', shared a late nineteenth- and early twentieth-century enthusiasm for progress and innovation. Yet in other ways the modernists were highly sceptical of 'progress': wary of threats to the integrity of the individual posed by a rationalised, materialist modern world. The industrial practices depicted by D.H. Lawrence in *Women in Love* (1922) – Taylorised, automated, and pre-Fordist – regimented working life more and more comprehensively, imposing ubiquitously the slogan 'time is money'. Time and history, especially after the nightmare experience of the First World War, seemed thoroughly compromised dimensions to the modernists. Preferring what Woolf called 'time in the mind' to 'time on the clock', they relied on memory to structure non-linear narrative forms which dominate modernist fiction from *Á la recherché du temps perdu* (1913–27) by Marcel Proust (1871–1922) to Lewis Grassic Gibbon's *A Scot's Quair* (1932–34) and beyond. Lanark is in several ways part of that 'beyond', envisaging later versions of the same problems, and offering comparable alternatives to them. 'Life's easy when you're a robot', Coulter reflects in Book One: 'You get up, dress, eat, go tae work, clock in etcetera etcetera automatically, and think about nothing but the pay packet on a Friday'.[12] □

Stevenson argues that like many modernist characters Lanark is unable to alter the conditions of his subjection within what is a hyper-industrialised and hyper-technologised world. It is in keeping with the prescriptive tendencies of modernism that Gray offers aesthetic rather than practical solutions to the forces which confronts his protagonist. When Lanark and Rima need to escape the from the core of this authoritarian universe, the Institute, they do so through a door marked 3124, the very order in which Gray asks us to read the books in his novel.

Let us consider for a moment the second approach, that which Stevenson traces to Thomas Docherty and the philosophical crisis confronting the emancipatory promises of the Enlightenment. This form of ideological critique has been most forcefully articulated in the twentieth century by German thinkers of the Frankfurt School like Theodore Adorno (1903–69), Max Horkheimer (1895–1973), and, later, by Jürgen Habermas (born 1929). They argued that if the Enlightenment did signal a grand narrative of progress, then this progress was from the sling shot to the atomic bomb. In 2,000 years of history mankind's major achievement was in developing new and more efficient ways of destroying his fellow man. For Adorno and Horkheimer in particular, the gas chambers of Auschwitz symbolise a scientific rationalism that had enabled mankind to brutally extinguish his fellow beings with unprecedented levels of efficiency:

■ Most contributors to the postmodern debate envisage this trajectory as a movement away from the 'happy match between the mind of man and the nature of things' which Theodore Adorno and Max Horkheimer attributed to the outlook of the late eighteenth century. Consolidated by the Enlightenment thinkers of the time, this optimistic outlook shaped the grandest of all narratives – defined by Jürgen Habermas as a 'project of modernity' which assumed that, universally, 'the arts and the sciences would promote not only the control of natural forces, but [...] moral progress, the justice of institutions, and even the happiness of human beings'. By the early twentieth century, any match between mind and nature, happy or otherwise, had been severely challenged by the work of thinkers such as the German philosopher Friedrich Nietzsche (1844–1900) and the French philosopher Harri Bergson (1859–1941). For Adorno and Horkheimer, the powers of reason, science, and technology emphasised by the Enlightenment and by the Industrial Revolution, had always been too narrowly bound by 'the rule of computation and utility'. In *Dialectic of Enlightenment*, written late in the Second World War, they concluded that 'the fully enlightened earth radiates disaster triumphant'. Enlightenment values not only failed to prevent the war, but seemed to many commentators sinisterly complicit with its worst disasters.[13] □

Stevenson locates such scientific scepticism as part of a tradition of Scottish writing that stretches back to Robert Louis Stevenson, particularly *The Strange Case of Dr. Jekyll and Mr. Hyde* (1886). This novel partakes in a tradition of technophobic writing that includes Mary Shelly's *Frankenstein* (1818), Aldous Huxley's *Brave New World* (1932) and climaxes, according to Stevenson, on the streets of Unthank in Alasdair Gray's *Lanark*:

■ Such views might be considered less relevant in Scotland, and to its literature, than almost anywhere else. A country so centrally responsible for the birth of the Enlightenment – and for fostering the Industrial Revolution thereafter – might be supposed the least likely to accede to postmodern accounts of its demise, or to share in the resistive literary history outlined above. Yet a moments thought – especially of the later consequences of the Industrial Revolution for Scottish life – suggests exactly the opposite case: that Scotland might have encountered particularly quickly, and painfully, the darker influences or disastrous 'radiation' emphasised by recent views of the Enlightenment and its legacies. There is evidence of this throughout Scottish Literature, and at an early stage in some of its classic pre-twentieth century texts. A descendant of heroically successful lighthouse engineers – presuming to order the waves with beacons they shone into the depths of the night – Robert Louis Stevenson might have had motives oedipal as well as historical for demonstrating darkness at the heart of enlightened reason and science. This demonstration at any rate duly appeared in 1886. *The Strange Case of Dr Jekyll and Mr Hyde* is of course generally interpreted in terms of religion – of Calvinist dualities of good and evil. But as Jekyll explains, it is 'scientific studies' which lead him further towards the 'mystic and transcendental': his reflections on the divided moral nature of humanity have not gone far, he records, before 'a side light began to shine on the subject from the laboratory table'. Hyde may be primarily a personification of evil, but he is also a kind of cousin to another kind of monster embodying fears of the incipient powers of science, described by Mary Shell[e]y in *Frankenstein* (1818): Jekyll is related equally clearly to its creator.[14] □

For Stevenson Scotland's unique history compels us to resituate its writing within the kinds of ideological debates foregrounded by postmodern aesthetics elsewhere. For Cairns Craig the argument is more forceful than this. There are grounds for claiming Scotland not only belongs to the family of postmodern literatures, but is also its point of origin, its great-grandfather so to speak.

The Scottish invention of the postmodern world

The ideological significance of the Enlightenment also forms the central tenet within Cairns Craig's assessment of Scotland's relationship to postmodern theory. For Stevenson such circumstances serve to locate Scottish writing within a series of general debates about Western culture. In contrast Craig argues that Scotland's place at the vanguard of this intellectual movement endows it a certain foundational status. Scotland becomes a point of origin for the kind of debates that have only recently be reconvened by literary critics under the banner of postmodern theory: 'The characteristics typical of much postmodernist literature, in other words, fit with key elements of the Scottish literary tradition, and do so from long before the invention of "postmodernism" as a critical term.'[15] There is of course a resonance here with more familiar narratives of Scottish ingenuity manifest over the centuries in the invention of new technologies like tarmac, the telephone and the pneumatic tyre. In *The Scottish Enlightenment* (2001) Arthur Herman argues that the philosophical and economic achievement of Hume, Smith et al gives some credence to the view that Scotland in fact invented the modern world! In the extract below Craig argues there has *always* been something peculiarly postmodern about Scottish literature. Far from joining the postmodern party late in the day, the early nineteenth century saw Scottish writers constructing a highly experimental and formally innovative mode of writing:

■ At the Walter Scott conference in Oregon in 1999, Jerome McGann pronounced Scott to be the first postmodernist, a judgement based on Scott's use of various metafictional techniques and his ironic combination of contradictory genres. The proposal was less surprising (to some, at any rate) than it might have been, given how regularly another Scottish novel of the early nineteenth century – James Hogg's *Confessions of a Justified Sinner* – is cited as prophetic of postmodernism in its use of multiple and conflicting narratives. Taken together, the implications of these prescient texts might suggest that there is something inherently postmodern about Scottish culture, or something in Scottish culture which leads its writers to exploit narrative strategies that we now identify as typical of postmodernism.[16] □

Craig illustrates his argument with a number of examples including the use of intertextuality in the poetry of Hugh MacDiarmid; the *Poems of Ossian* 'discovered', in actual fact forged, by James MacPherson in the 1760s; and most significantly in the historical fiction of Sir Walter Scott:

■ Scotland's most important contribution to nineteenth-century literature, Walter Scott's invention of the 'historical novel', can be seen to rest not in the originality of the means by which he represented the *reality* of the past, but by his evocation of competing historical narratives, each of which will survive the trial of history. Postmodernist theorists such as Hayden White have argued that all history writing is actually shaped by literary genres and that the 'truth' which the historian seeks is always structured according to the dictates of fiction.[17] □

Craig also locates Muriel Spark's debut novel *The Comforters* (1957) within what Brian McHale defines the ontological uncertainty characteristic of postmodern fiction. Ontology is a branch of philosophical enquiry concerned with questions of being and the nature of reality. For McHale one of the features of postmodern writing lies in obfuscating the boundaries between fiction and the 'real' world, i.e. the one inhabited by the reader and the author.

■ In Spark's earliest novel, *The Comforters*, published in 1957, Caroline, the central character, is constantly aware of a typewriter and of voices that anticipate the events of her own life: 'But the typewriter and the voices – it is as if a writer on another plane of existence was writing a story about us.' As soon as she had said these words, Caroline knew that she had hit on the truth'. *The Comforters*, which gestures in the name of one of its central characters – Mrs Hogg – to its connection with *Confessions of a*

Justified Sinner, conforms to [Brian] McHale's conception of the conflicting ontological levels. Others of Spark's novels, such as *The Prime of Miss Jean Brodie*, 'play' with conceptions of history and of fictionality in ways that fit with Linda Hutcheon's famous definition of the postmodern as 'historiographic metafiction'.[18] ☐

In the second part of his essay Craig addresses the objections voiced by many Scottish authors regarding the aesthetic politics of postmodern theory. He cites thinkers like Jean-Franois Lyotard (1924–98) and Frederic Jameson, and their reading of postmodernism as the cultural counterpart to global capitalism and the age of rampant consumerism:

■ Postmodernism, in this sense, has come to be identified not as a generic or stylistic issue but as the cultural expression of the changing nature of modern capitalism. As such, postmodernism is nothing other than the power relations of capitalism which function, in the contemporary world, through the process of Americanisation and globalisation – two words which are, unfortunately, almost synonymous.[19] ☐

Under such coda art is deprived of its ability to critique society. The art object becomes merely another commodity, its value determined in the narrowest possible sense by its value in the market place. Craig looks to the work of Linda Hutcheon to reconcile the antagonism between the Leftism of certain Scottish writers and the kind of political paralysis and moral relativism often associated with postmodern theory. For Hutcheon, the self-awareness and narrative scepticism of postmodern fiction in fact destabilises the power of structures of late capitalism. It is able to do so through highlighting the ultimate contingency of all discourses.

■ Scottish writers such as Muriel Spark (a Catholic convert), or Alasdair Gray (who declares himself to be anachronistically in favour of a Scottish Co-operative Workers Republic), are hardly likely to see their own use of post-modernist techniques as implying commitment to such conceptions of the world. We can integrate this opposition into a theory of the postmodern by suggesting, as Linda Hutcheon does in *The Politics of Postmodernism*, that the postmodern condition (globalising capitalism) is not identical with post-modernism in art, which actually develops as a resistance to the former. For Hutcheon, 'critique is as important as complicity in the response of cultural postmodernism to the philosophic and socio-economic realities of postmod-ernity', thereby allowing writers like Spark or Gray to be postmodern*ist* in their opposition to postmodern*ism*. On the other hand, it might be better to say that their style is peculiarly Scottish – rooted in stylistic devices which happen to have become typically post-modernist – and that their resistance is to a world system which sees small and marginal cultures as irrelevant to its logic.[20] ☐

For Craig postmodern theory allows us as to recognise and reassess the importance of Scottish culture. For other critics though, postmodern theory encourages the crossing of boundaries and the denial of pre-existing categories. One of the most significant categories to come under fire within Scottish criticism has been the nation. In the era of globalisation the nation becomes only one of a number of competing forces vying for our allegiance. For critics like Eleanor Bell it is increasingly making more sense for us to think of ourselves as existing in a postnational era.

Postmodernity and postnationalism

Whereas Craig argues that postmodern theory affirms a distinctive and exemplary literary tradition in Scotland, Eleanor Bell takes a very different view. Similar to a critic like Christopher Whyte, Bell maintains that Scottish studies has been immured within a critical discourse delineated by questions of nation and nationalism. Reading local writers in terms of their unique Scottish characteristics can only foster a distorted and introverted perception of the literary terrain:

■ For too long the discipline [of Scottish studies] has been posited in parochial, stereotypical, cultural nationalist terms without recourse to the possible reverberations and limitations of such constructions [...] [T]here is a certain factor of reducibility at work, where texts produced by Scottish authors must in the first instance be explained in terms of their Scottishness [...] such approaches tend to perpetuate the introversion of a discipline that in actuality needs to expand its conceptual boundaries.[21] □

Bell argues that postmodern theory offers the possibility of reinterpreting Scottish literature beyond such parochial, stereotypical and limiting terms. Her book *Questioning Scotland* (2004) contains a full working out of this thesis. The work of the Irish philosopher Richard Kearney provides one of the building blocks of Bell's argument. Kearney maintains that we live in a postnational era. Intimately bound up with the decentred nature of postmodern theory, 'postnationalism' suggests a more appropriate framework for thinking about the power structures of the modern world:

■ It has been suggested [...] that postmodern theory can have radical implications for politics. One frequently encounters the claim, for instance, that the postmodern critiques of the centre, as logos, arché, origin, presence, identity, unity or sovereignty – challenge the categories of established power. The most often cited examples here relate to the critique of totalitarianism, colonialism and nationalism. The postmodern theory of power puts the 'modern' concept of the nation-state into question. It points toward a decentralising and dissemination of sovereignty which, in the European context at least, signals the possibility of new configurations of federal-regional government.[22] □

For Bell postnationalism is a useful way of theorising the complex matrix of regional, national and international power (Holyrood-Westminster-Brussels) that Scotland found itself borne into in 1998. Such dispersals of sovereignty are, of course, compounded by the increasing influence of global capitalism and multi-national corporations. *Questioning Scotland* focuses on the work of Edwin Morgan and Alasdair Gray in its attempts to counterbalance the nationalist tendencies of earlier Scottish criticism. Bell argues that it has been Scottish writers, as opposed to Scottish critics, that have been most alert to these kinds of reconfigurations. Few writers are as deserving of such a description as Muriel Spark. For Spark, both her life and fiction have consistently sought to resist orthodox thinking, to transcend boundaries and test the limits of artistic possibility.

Muriel Spark

Within post-war fiction, Muriel Spark is one of the most long-standing practitioners of a recognisably postmodern aesthetic. Her prodigious literary career began in 1957 with the publication of *The Comforters*. Since then Spark has written 21 novels, four short story collections, three volumes of poetry, and several collections of critical essays. Her most renowned novel is *The Prime of Miss Jean Brodie*, the story of an irresistible Edinburgh school mistress and her excessive influence over the girls in her charge. In 1969 *The Prime of Miss Jean Brodie* was made into a highly successful film starring Maggie Smith. Another of Spark's novels *The Drivers' Seat* (1970) was also made into a film with Elizabeth Taylor in the lead role as the traumatised and unstable Lise. Spark is the most internationally recognised Scottish writer of the post-war era. Her work has been translated over 300 times and not only is it published in all the major European languages it is also available in Japanese! Unsurprisingly, Spark is also the most written about Scottish writer of recent generations. At last count there were 17 monographs devoted to her work. Until quite recently the majority of this secondary literature remained relatively uninterested in the Scottish aspects of Spark's fiction. This is perhaps related to both the variety of locations in which her novels are set, as well as the author's own global perambulations. Since she was 19, Spark spent most of her life living outside of Scotland. Although born and raised in Edinburgh, from 1937–43 she lived in Rhodesia, then in London and New York, before moving to Rome in 1967, then Tuscany in 1979, where she remained until she died.

One of the predominant tendencies within Sparkian criticism has been to focus on the religious undertones within her fiction. The author's conversion to Catholicism in 1954 has encouraged a number of critics to read her work as the product of a self-consciously Catholic writer. Frank Kermode for example calls Spark 'an unremittingly Catholic novelist committed to immutable truths.'[23] Similarly, David Lodge reads *The Prime of Miss Jean Brodie* as a contest, 'between the Catholic God who allows free will and the Calvinistic one who doesn't.'[24] In *The Faith and Fiction of Muriel Spark* (1982) Ruth Whittaker maintains 'the theme of all [Spark's] work [is] the relationship – shown openly or implied – between the secular and the divine, between man's temporal viewpoint and God's eternal vision.'[25] More recent criticism has tended to shy away from such ecumenical interpretations. In his introduction to *Theorizing Muriel Spark* (2002) Martin McQuillan addresses the counter intuitive nature of such overt religiosity: 'Writing is not a theological activity, it purposely undermines essential and stable meanings, which presuppose and seek a single and authoritative centre. Meaning is always plural; writing cut adrift from its source and origin.'[26] McQuillan's own book seeks to read Spark's work through a variety of lenses made possible by the discourse of literary theory:

> ■ *Theorizing Muriel Spark* is the first serious attempt to engage the writing of Muriel Spark in a sustained theoretical reading. It has particular emphasis on gendered, psychoanalytic, postcolonial and deconstructive reading strategies. The collection of essays analyzes Spark's work in relation to French feminism, queer theory, autobiography, cultural hybridity, migration, nationalism, spectrality, economics and materialism.[27] □

The question of Spark's postmodernism sits neatly within such attempts to place her work within this more complex and robust form of critical analysis.

For Randall Stevenson the postmodern trickery of Spark's fiction is influenced by a number of European developments within the novel, particularly Alan Robbe-Grillet and the French *nouveau roman* of the 1950s. He comments:

> ■ Postmodernist 'prophecy' was probably first clearly fulfilled in Scottish writing in the work of Muriel Spark. Influenced less directly by Irish than French authors, though ones who emphasised their own descent from modernism, Spark was particularly indebted to the *nouveau roman* of the 1950s, whose

self-reflexive interests in 'the problems of writing' and the nature of narrative imagination followed, as its leading author Alain Robbe-Grillet explained,
'after Joyce' and the work of his modernist contemporaries.[28] □

The relevance of such international contexts coincides with the avowed
cosmopolitanism with which Spark lived her life. In keeping with his
overall argument, Stevenson reads Spark's interest in the formal limits of the novel as continuing and developing the kind of innovations
enacted by modernist practitioners of the 1920s. He acknowledges a
coincidence between this wider context and the recognisably Scottish
aspects of Spark's work; most notably the Calvinist undercurrents
within *The Prime of Miss Jean Brodie* and the main character's self-cer-
tainty regarding her own manifest destiny. Spark's fictions engender a
specifically Scottish dimension to postmodern writing, whilst also placing such developments within a wider conversation about the novel
as a literary form.

■ The central figure of *The Prime of Miss Jean Brodie* (1961), for example,
clearly belongs to a context of specifically Scottish education, and Scottish
religion – tyrannical control of her pupils demonstrating how completely she
'thinks she is the God of Calvin'. Yet her penchant for forcing reality into
accord with her vision – for fictions, art, and 'making patterns with facts'
generally – also contributes to a role as an author-analogue, raising questions about the nature and ethics of writing familiar to the *nouveau roman*
and postmodernist literature generally. Questions of this kind are considered throughout Spark's work: in *The Comforters* (1957), for example, or *The
Driver's Seat* (1970), which concern themselves with the capacity of authors
or author-surrogates to organise life into what the former novel calls 'a
convenient slick plot' [...] Spark's heroine in *The Comforters* is only mildly
disturbed, while working on her novel about 'characters in a novel', by [a]
persistent faint sound of typing, eventually attributed to 'a writer on another
plane of existence' somehow engaged in creating *her* life.[29] □

What Stevenson refers to as specifically *postmodern* 'problems of
writing', Margery Palmer McCulloch submits to a more religiously orientated analysis. For McCulloch rather than a criticism indebted to
the rhetoric of postmodern theory, it is Calvinism and its notion of
pre-destination, that remain fundamental to understanding the textual strategies of *The Prime of Miss Jean Brodie*. She argues that questions
of narrative authority, determinism and free will evince a specifically
Scottish undertone within the author's work. Set in 1930s Edinburgh,
the novel depicts a group of school girls who fall under the influence
of the charismatic school teacher Jean Brodie. 'The Brodie set', as they
are known, are offered as a parody of the Calvinist notion of the elect.

This doctrine maintained that God's will was absolute and that he has already chosen those who will be saved ('the elect') and those who will be damned. Under such rigid metaphysics human choice and free will are rendered ultimately meaningless. Just as Miss Brodie plays the role of a tyrannical God over her set, McCulloch asks us to consider Spark's own position as author/authority figure *vis a vis* the novel. One of the main narrative techniques in the text is the use of prolepsis, where future events are referred to in anticipation of their actual happening. The novel disrupts traditional ideas about plot and teleology, where the narrative unfolds chronologically to a point of climactic disclosure at the end of the book. Instead, near the beginning we are told that the story will end with the betrayal of Miss Brodie by one of her girls, Sandy Stranger. For McCulloch the use of prolepsis echoes the predestined human journey maintained by Calvinist religious teaching: 'Spark is her own Calvinist God and she plots and plans nasty surprises for her characters.'[30] This sense of narrative determinism has important metaphysical consequences for how the novel subsequently encourages us to perceive human existence: '[I]f our course is set before we start out in life and no good works can change God's decision, then what is the point of self-discovery and self-development as these themes are played out, for example, in the novels of Jane Austen and George Eliot?'[31] The fact that several of the characters in the novel defy Miss Brodie's prescriptions about their future might be read as a reassertion of the fundamental power of free will and a rebuttal of such notions of pre-destination. For McCulloch this resistance instead evinces Spark's own trumping of Miss Brodie as the ultimate authority figure within this fictional world:

■ In her narrative form, then, Spark employs her Scottish heritage in a detached, witty, ironic, and ambivalent way, while philosophically she again playfully subverts Calvinist determinism in her authorial rewriting of scenarios – something not possible in the actual context of the elect and the damned. There are in fact two Calvinist God-authors in *The Prime of Miss Jean Brodie*: Spark herself, manipulating fictional form, making patterns with facts, showing us how she creates and controls her characters, leading them to the end *she* has predestined; and her creation, Miss Jean Brodie, who attempts to predetermine the lives her chosen girls will lead.[32] □

In *Postmodernist Fiction* (1987) Brian McHale maintains one of the preoccupations of postmodern fiction is with questions of ontological uncertainty. It is a mode of writing interested in blurring the boundary between the 'real' world and our textual representations of it. Postmodern fiction regularly depicts 'reality' encroaching upon the world of the novel – we might wish to think about Lanark meeting his author in Alasdair Gray's novel, or Caroline in *The Comforters* hearing her thoughts being typed on another plane of existence. As we saw for Cairns Craig, Scottish literary history is replete with examples of this ontological uncertainty; these include the poems of Ossian and their dubious authenticity, and likewise the blend of history and fiction that characterises the work of Sir Walter Scott. For Bryan Cheyette *The Prime of Miss Jean Brodie* is acutely interested in problematising the distinction between the real and the fabulous. However, if a novel like *The Comforters* sees the real world intruding upon the fictional, in *The Prime* it is the human habit of fictionalising real life that comes under scrutiny. As Margery Palmer McCulloch argues, Miss Brodie herself becomes a metaphor for the author's own commanding influence over the world of her fiction. As the story unfolds Sandy Stranger and Jenny Gray realise Miss Brodie's own habit of rewriting her past in order that it might cohere with the reality of her present. As the teacher's affections alter during the novel her fiancé Hugh Carruthers, who died tragically on Flanders Field during World War I, begins to resemble the art teacher Teddy Lloyd and subsequently assumes the qualities of Gordon Lowther, the music master. Jenny and Sandy realise that Miss Brodie is deliberately manipulating reality. She is making her new love story fit the old. It is in this realisation that the seeds of Sandy's betrayal are sown. The excesses of Miss Brodie's prime, her belief that she can defy reality and act with immunity are considered to be beyond the pale. Cheyette describes her as a 'mythomaniac', someone who fictionalises everything that she encounters. Any outright condemnation of Jean Brodie is, however, made more difficult when we realise that other characters also partake in such ready fictionalising. Cheyette comments: 'such pattern-making is the very essence of the art of fiction. As a writer and artist, respectively, both Sandy Stranger and Teddy Lloyd also aestheticize reality, or "transfigure the common-place" according to the title of Sandy's "odd psychological treatise" on the "nature of moral perception".'[33] It is in this contradiction that much of Miss Brodie's enduring appeal can be found. On the one hand she is to be condemned for the wanton abandonment of reality. At the same time her ability to romanticise the repressive and dour world of 1930s Edinburgh is irresistibly appealing.

■ As well as being close to Spark in terms of her life-history, she is the most unlovable of heroines, and when she dismisses Brodie as a 'tiresome woman' the reader's sympathy is undoubtedly on the side of her more seductive and nuanced teacher [...] Brodie is both attractive and dangerous and impossible, finally, to pin down. By the end, she is most closely identified with her famous ancestor, Deacon William Brodie [1741–88], a respectable 'man of substance' who was a 'night burglar', a bigamist, and died 'cheerfully on a gibbet of his own devising'. As Velman Richard has noted, William Brodie was the historical source for Robert Louis Stevenson's *The Strange Tale of Dr Jekyll and Mr Hyde* (1886) which is also centrally concerned with the doubleness of its protagonist.[34] ▢

Cheyette's remarks about Deacon William Brodie foreground a set of specifically Scottish influences at work in Spark's fiction. This can be read as symptomatic of a recent critical trend to relocate this enigmatic and elusive writer within a number of recognisably Scottish contexts. Gerry Carruthers, for example, highlights the moral ambiguity of Jean Brodie by connecting her to a number of important Scottish figures from the past. Spark's book does not present the reader with a secure vantage point from which we might pass moral judgement on her characters. Far from being a crudely drawn villain, Carruthers reads Jean Brodie as a figure of her time. One of the many Great War spinsters, she lives in a 1930s Edinburgh that forecloses on the possibilities of female experience:

■ Brodie's interaction with the world is carefully detailed through the pressures which operate on her as a 'schoolmarm' of her period and also through her attempts to refurbish the narrative of her own life and fabricate narratives in the lives of the girls she teaches [...] This oxymoronic identity is explained by the fact that while such women might indulge in a degree of freethinking, their spinsterhood is thrust upon them by a combination of their Presbyterian background and the carnage of the Great War.[35] ▢

For Carruthers Spark's narrative is best located at the intersection of a number of specifically Scottish avenues; these include the educational idea of the democratic intellect, and such iconic figures as Mary Queen of Scots, John Knox (c. 1514–72)and Robert Burns:

■ Jean Brodie might almost be read as an exemplar of the 'democratic intellect' as she refuses to respect curricular boundaries and appropriates all school studies under the concern of experience. At the same time though, her sense of her experiential superiority over her girls leads to her totalitarian attempts to control her pupils' destinies. Her contrasting nature is visible too in the way she can be read as a representation of an ambivalent Scotland itself, as she identifies with Mary, Queen of Scots and abhors John Knox, and, at the same time, acts, in the perception of Sandy Stranger, 'Like the God of Calvin'. But if her psychology is sociologically and culturally infused, it is also highly personal; she projects her interests into her own life, remoulding her dead lover Hugh, who has been killed in the war, into a cross between her ideal lover and Robert Burns, and elevating her rival lovers Teddy Lloyd and Gordon Lowther into something like principles of art and music, the subjects they teach.[36] ▢

For Carruthers the identification of Jean Brodie at the end of the novel with her namesake Deacon William Brodie is heavily ironic. Deacon Brodie was an eighteenth century cabinet maker in Edinburgh, a pillar of the community by day and a thief and fornicator by night. This sense of dualism reverberates within Spark's depiction of her heroine as we are simultaneously compelled and repelled by Jean Brodie. Her refusal to bow to conservative social values is just as inspiring as her excessive influence over the girls is deeply troubling. At one stage she encourages Emily Hammond to run off and fight in the Spanish civil war where she is quickly killed. Miss Brodie also attempts to replace herself in the bed of the art master Teddy Lloyd with one of her pupils Rose Stanley. The comment in Spark's novel that William Brodie 'hanged on the gibbet of his own devising' could equally be applied to the schoolmistress whose own fate was very much a product of her highly individual response to the circumstances she found herself in. For Carruthers: 'Spark's fiction presents a woman who cannot be judged with any complete certainty, who is on the one hand precisely located in social and cultural history, and on the other, functions within Spark's characteristic demonic framework.'[37]

In both her life and her artistic output Muriel Spark continually sought to press against boundaries and defy conventional expectations. Her fictions resist simple categorisation as the work of a Scottish writer, a female writer, a Catholic writer and so on. It is the interest in questions of authority and control, in the relationship between fiction and everyday reality, where her enduring legacy is perhaps most keenly felt. One of the writers of recent years who can be seen to partake in a similar project is A.L. Kennedy. In a similar vein Kennedy's work deliberately operates in the interstices between our everyday assumptions about the real and the fabulous. In her second novel set in contemporary Glasgow, *So I Am Glad* (1995), radio announcer Jennifer Wilson becomes involved with a man who mysteriously appears one day in her flat. In a certain light he can be seen to omit a slightly blue glow. What is even more marvellous is that he claims to be the seventeenth century French dramatist Cyrano de Bergerac. There are other parallels between the work of Spark and Kennedy. Both writers make use of the kinds of formal trickery that have become the hallmark of postmodern fiction. Like Spark, Kennedy has also sought to transcend any narrow identification to do with questions of gender or nationality within her work.

A. L. Kennedy

Alison Louise Kennedy is one of the most highly acclaimed Scottish authors writing today. In 1993 she appeared in *Granta* magazine's

'Twenty Best Young British Novelists' alongside figures such as Jeanette Winterson, Hanif Kureshi and Louis de Bernières. Other Scottish writers, Iain Banks and Candia McWilliam, also appeared in this top 20. The 1993 list was a follow-up to an original 'hit parade' published in1983, which featured such luminaries as Martin Amis, Salman Rushdie and Ian McEwan. Kennedy's literary ascent in the following years is attested to by the fact that she was the only writer from the 1993 list to reappear on a similar list in 2003. This time her contemporaries would include writers like Monica Ali and Zadie Smith. One of the notable things about Kennedy is that, like Spark, she has been consistently subsumed within a larger canon of what is sometimes called 'British literature'.[38] Born in Dundee in 1965, she made her literary debut with the short story collection *Night Geometry and the Garscadden Trains* (1991). Since then she has published five novels, three further short story collections and several works of non-fiction. Kennedy won the Mail on Sunday/John Llewellyn Rhys Prize for *Night Geometry*, the Somerset Maugham Award for her debut novel *Looking for the Possible Dance* (1993), and the Encore award for her second novel *So I am Glad*. Within her own comments about her work there is always a tendency for Kennedy to resist what she regards as the reductive categorisations often espoused by literary critics. One of the more popular tendencies is to read Kennedy's work alongside that of Janice Galloway, the two women providing a female counterpoint to the influence of male writers like Gray and Kelman.[39] When asked if she felt that she belonged to a Glasgow school of writing, alongside Gray and Kelman, Kennedy herself remained highly cautious:

> ∎ I probably don't fit because I'm too young and I'm the wrong sex. I've probably got more in sympathy with Alasdair because he does weird stuff. And Jim's straight down the line – he has particular aims and linguistic aims that he wants to use. I don't think I got so much tacked on with Jim and Alasdair but with the younger Scottish authors, buts that's really because they're all published by the same publisher and it's easier for them to market five people all at once. But it is about marketing. I mean that would include people like Bernard MacLaverty, who's very lyrical and actually Irish, it just so happens that he lives here. But he's very different from Irvine Welsh, who tends to be categorised as a Glasgow writer and actually he's an Edinburgh/Leith writer. There's all kinds of weird misunderstandings. Basically we all know each other, but there isn't that much of a scene where everybody meets. And you know, I suppose we read each other but not that much. The thing that would tie most Scottish writers together is that they all read American authors and they all read European authors.[40] □

For Kennedy it is the author's individual creative voice that ought to be the primary point of identification, rather than critical labels denoting gender, place or class. As alluded to in Chapter One, there is need for care in any reading of contemporary Scottish literature as a school or movement with some kind of coherent agenda. Having said this, there is scope for reading Kennedy's own affinities with the likes of Alasdair Gray in terms of a mutual interest in the experimental techniques of postmodern writing. It is this aspect of the author's work that we will focus on below.

As we saw earlier, both Randall Stevenson and Eleanor Bell employ postmodern theory as a way of counteracting what they deem to be parochial or immuring tendencies within the idea of a national literary tradition. Objections to such critical reductionism characterise Kennedy's own comments about the importance of Scotland in her work. In her essay 'Not changing the world' the author attempts to distinguish between her own measured, conditional engagement with ideas of place and what she views as other, more 'poisonous' forms of nationalism.

> ■ I have a problem. I am a woman. I am heterosexual, I am more Scottish than anything else and I write. But I don't know how these things inter-relate [...] So here is my problem. I have been asked for a personal response on my writing, Scottishness in literature and Scottishness in my work, but my method of making it does not stem from literary or national forms and traditions.[41] □

For Kennedy any notion of a national literature can be applied only in a loose sense to her work. She describes her writing as 'fiction with a thread of Scottishness', as a way to imagine the relationship between her work and the place in which it is set:

> ■ Because I love Scotland I will always seek to write about it as enough of an outsider to see it clearly. By sharing my intimate, individual human-ity – Scottishness included – I hope to communicate a truth beyond poi-sonous nationalism or bigotry [...] If I respect my reader and am willing to enter into a relationship of trust, if not love, with them, I would prefer not [to] be labelled and categorised in return.[42] □

Kennedy's reluctance to be labelled and categorised resonate with those made by authors like Kelman, Gray and Leonard elsewhere in this Guide. She encourages her audience to read with integrity, to approach her work with honesty and not hide behind pre-conceived notions about what she as a female Scottish author is writing about. These comments resonate in particular with Eleanor Bell's critical take on contemporary Scottish literature. We might recall that for Bell a postmodern/postnational Scotland is capable of maintaining its distinctive character whilst also avoiding the more introverted and jingoistic aspects of nationalism. As we discussed earlier one of the recurring motifs within much postmodern fiction is the desire to question narrative authority. In this perspective the nation becomes merely one among many discourses vying for our attention in the act of interpreting the text. In her essay 'Scotland and Ethics in the Work of A.L. Kennedy' Bell argues it is the author's use of 'magic realism and postmodern hyper-reality' which allow her to transcend any narrow engagement with the politics of national identity. Kennedy does not offer an obsessional fiction, intent on encompassing the country as a whole. Her writing is both ethically and politically sensitive, but at the same time it resists promulgating any stereotypical forms of Scottish life. Scotland, when it is there, is not a known quantity. Instead it is a place to be discovered, charted and mapped out. As much as Kennedy's characters reside in Scotland, and Glasgow in particular, they also benefit from travelling to other places. It is such encounters that enable them to expand upon their own self-knowledge and deepen their understanding of their own identity. Bell comments:

■ There is an evident need in [Kennedy's] texts to open up the concept of national boundaries, and it is therefore in the in-between spaces, between Scotland and the rest of Europe, that real awareness is generated for these characters. In order to avoid national self-obsession here, characters are visibly transported to a different location from where they can evaluate their own culture.[43] □

Although Kennedy is sceptical of cosy national canons and what she identifies as 'poisonous nationalism', it is possible to detect some common ground between her own fiction and the work of other Scottish writers. For Douglas Gifford Kennedy belongs to a generation of Scottish writers who now wear their sense of place lightly and with confidence. Moreover, it is the blend of the fantastic and the real, and the deferred narrative resolution of these worlds, that links Kennedy's writing with that of people like Alasdair Gray and Muriel Spark. Gifford argues that the fusion of the real with the fantastic in a novel like *So I Am Glad* ought to be seen alongside a number of recent Scottish texts interested in this type of juxtaposition:

■ Once again a new kind of treatment of fantasy and the supernatural accepts few or no limitations to its scope, and is no longer contained by traditional folk and Gothic rules. In many ways [*So I Am Glad*] develops the contemporary rediscovery of magic and myth splendidly, extending the worlds of Gray's *Lanark* and *Poor Things* (1992), Lochhead's *Dreaming Frankenstein* (1985), or Morgan's *Sonnets from Scotland* (1984), until the Scottish and mainly urban present intermingles with anything and anywhere the author cares to imagine.[44] □

We might recall here Randall Stevenson's interest in the specifically Scottish genealogy of such literary techniques stretching back through such works as Robert Louis Stevenson's *The Strange Case of Dr Jekyll and Mr Hyde*. Gifford also locates such tropes within a much deeper Scottish heritage, one that contains Stevenson but goes further back to include the likes of James Hogg.

■ The domestication of the nobly comic French spirit in such an unlikely setting is audaciously effective; to see Savinien Cyrano de Bergerac weeding a scrubby Glasgow garden has its charm; and to witness the growing tenderness between damaged Jennifer and disorientated Cyrano is equally pleasing. And Kennedy keeps the reader guessing for long as to the legitimacy of Cyrano, in the tradition of ambivalence which is the hallmark of the Scottish novel from Hogg and Stevenson to Spark and Gray [...] The novel deliberately echoes older Scottish fiction of the supernatural, with its doppelgängers and dualisms, always with its insistence that these are echoes, and not rules or conventions to be adhered to.[45] □

The extract below is taken from Sarah Dunnigan's essay 'A.L. Kennedy's Longer Fiction: Articulate Grace' (1997). Although she does not explicitly use the term postmodern, Dunnigan discusses a number of themes within Kennedy's work that are closely affiliated to this mode of writing. She describes Kennedy as 'an elusive rather than an evasive writer', someone who deliberately refuses to be pinned down by any literary philosophy or set of beliefs pertaining to the politics of gender or nationalism. She quotes Kennedy herself: 'When I write, my aim is to communicate, person to person. I am a human being telling another human being a story which may or may not be true, but which hopefully has a life and truth and logic of its own.'[46] For Dunnigan, Kennedy's fictions are 'narratologically complex'. Displaying an inheritance from the likes of James Joyce, Kennedy makes extensive use of indirect discourse in presenting the interior lives of her characters. The effect is to undermine the authority of any third person narrator as the purveyor of ultimate meaning within the text. In Randall Stevenson's assessment of postmodernism he argued for a development of key modernist tropes, one of which was a retreat from notions of 'time on the clock' to more subjective accounts, premised on ideas of 'time on the mind'. For Dunnigan, Kennedy's fictions can also be seen to forgo conventional chronologies, oscillating between past and present, in what she identifies as a Proustian aesthetic. Kennedy is only marginally concerned with questions of gender and nation. Instead her work focuses on a very postmodern project as it seeks to deconstruct the very act of writing itself.

■ Most of Kennedy's fictions construct their own metafictions or metanarratives. This is exemplified not only by their artistic formalism but in the process by which the act of writing is deconstructed by Kennedy's protagonists, usually for its emotionally sacrificial nature [...] [Kennedy's] novels also share a fascination with the text, the created object or artefact. Whether the earlier work is memoir, testament, fiction, document, there are other smaller 'texts' encompassed within the larger which play upon the concepts of writing, communication, language. Jennifer's letter to Savinien writes her miraculous love into being, textual shape or form, while she never allows Savienen, its recipient, to read it. Instead, as part of the interior narrative, she lays it bare upon the page for her voyeuristic readers as witnesses: 'Think of what follows as the letter I would have written then and it will serve you and the story perfectly well. Indulge me for a page'.[47] □

It is such narrative trickiness, the constant meta-fictional musing, which perhaps encourages us to read Kennedy alongside other post-modern writers and beyond a canon constructed from contemporary Scottish writers. The author is emblematic of many of the developments within Scottish literature that this Guide has attempted to chart. Whilst achieving considerable international acclaim, her latest novel *Day* (2007) won a number of prizes including the Costa Coffee Award for fiction, her writing continues to probe and test the very vocabulary with which critics attempt to write about literature. It is this sense of a fluid, evolving and constantly changing literature that critics of the last 30 years have sought to understand. As we move into the twenty-first century a number of critical projects have begun to re-examine the history of Scottish literature and supplement existing scholarship with detailed reassessments of the work of key authors. The three volume *Edinburgh History of Scottish Literature* (2007) and the forthcoming *Edinburgh Companion* series attest to an enduring fascination with Scottish literature. These volumes, along with other key publications, suggest a number of avenues of inquiry that the subject is heading toward in the coming years. It is these that we turn to in order to offer some concluding remarks.

Conclusion

Scottish studies today

The individual chapters of this Guide have charted the key themes that have emerged in response to Scottish literature over the past 30 years. In terms of the relationship between literature and place, we saw that certain critics have sought to resist whilst others have sought to re-inscribe the nation as a fundamental unit of signification. Such theoretical manoeuvres coincide with the revival of the national question within the peripheral regions of the United Kingdom and, in the late 1990s, the establishment of devolved parliaments in Edinburgh, Cardiff and Belfast. In Scotland the future trajectory of the debate remains open-ended. Is devolution a half-way house on the road to independence, or the final stopgap to shore up a disintegrating British union? Such a question remains to be answered. At present an SNP Government sits in Holyrood on an election manifesto that includes, among other things, a referendum on outright independence from the United Kingdom. In terms of literature, as the work of Cairns Craig, Robert Crawford and others has made clear, if the nation is to continue to partake in the discussion about Scottish literature, it must look to do so in a complex and theoretically sophisticated way. The politics of national identity can no longer be constructed in reaction to oversimplified stories of historical subjugation. Increasingly there is a popular awareness of the dynamism of Scotland's past and the importance of its interaction with other cultures, beyond that of its immediate southern neighbour. Moreover, in the twenty-first century, with narratives of globalisation, multi-culturalism and consumerism, we are interrogating a highly complex cultural terrain. In this rapidly changing climate it remains to be seen whether the nation, as a political and ideological unit, can continue to influence how we think about individuals, communities and their relationship to one another.

Scottish Studies has sought to both incorporate and transcend the nation as an object of philosophical inquiry. Questions about sexuality, race, technology and crime are just as important to the critical imagination as any discussion of what it might mean to be a twenty-first-century Scot. In recent decades Scottish writing has emerged as a rich and diverse cultural terrain. Postcolonial theory has opened the door to a discussion whereby contradiction, paradox and discontinuity are no longer anomalous or peculiarly Scottish phenomena. They are now recognised as part of the inescapable condition out of which modern experience is fashioned. T. S. Eliot's accusation of literary parochialism in 1919 seems even less credible than before with Scottish writing part of a global literary culture. A recent collection of essays, *Beyond Scotland* (2004), takes such assertions as their point of departure. For its editors, Gerry Carruthers, David Goldie and Alastair Renfrew the future of Scottish Studies lies in the continued disaggregation of political and cultural nationalism. Historic searches for an over-determined, essentialist notion of national identity have been limiting and ultimately self-defeating. They argue that the quest for a sense of national authenticity has been an enduring preoccupation of the Scottish critics and not the country's poets, playwrights and novelists. Carruthers, Goldie and Renfrew maintain that assertions of cultural 'independence' are highly problematic, predicated as they are on a fundamentally misguided understanding about what culture is and how it functions. Instead, they suggest that the term 'interdependence' offers a more accurate way of describing modern Scottish culture. Such conceptualising eludes false oppositions and forces us to recognise the intimate and deep connections between Scotland and other places.

■ Interdependence is not the opposite of independence, but in fact reveals the folly of recourse to the latter term in the cultural domain. Independence is little more than an illusion or an aspiration that has been projected onto the cultural sphere through its persistent lack in the political sphere. The philosophy of 'ourselves alone', rather than entrenching a coherent sense of national identity, is more likely to deform the very idea of Scottishness itself – to mistake a complex, forward-looking, heterogeneous identity for one that is narrow and reductive in its nativism[1]. □

As an object of enquiry, Scottish literature is currently enjoying an unprecedented amount of critical interest. Its official coming of age as a subject of serious study is symbolised in the publication of the prestigious *Edinburgh History of Scottish Literature* (2007). Arriving 20 years after the landmark Aberdeen *History of Scottish Literature* (1987), this collection comprises three volumes and over 100 essays covering six centuries of literary evolution. In a sense these two histories, the Aberdeen and the Edinburgh, act as bookends for us, coming as they do at either end of the critical transformations outlined in this Guide. Edited by Ian Brown, Thomas Owen Clancy, Susan Manning and Murray Pittock, one of the most significant achievements of the *Edinburgh History* is its redress of the neglect of Gaelic writing and its place within the Scottish canon. Whereas Gaelic literature has been treated, often unconsciously, with a degree of tokenism by monolingual critics of Scottish literature, the *Edinburgh History* decisively resituates the language, creating a space in which the widest possible story of Scotland's literary development can begin to be retold. The *Edinburgh History* describes the late twentieth century as a period when critics looked to establish and defend a canon of Scottish literary texts. This formative process, of course, finds precedence in the establishment of English Literature as an academic subject in the late nineteenth century. A similar course of institutionalisation occurred within Irish literary studies in the mid-twentieth century. For certain critics the canon formation within Scottish literature during the 1980s occurred in problematic isolation from many of the developments that were revolutionising literary studies elsewhere. The arrival and absorption of 'Theory' within the academy saw the very notion of canonicity come under increasing scrutiny. As Scottish critics sought to re-assert the cultural hegemony of the nation, literary theorists were calling into question the very validity of all such prescriptive ideologies. As the *Edinburgh History* makes clear, at the dawn of the twenty-first century, Scottish Studies is moving towards a more confident engagement with many of these theoretical ideas. The *International Journal of Scottish Literature*, edited by Scott Hames and Eleanor Bell, is one of the places where such intellectual ambitions have found an important outlet. The journal's manifesto asks:

■ How have recent theoretical developments altered our conceptions of the nation, or of national literature? How has Scottish literature been perceived at an international level, and how do Scottish writers and critics engage with non-Scottish literary contexts? What can the discipline gain from establishing more comparative links?[2] □

Scottish Studies is beginning to deconstruct many of the theoretical building blocks, including the notion of a national canon, that lay at the heart of its resuscitation in the 1980s. Following in the wake of their *Edinburgh History*, Edinburgh University Press have commissioned a series of critical companions that will provide in-depth re-evaluations of key authors, genres and periods of Scottish literary history. These new companions will include individual volumes dedicated to the work of Muriel Spark, Irvine Welsh and contemporary Scottish poetry.

Published on the tenth anniversary of devolution, the *Edinburgh Companion to Contemporary Scottish Literature* (2007) edited by Berthold Schoene, is the most recent assessment of the state of Scottish writing. Schoene's *Companion* is concerned with how and in what ways Scottish writing has developed in the wake of the country's emergence from its subnational existence. In an ironic move, Schoene takes the highly significant date of 1997 as a point of departure and argues that it no longer makes sense to read Scottish literature through a critical paradigm, the parameters of which are defined by questions of nation and nationalism. He maintains that post-devolution Scotland must cease, once and for all, to define itself in opposition to all things English. In doing so Schoene concurs with Michael Gardiner's observation that the histories of the two nations are irrevocably intertwined and that, on the whole, these countries have had quite good relations with each other. The *Edinburgh Companion to Contemporary Scottish Literature* evinces a widening of the critical debate, one that relegates questions of national identity as merely one of a number of issues that pertain to reading Scottish literature.

■ [W]hile discussions of Scottish nationalism and nationhood feature prominently in the present volume, they are conducted invariably with reference to other debates on contemporary 'identity', such as class, sexuality and gender, globalisation and the new Europe, cosmopolitanism and postcoloniality, as well as questions of ethnicity, race and postnational multiculturalism. The problematisation of 'Scottishness' is enhanced further by adding an international perspective, incorporating 'foreign' viewpoints and analysing the reception of Scottish literature, as well as dominant images of Scottishness, both in Europe and overseas.[3] □

Schoene's volume is as much interested in the internal differences that constitute the contemporary Scottish cultural terrain. The juxtaposition of urban and rural landscape remains a central issue. The *Companion* also reflects a highly modern approach in which the study of 'literature' can no longer remain confined to the traditional field of poetry, prose and drama. The role of film and television, popular writing, including crime and children's fiction, are all included in the debate: 'Literary production and critical practice are placed within the broadest possible cultural context, including history, economics, national and international politics, as well as the literary marketplace and literature's relationship with the media and issues of topical significance, such as ecology or town-planning.'[4]

Unfortunately, whilst the criticism of Scottish literature is thriving with unprecedented vigour, the same cannot be said for life on the creative side of the fence. Scottish authors are confronted by the same market forces that leave the majority of contemporary writers struggling to survive. The BOGOF ('Buy One Get One Free') ethos of late capitalist consumer culture means that writing is a profession whose benefits are bestowed only at the very top of the literary food chain. The top 10 per cent of British writers earn over 50 per cent of the total income of all British writers. The average earnings of a writer in Britain today are

33 per cent below the national average wage with over 60 per cent of writers needing to work at a second job in order to survive[5]. In these circumstances many Scottish writers have had to find work in one of the most burgeoning areas within the modern University, the teaching of creative writing as part of English Literature courses. Almost all of the writers featured in this Guide have at one time been employed within the Higher Education system in this way. The latter decades of the twentieth century have seen the profile of Scottish writing significantly altered. The critical neglect of the 1970s and the fear of London-based publishers is no longer the reality it once was. Under the pressure of full economic costing, the kind of technical innovations that defined much Scottish writing since the 1970s are themselves under threat. Publishers regularly refuse to print books with illustrations or unconventional type settings due to the additional costs. We might ask what would have happened to Alasdair Gray's *Lanark* or Janice Galloway's *The Trick is to Keep Breathing* if such economic straitjackets had been in place 20 or 30 years ago. It would seem that the challenges we identified at the start of this Guide, to create literature out of whatever subject matter one chooses, and to write in whatever manner one chooses, remain an overriding concern confronting Scottish writers at the dawn of the twenty-first century.

Notes

INTRODUCTION

1. Colm. Toíbín (ed.), *The Penguin Book of Irish Fiction* (London: Penguin, 2001), p. xxxii.
2. John Hodge, *Trainspotting and Shallow Grave: The Screenplay* (London: Faber, 1996), p. 46.
3. J. Kelman, 'Elitist slurs are racism by another name', *Scotland on Sunday* (16 October 1994), Spectrum, p. 2.
4. James Kelman, *How Late It Was, How Late* (London: Secker & Warburg, 1994), dedication.
5. P. Kravitz (ed.), *The Picador Book of Contemporary Scottish Fiction* (London: MacMillan, 1997), p. xxiii.
6. Kravitz (1997), p. xxiii.
7. P. Kravitz, 'Editorial', *Edinburgh Review* 69 (1984), p. 2.
8. J. Kelman, 'The Importance of Glasgow in my Work', *Some Recent Attacks: Essays Cultural and Political* (Stirling: AK Press, 1992), p. 78.
9. Kravitz (1997), p. xii.
10. G. Wallace, 'Introduction' in R. Stevenson and G. Wallace (eds), *The Scottish Novel Since the Seventies* (Edinburgh: Edinburgh University Press, 1993), p. 4.
11. See http://books.guardian.co.uk/authors/author/0,,-209,00.html
12. A. Bold, *Modern Scottish Literature* (London: Longman, 1983), pp. 1–2.
13. T. M. Devine, *The Scottish Nation: 1700–2000* (London: Penguin, 1999), pp. 608–9.
14. R. Crawford, 'Bakhtin and Scotlands' in *Scotlands* 1 (1994), p. 55.
15. C. Whyte, 'Masculinities in Contemporary Scottish Fiction', *Forum for Modern Language Studies* 34: 2 (1998), p. 274.
16. Foreword to C. Beveridge and R. Turnbull, *The Eclipse of Scottish Culture* (Edinburgh: Polygon, 1989), p. 1.

ONE   NATION AND NATIONALISM

1. I. A. Bell, 'Imagine Living There: Form and Ideology in Contemporary Scottish Fiction' in S. Hagemann (ed.), *Studies in Scottish Fiction: 1945 to the Present* (Frankfurt am Main; New York: Peter Lang, 1996), p. 219.
2. L. McIlvanney, 'The Politics of Narrative in the Post-War Scottish Novel', in Z. Leader (ed.), *On Modern British Fiction* (Oxford: Oxford University Press, 2002), p. 184.
3. D. Gifford, 'Breaking Boundaries: From Modern to Contemporary in Scottish Fiction' in Brown, Clancy, Manning and Pittock (2007), pp. 237–52.
4. T. Nairn, *The Break-up of Britain* (London: NLB, 1981), p. 71.
5. Michael Gardiner, *The Cultural Roots of British Devolution* (Edinburgh: Edinburgh University Press, 2004), p. x.
6. T. Toremans, 'An Interview with Alasdair Gray and James Kelman', *Contemporary Literature* 44: 4 (Winter 2003), p. 570.
7. Toremans (2003), p. 569.
8. R. Stevenson and G. Wallace, *Scottish Theatre Since the Seventies* (Edinburgh: Edinburgh University Press, 1996), p. 5.
9. Stevenson and Wallace (1993), p. 1.
10. Stevenson and Wallace (1993), pp. 1–2.
11. Stevenson and Wallace (1993), p. 3.

12. Stevenson and Wallace (1993), pp. 3–4.

13. D. Gifford, *Scottish Literature in English and Scots* (Edinburgh: Edinburgh University Press, 2002), pp. 732, 973.

14. D. Gifford, 'At Last – The Real Scottish Literary Renaissance?' in *Books in Scotland* 34 (1990), p. 1.

15. Gifford (1990), p. 1.

16. Gifford (1990), p. 4.

17. Gifford (1990), p. 4.

18. D. O'Rourke (ed.), *Dream State: The New Scottish Poets* (Edinburgh: Polygon, 1994), pp. 280–1.

19. O'Rourke (1994), p. 281.

20. O'Rourke (1994), p. 281.

21. A. Gray, 'A Modest Proposal for By-Passing a Predicament', *Chapman* 35–6 (1983), pp. 7–9.

22. Kravitz (1993), pp. xiii–xiv.

23. Catherine Lockerbie, 'Lighting up Kelman', *The Scotsman* (19 March 1994), Weekend, p. 2.

24. J. Kelman, '...And the Judges Said...' (London: Vintage, 2002), p. 120.

25. T. Brennan, 'The National Longing for Form', in Homi Bhabha (ed.), *Nation and Narration* (London: Routledge, 1990), p. 44.

26. C. Craig, *Out of History: Narrative Paradigms in Scottish and English Culture* (Edinburgh: Polygon, 1996), p. 11.

27. Craig (1996), pp. 11–12.

28. G. Gregory Smith, *Scottish Literature: Character and Influence* (London: Macmillan, 1919), p. 23.

29. Craig (1996), p. 16.

30. Craig (1996), p. 16.

31. D. Gifford, *The Dear Green Place: The Novel in the West of Scotland* (Glasgow: Third Eye Centre, 1985), p. 14.

32. Kelman (2002), p. 64.

33. Craig (1996), p. 16.

34. Craig (1996), pp. 16–18.

35. C. Craig, *The Modern Scottish Novel: Narrative and the National Imagination* (Edinburgh: Edinburgh University Press, 1999), pp. 31–2.

36. Craig (1999), p. 33.

37. D. Gifford and A. Riach (eds), *Scotlands: Poets and the Nation* (Manchester: Carcarnet, 2004), p. xvii.

38. M. Walker, *Scottish Literature Since 1707* (Edinburgh: Addison Wesley Longman, 1996), p. 1.

39. C. Whyte, *Modern Scottish Poetry* (Edinburgh: Edinburgh University Press, 2004), p. 8.

40. Whyte (2004), p. 8.

41. Whyte (2004), p. 8.

42. C. Sassi, *Why Scottish Literature Matters* (Edinburgh: The Saltire Society, 2005), p. 9.

43. P. Mores, *Alasdair Gray: Critical Appreciations and a Bibliography* (Boston Spa & London: The British Library, 2002), p. ix.

44. Quoted in Mores (2002), pp. 2–3.

45. BBC, *Collective*, 29 November 2007, <http://www.bbc.co.uk/dna/collective/A3583325>

46. K. Williamson, 'Under the Influence', in Moores (2002), p. 165.

47. Williamson (2002), p. 166.

48. R. Crawford and T. Nairn (eds), *The Arts of Alasdair Gray* (Edinburgh: Edinburgh University Press, 1991), p. 7.

49. C. Craig, 'Going Down to Hell is Easy: Lanark, Realism and The Limits of the Imagination', in Crawford and Nairn (1991), p. 90.

50. Craig (1991), p. 90.
51. Craig (1991), pp. 90–1.
52. Craig (1991), pp. 93, 94.
53. Gifford (2002), p. 734.
54. Gifford (2002), p. 734.
55. A. Gray, *Mavis Belfrage: A Romantic Novel with Five Shorter Tales* (London: Bloomsbury, 1996), pp. 152–3.
56. R. Stevenson, 'Alasdair Gray and the Postmodern', in Crawford and Nairn (1991), pp. 48–9.
57. Stevenson (1991), p. 52.

TWO LANGUAGE

1. C. Craig, *The Modern Scottish Novel: Narrative and the National Imagination* (Edinburgh: Edinburgh University Press, 1999), p. 79.
2. C. Craig (1999), p. 79.
3. O'Rourke (1994), p. 2.
4. C. A. Duffy, *The Other Country* (London: Anvil Press Poetry, 1990), p. 54.
5. Kelman (1994), p. 2.
6. D. McLean, 'An interview with James Kelman', *Edinburgh Review* 71 (1985), p. 69.
7. Welsh (1993), p. 3.
8. Welsh (1993), p. 167.
9. A. Kelly, *Irvine Welsh* (Manchester: Manchester University Press, 2005), pp. 53–4.
10. R. Watson, 'Living with the Double Tongue: Modern Poetry in Scots', I. Brown, T. Clancy, S. Manning and M. Pittock (eds), *Edinburgh History of Scottish Literature Vol 3* (Edinburgh: Edinburgh University Press, 2007), p. 163.
11. J. D. McClure, *Language, Poetry and Nationhood: Scots as a Poetic Language from 1878 to the Present* (East Linton: Tuckwell Press, 2000), p. 4.
12. R. Crawford, *Devolving English Literature* (Edinburgh: Edinburgh University Press 1992), p. 18.
13. Craig (1996), p. 12.
14. H. MacDiarmid, *Selected Poems* (London: Penguin, 1994), p. 152.
15. L. G. Gibbon, *The Intelligent Man's Guide to Albyn* (London: Jarrolds, 1934), p. 165.
16. E. Muir, *Scott and Scotland: the Predicament of a Scottish Writer* (Edinburgh: Polygon, 1984), pp. 8–9.
17. Stevenson and Wallace (1996), p. 5.
18. Stevenson and Wallace (1996), p. 5.
19. T. Leonard, *Reports from the Present: Selected Works 1982–94* (London: Jonathan Cape, 1995), p. 54.
20. Leonard (1995), p. 52.
21. Leonard (1995), pp. 47–62.
22. T. Leonard, *Intimate Voices: Selected Work 1965–1983* (London: Vintage, 1995), back cover.
23. Leonard (1995), back cover.
24. McClure (2000), p. 168.
25. McClure (2000), pp. 168–75.
26. McClure (2000), pp. 168–75.
27. B. Kay, *Scots: The Mither Tongue* (Edinburgh: Mainstream Publishing, 1986), p. 134.
28. Watson (2007), p. 163.
29. Leonard (1995), p. 95.
30. Crawford (1993), pp. 284–5.
31. Quoted in M. Macleod and M. Wilson, 'In the Shadow of the Bard: The Gaelic Short Story, Novel and Drama since the early Twentieth Century', in Brown, Clancy, Manning, Pittock (2007), pp. 273–82.

32. R. Black, 'Thunder, Renaissance and Flowers: Gaelic Poetry in the Twentieth Century' in C. Craig (ed.), *The History of Scottish Literature Vol 4* (Aberdeen: Aberdeen University Press, 1987), pp. 195–6.

33. I. C. Smith, *Collected Poems* (Manchester: Carcanet, 1992), p. 102.

34. Whyte (2004), pp. 20–1.

35. Douglas Gifford, Sarah Dunnigan and Allan MacGilvaray, *Scottish Literature in English and Scots* (Edinburgh: Edinburgh University Press, 2002), p. 767.

36. Thomson (1974), pp. 249–50.

37. D. MacAulay (ed.), *Modern Scottish Gaelic Poems* (Edinburgh: Canongate, 1995), pp. 47–9.

THREE   GENDER

1. M. Gray, *A Dictionary of Literary Terms* (New York: Longman, 1992), p. 118.

2. S. Hagemann, 'From Carswell to Kay: Aspects of Gender, the Novel and the Drama', in Brown, Clancy, Manning, Pittock (2007), pp. 214–15.

3. Quoted in M. Bain, 'Scottish Women in Politics' in *Chapman* 27/28 (1980), p. 3.

4. D. McMillan and M. Byrne (eds), *Modern Scottish Women Poets* (Edinburgh: Canongate, 2003), pp. xxii–xxiii.

5. McMillan and Byrne (2003), p. xxiii.

6. W. Findlay, 'Interview with Margaret Atwood' in *Cencrastus* 1 (Autumn 1979), p. 2.

7. D. Gifford and D. McMillan (eds), *A History of Scottish Women's Writing* (Edinburgh: Edinburgh University Press, 1997), p. xix.

8. Gifford and McMillan (1997), p. ix.

9. E. Showalter, *Sister's Choice: Tradition and Change in American Women's Writing* (Oxford: Clarendon Press, 1991), pp. 2–3.

10. M. Reizbaum, 'Canonical Double Cross: Scottish and Irish Women's Writing', in K. R. Lawrence (ed.), *Decolonizing Tradition: New Views of Twentieth-Century 'British' Literary Canons* (Chicago: University of Illinois Press, 1992), p. 165.

11. Reizbaum (1992), p. 166.

12. Reizbaum (1992), p. 171.

13. J. Galloway (ed.), *Meantime: Looking Forward to the Millennium* (Edinburgh: Polygon, 1991), pp. 5–6.

14. Galloway (1991), p. 6.

15. C. Whyte (ed.), *Gendering the Nation: Studies in Modern Scottish Literature* (Edinburgh: Edinburgh University Press, 1995), pp. ix–xi.

16. C. Whyte, 'Gender and Nationality' in *Cencrastus* 42 (Winter 1991/1992), p. 46.

17. Simon Kovesi, *James Kelman* (Manchester: Manchester University Press, 2007), pp. 36–60.

18. A. Christianson, 'Gender and Nation: Debatable Lands and Passable Boundaries', in G. Norquay and G. Smyth (eds), *Across the Margins: Cultural Identity and Change in the Atlantic Archipelago* (Manchester: Manchester University Press, 2002), p. 67.

19. Christianson (2002), p. 68.

20. Quoted in Christianson (2002), p. 87.

21. A. Christianson and A. Lumsden, *Contemporary Scottish Women Writers* (Edinburgh: Edinburgh University Press, 2000), p. 6.

22. Christianson and Lumsden (2000), p. 6.

23. Christianson and Lumsden (2000), p. 5.

24. J. Hendry, 'Twentieth-century Women's Writing: The Nest of Singing Birds', in Craig (1987), p. 291.

25. Hendry (1987), p. 291.

26. C. Kerrigan (ed.), *An Anthology of Scottish Women Poets* (Edinburgh: Edinburgh University Press, 1991), p. 1.

27. Gifford and McMillan (1997), p. xiv.

28. D. McMillan and M. Byrne (eds), *Modern Scottish Women Poets* (Edinburgh: Canongate, 2003), p. xxxv.

29. M. P. McCulloch, *Liz Lochhead's Mary Queen of Scots Got Her Head Chopped Off* (Glasgow: ASLS, 2000), p. 7.

30. J. Kay, *The Adoption Papers* (Bloodaxe Books: Newcastle, 1991), p. 25.

31. R. Crawford, 'The Two-faced Language of Lochhead's Poetry', in R. Crawford (ed.), *Liz Lochhead's Voices* (Edinburgh: Edinburgh University Press, 1993), pp. 57–8.

32. A. Varty, 'The Mirror and the Vamp', in Gifford and McMillan (1997), p. 645.

33. Quoted in C. Nicholson, *Poem, Purpose and Place: Shaping Identity in Contemporary Scottish Verse* (Edinburgh: Polygon, 1992), p. 223.

34. Quoted in Nicholson (1992), p. 204.

35. For an explanation of the principles underlying *écriture féminine* see Toril Moi, *Sexual/textual politics: feminist literary theory* (London: Metheun, 1985).

36. C. Whyte, *Modern Scottish Poetry* (Edinburgh: Edinburgh University Press, 2004), p. 187.

37. Whyte (2004), p. 188.

38. Whyte (2004), p. 188.

39. Nicholson (1992), p. 207.

40. Jen Harvie and Jan McDonald, 'Putting New Twists to Old Stories: Feminism and Lochhead's Drama', in Robert Crawford and Anne Varty (eds), *Liz Lochhead's Voices* (Edinburgh: Edinburgh University Press, 1993), p. 127.

41. McDonald and Harvie (1993), p. 127.

42. Nicholson (1992), p. 204.

43. C. L. March, 'Interview with Janice Galloway', in *Edinburgh Review* 101 (1990), p. 87.

44. M. Metzstein, 'Of Myths and Men: Aspects of Gender in the Fiction of Janice Galloway', in Stevenson and Wallace (1993), p. 136.

45. Metzstein (1993), p. 144.

46. Metzstein (1993), pp. 145–6.

47. March (1999), p. 90.

48. Gifford and McMillan (1997), p. 607.

49. J. Galloway, 'Different Oracles: Me and Alasdair Gray', *Review of Contemporary Fiction* 15:2 (Summer 1995), p. 193.

50. Gifford and McMillan (1997), p. 608.

51. M. McGlynn, 'Janice Galloway's Alienated Spaces', *Scottish Studies Review* 4:2 (Autumn 2003), p. 84.

52. A. Christianson, 'Lies, notable silences and plastering the cracks: the fiction of A. L. Kennedy and Janice Galloway', in *Gender and Scottish Society: Polities, Policies and Participation* (report of conference held at University of Edinburgh, 31 October 1997), p. 138.

53. G. Norquay, 'The Fiction of Janice Galloway: "Weaving a Route through Chaos"' in G. Norquay and G. Smyth (eds), *Space and Place: the Geographies of Literature* (Liverpool: John Moores University Press, 1997), pp. 323–4.

54. Norquay (1997), p. 325.

55. C. L. March, *Rewriting Scotland: Welsh, McLean, Warner, Banks, Galloway and Kennedy* (Manchester: Manchester University Press, 2002), p. 110.

FOUR CLASS

1. A. Kelly, *Irvine Welsh* (Manchester: Manchester University Press, 2005), pp. 6–7.

2. Quoted in David Cannadine, *Class in Britain* (New Haven: Yale University Press, 1998), p. 4.

3. Anthony Blair, *New Britain: My Vision of a Young Country* (London: Forth Estate, 1996), pp. 30, 38, 58–9.

4. Anthony Giddens, *The Third Way: The Renewal of Social Democracy* (Cambridge: Polity Press, 1998), p. 24.

5. G. Wallace and R. Stevenson (eds), *The Scottish Novel Since the Seventies* (Edinburgh: Edinburgh University Press, 1993), p. 3.

6. A. Gray, *Lanark* (London: Picador, 1994), p. 243.

7. W. McIlvanney, *Surviving the Shipwreck* (Edinburgh: Mainstream, 1991), p. 25.

8. J. Kelman, 'Elitism and English Literature, Speaking as a Writer', in *"and the judges said. . "* (London: Vintage, 2003), p. 64.

9. R. Stevenson and G. Wallace (ed.), *Scottish Theatre Since the Seventies* (Edinburgh: Edinburgh University Press, 1996), p. 7.

10. Edwin Muir, *Scottish Journey* (Edinburgh: Mainstream Publishing, 1996), pp. 102–3.

11. Edwin Muir, 'Extracts from a Diary, "Summer 1939"' in *The Story and the Fable* (London: George G. Harrap, 1940), p. 263.

12. D. Gifford, *The Dear Green Place: The Novel in the West of Scotland* (Glasgow: Third Eye Centre, 1985), pp. 5–6.

13. Gifford (1985), p. 8.

14. C. Craig, 'Going Down to Hell is Easy: Lanark, Realism and The Limits of the Imagination' in Crawford (1993), p. 96.

15. D. Dunn, 'Divergent Scottishness: William Boyd, Allan Massie, Ronald Frame' in Stevenson and Wallace (1993), pp. 149–50.

16. E. R. Jackson and W. Maley, 'Committing to Kelman: the Art of Integrity and the Politics of Dissent' in *Edinburgh Review* 108 (2001), pp. 22–3.

17. Jackson and Maley (2001), p. 22.

18. J. Neuberger, 'Cooking the Booker', *Evening Standard* [London] (13 October 1994), p. 27.

19. Kelman (1994), p. 2.

20. S. Jenkins, 'An Expletive of a Winner', *The Times* (15 October 1994), p. 20.

21. A. Clarke, 'A Prize insult to the courage of Scotland's finest', *Mail on Sunday* (23 October 1994), p. 10.

22. G. Warner, 'Time for a disaffection from literary slumming', *Sunday Times* (25 September 1994), p. 7.

23. Quoted in S. Wavell, 'Scots bewail 4,000-expletive blot on national character', in *Sunday Times* (16 October 1994), p. 5.

24. Wavell (1994), p. 5.

25. Quoted in Wavell (1994), p. 5.

26. A. Good, *The Scotsman* (20 October 1994), Letters, p. 14. See also J. Wilson, *The Scotsman* (18 October 1994), Letters, p. 16.

27. W. Maley, 'Swearing Blind: Kelman and the Curse of the Working Classes', *Edinburgh Review* 95 (1996), pp. 105–12.

28. C. Craig, 'Resisting Arrest: James Kelman', in Stevenson and Wallace (1993), p. 100.

29. Craig (1993), p. 101.

30. Craig (1993), p. 102.

31. Craig (1993), p. 104.

32. Craig (1993), pp. 105–6.

33. J. Kelman, *Some Recent Attacks: Essays Cultural and Political* (Stirling: AK Press, 1992), p. 84.

34. Kelman (1992), p. 84.

35. Kelman (1992), p. 84.

36. Simon Baker, '"Wee stories with a working-class theme": The Reimagining of Urban Realism in the Fiction of James Kelman', in J. Schwend and H. Drescher (eds) *Studies in Scottish Fiction: Twentieth Century* (Frankfurt am Main: P. Lang, 1990), p. 238.

37. Kelman (2003), p. 62.

38. Quoted in M. McGlynn, '"Middle-Class Wankers" and Working-Class Texts: The Critics and James Kelman', in *Contemporary Literature* 43:1 (Spring 2002), p. 53.

39. McGlynn (2002), p. 60.

40. K. McNeill, 'An Interview with James Kelman', in *Chapman* 57 (1989), pp. 2–12.

41. McGlynn (2002), pp. 69–70.

42. McGlynn (2002), p. 70.

43. D. Bönkhe, *Kelman Writes Back: Literary Politics in the Work of a Scottish Writer* (Leipzig: Galda and Wilch, 1999), p. 11.

44. Bönkhe (1999), p. 34.

45. L. Nicoll, 'This Is Not A Nationalist Position: James Kelman's Existential Voice' *Edinburgh Review* 103 (2000), pp. 79–84; 'Gogol's Overcoat: Kelman Resartus', *Edinburgh Review* 108 (2001), pp. 116–24.

46. Nicoll (2000), p. 79.

47. Nicoll (2000), p. 81.

48. Nicoll (2000), p. 81.

49. Quoted in Nicoll (2000), p. 81.

50. Nicoll (2000), p. 81.

51. L. G. Gibbon, *A Scots Hairst* (London: Hutchinson & Son, 1967), p. 87.

52. Allan McMunnigall and Gerard Carruthers, 'Locating Kelman: Glasgow, Scotland and the Commitment to Place' *Edinburgh Review* 108 (2001), pp. 56–7.

53. McMunnigall and Carruthers (2001), p. 57.

54. McMunnigall and Carruthers (2001), p. 57.

55. Interview with Irvine Welsh by Aaron Kelly in *Edinburgh Review* 113 (2004), pp. 7–17.

56. R. A. Morace, *Irvine Welsh's Trainspotting: A Readers Guide* (London: Continuum, 2001), p. 22.

57. D. Milne, 'The Fiction of James Kelman and Irvine Welsh: Accents, Speech and Writing' in R. J. Lane, R. Mengham and P. Tew (eds), *Contemporary British Fiction* (Cambridge: Polity Press, 2003), p. 162.

58. C. Whyte, 'Imagining the City: The Glasgow Novel', in J. Schwend and H. W. Drescher (eds), *Studies in Scottish Fiction: Twentieth Century* (Frankfurt: Peter Lang, 1990), p. 317.

FIVE POSTCOLONIALISM

1. J. McLeod, *Beginning Postcolonialism* (Manchester: Manchester University Press, 2000), p. 17.

2. J. Galloway, 'Tongue in my Ear: on writing and not writing *Foreign Parts*', in *The Review of Contemporary Fiction* (Chicago: Dalkey Archive Press, 1995) – http://www.galloway.1to1.org/ear.html –

3. Welsh (1993), p. 78.

4. A. O'Hagan, 'Scotland's fine mess', *The Guardian*, Weekend Section (23 July 1994), p. 24.

5. F. O'Toole, 'Imagining Scotland' in *Granta* 56 (Winter 1996), pp. 70–1.

6. T. M. Devine, *Scotland's Empire 1600–1815* (London: Allen Lane, 2003), pp. 230–1.

7. Devine (2003), p. xxiii.

8. B. Ashcroft, G. Griffiths and H. Tiffin, *The Empire Writes Back: Theory and Practice in Post-Colonial Literatures* (London: Routledge, 2002), p. 31.

9. C. Beveridge and R. Turnbull, *The Eclipse of Scottish Culture* (Edinburgh: Edinburgh University Press, 1989), p. 1.

10. Beveridge and Turnbull (1989), p. 3.

11. Beveridge and Turnbull (1989), p. 3.

12. B. Schoene-Harwood, '"Emerging as the Others of Our Selves": Scottish Multiculturalism and the Challenge of the Body in Postcolonial Representation' *Scottish Literary Journal* 25:1 (1998), pp. 54–72

13. B. Schoene, 'A Passage to Scotland: Scottish Literature and the British Postcolonial Condition', *Scotlands* 2:1 (1995), p. 107.

14. Schoene (1995), p. 108.
15. Schoene (1995), p. 108.
16. Schoene (1995), p. 109.
17. Schoene (1995), p. 119.
18. Schoene (1995), p. 121.
19. Ngũgĩ wa Thiong'o, 'The Language of African Literature', *New Left Review*, 150 (March/April 1985), p. 19.
20. Schoene (1995), p. 121.
21. Quoted in Berthold Schoene, '"Emerging as the Others of Ourselves": Scottish Multiculturalism and the Challenge of the Body in the Postcolonial Condition', *Scottish Literary Journal* 25:1 (1998), p. 56.
22. Schoene (1998), p. 56.
23. H. G. Klaus, '1984 Glasgow: Alasdair Gray, Tom Leonard, James Kelman', *Études Écossaises* 2 (1992), pp. 31–2.
24. M. Gardiner, 'Democracy and Scotland's Postcoloniality', *Scotlands* 3.2 (1996), p. 25.
25. Gardiner (1996), p. 26.
26. M. Gardiner, 'Interdisciplinarity after Davie: Postcolonial Theory and Crises of Terminology in Scottish Cultural Studies', *Scottish Studies Review* 2:1 (2001), pp. 24–38.
27. C. Craig, 'Postcolonial Hybridity in Scotland and Ireland' in E. Longley, E. Hughes and D. O'Rawe (eds), *Ireland (Ulster) Scotland: Concepts, Contexts, Comparisons* (Belfast: Cló Ollscoil na Banríona, 2003), p. 231.
28. Quoted in Craig (2003), p. 233.
29. A. Renfrew, 'Brief Encounters, Long Farewells: Bakhtin and Scottish Literature', *International Journal of Scottish Literature*, Issue 1 (2006). http://www.ijsl.stir.ac.uk/issue1/renfrew.htm
30. A. Kelly, 'In conversation with Irvine Welsh', *Edinburgh Review* 113 (2004), p. 9.
31. S. Redhead, *Repetitive Beat Generation* (Edinburgh: Rebel Inc., 2000).
32. W. Maley, 'Subversion and squirrility in Irvine Welsh's shorter fiction' in Dermot Cavanagh and Tim Kirk (eds), *Subversion and Scurrility: Popular Discourse in Europe from 1500 to the Present* (Aldershot: Ashgate, 2000), p. 192.
33. R. Morace, *Trainspotting: A Reader's Guide* (New York: Continuum, 2001), p. 19.
34. K. MacNeil, *The Stornoway Way* (London: Hamish Hamilton, 2005), cover.
35. Quoted in E. Young, 'Blood on the tracks', *The Guardian* (14 August 1993), p. 33.
36. Kelly (2005), pp. 61–6.
37. Martin Brüggernmeier and Horst W. Drescher, 'A subculture and its characterisation in Irvine Welsh's *Trainspotting'*, *Anglistik & Englischuntericht* 63 (Winter 2000), p. 139.
38. Kelly (2005), p. 64.
39. Kelly (2005), p. 64.
40. Antonio Gramsci, *Selections from the Prison Notebooks*. ed. and trans. Quentin Hoare and Geoffrey Nowell Smith (London: Lawrence and Wishart, 1996), pp. 54–5.
41. Homi K. Bhabha, *The Location of Culture* (London: Routledge, 1994), p. 86.
42. Welsh (1993), p. 167.
43. Welsh (1993), pp. 187–8.
44. Kelly (2005), p. 46.
45. Jean-Francois Lyotard, *The Postmodern Condition* (Manchester: Manchester Unversity Press, 1984), p. 76. Alex Callinicos, *Against Postmodernism: A Marxist Critique* (Oxford: Polity Press, 1992), p. 162.
46. Callinicos (1992), p. 162.
47. E. Finlay, 'The Bourgeois Values of Irvine Welsh', *Cencrastus* (2003), p. 5.
48. Kelly (2005), p. 68.
49. John Hill, *British Cinema in the 1980s* (Oxford: Oxford University Press, 1993), p. 13.
50. John Hodge, *Trainspotting and Shallow Grave: The Screenplays* (London: Faber, 1996), p. 78.
51. W. Self, 'Carry On up the hypodermic', *The Observer* (11 February 1996), p. 6.

52. Self (1996), p. 6.
53. Mark Leonard, *Britain TM: Renewing Our Identity* (London: Demos, 1997), p. 56.
54. Irvine Welsh, *Marabou Stork Nightmares* (London: Jonathan Cape, 1995), p. 80.
55. E. Jackson and W. Maley, 'Birds of a Feather?: A Postcolonial Reading of Irvine Welsh's "Marabou Stork Nightmares" (1995)' *Revista Canaria de Estudios Ingleses*, 41 (November 2000), pp. 187–8.
56. Kelly (2005), p. 113.
57. Kelly (2005), p. 116.

SIX POSTMODERNISM

1. S. Malpas, *The Postmodern* (London: Routledge, 2005), p. 4.
2. See for example Hutcheon, *A Poetics of Postmodernism*; Brian McHale, *Postmodernist Fiction* (London: Methuen, 1987).
3. See for example Thomas Docherty, 'Introduction' in Thomas Docherty (ed.), *Postmodernism: A Reader* (Hemel Hempstead: Harvester Wheatsheaf, 1993).
4. Malpas (2005), p. 9.
5. Fredric Jameson, *Postmodernism, or, The Cultural Logic of Late Capitalism* (Durham: Duke University Press, 1991), p. xix.
6. M. McGlynn, '"Middle-Class Wankers" and Working-Class Texts: the Critics and James Kelman', *Contemporary Literature* 43:1 (Spring 2002), p. 82.
7. Toremans (2003), p. 567.
8. Toremans (2003), p. 567.
9. R. Stevenson, 'A Postmodern Scotland?' in G. Carruthers, D. Goldie and A. Renfrew (eds), *Beyond Scotland: New Contexts for Twentieth Century Scottish Literature* (Amsterdam: Rodopi, 2004), p. 209.
10. Quoted in Stevenson (2004), p. 210.
11. Stevenson (2004), p. 212.
12. Stevenson (2004), pp. 212–13.
13. Stevenson (2004), pp. 217–18.
14. Stevenson (2004), p. 228.
15. C. Craig, 'Beyond Reason – Hume, Seth, Macmurray and Scotland's Postmodernity' in Bell and Miller (2004), pp. 249–50.
16. Craig (2004), p. 251.
17. Craig (2004), p. 252.
18. Craig (2004), p. 252.
19. Craig (2004), p. 260.
20. Craig (2004), p. 284.
21. E. Bell, *Questioning Scotland: Literature, Nationalism, Postmodernism* (Basingstoke: Palgrave MacMillan, 2004), p. 3.
22. Quoted in Bell (2004), pp. 4–5.
23. F. Kermode, 'Muriel Spark', *Modern Essays* (London: Fontana, 1990), p. 268.
24. D. Lodge, *The Art of Fiction* (Hammondsworth: Penguin, 1992), p. 76.
25. R. Whittaker, *The Faith and Fiction of Muriel Spark* (MacMillan: Basingstoke, 1982), p. 1.
26. M. McQuillan (ed.), *Theorizing Muriel Spark* (Vasingstoke: Palgrave McMillan, 2002), p. 4.
27. McQuillan (2002), inside cover.
28. Stevenson (2004), p. 213.
29. Stevenson (2004), p. 213.
30. M. P. McCulloch, 'Calvinism and Narrative Discourse in Muriel Spark', in N. Macmillan and K. Stirling (eds), *Odd Alliances: Scottish Studies in European Contexts* (Glasgow: Cruithne Press, 1999), p. 90.
31. McCulloch (1999), p. 91.

32. McCulloch (1999), p. 92.
33. B. Cheyette, *Muriel Spark* (Devon: Northcote House, 2000), p. 54.
34. Cheyette (2000), pp. 57–8.
35. G. Carruthers, 'The Remarkable Fictions of Muriel Spark', in Gifford and McMillan (1997), p. 514.
36. Carruthers (1997), p. 516.
37. Carruthers (1997), p. 516.
38. Kennedy is the only Scottish writer to feature in the collection of essays *Contemporary British Women Writers* (2004).
39. A notable example of this is A. Christianson, 'Lies, Notable Silences and Plastering the Cracks: The Fiction of A.L. Kennedy and Janice Galloway', in *Gender and Scottish Society: Polities, Policies and Participation* (Proceedings from a Conference at Edinburgh University, 1998), pp. 136–40.
40. C. March, 'Interview with A. L. Kennedy', *Edinburgh Review* 101 (1999), p. 112.
41. A. L. Kennedy, 'Not changing the world' in I. A. Bell, *Peripheral Visions: Images of Nationhood in Contemporary British Fiction* (Cardiff: University of Wales Press, 1995), p. 100.
42. Kennedy (1995), p. 101.
43. E. Bell, 'Scotland and Ethics in the Work of A.L. Kennedy', *Scotlands* 5:1 (1998), pp. 105–6.
44. Gifford and McMillan (1997), p. 619.
45. Gifford and McMillan (1997), p. 620.
46. Quoted in S. Dunnigan, 'A. L. Kennedy's Longer Fiction: Articulate Grace', in Christianson and Lumsden (2000), p. 144.
47. Dunnigan (2000), p. 145.

CONCLUSION

1. G. Carruthers, D. Goldie and A. Renfrew (eds), *Beyond Scotland: New Contexts for Twentieth-Century Scottish Literature* (Amsterdam: Rodopi, 2004), pp. 14–15.
2. Eleanor Bell and Scott Hames, 'About IJSL', *International Journal of Scottish Literature* (2006). http://www.ijsl.stir.ac.uk/about.htm (accessed 12/05/2008).
3. B. Schoene (ed.), *The Edinburgh Companion to Contemporary Scottish Literature* (Edinburgh: Edinburgh University Press, 2007), p. 2.
4. Schoene (2007), p. 2.
5. Centre for Intellectual Property Policy and Management, 'Research Into Authors' Earnings' (Published 8 March 2007). http://www.prnewswire.co.uk/cgi/news/release?id=194429 (accessed 12/05/2008).

Select Bibliography

MONOGRAPHS

Bell, Eleanor, *Questioning Scotland: Literature, Nationalism, Postmodernism* (Basingstoke: Palgrave Macmillan, 2004).

Beveridge, Craig and Ronald Turnbull, *The Eclipse of Scottish Culture* (Edinburgh, Polygon, 1989).

Bold, Alan, *Modern Scottish Literature* (London: Longman, 1983).

Craig, Cairns, *The Modern Scottish Novel: Narrative and the National Imagination* (Edinburgh: Edinburgh University Press, 1999).

Craig, Cairns, *Out of History: Narrative Paradigms in Scottish and English culture* (Edinburgh: Polygon, 1996).

Crawford, Robert, *Devolving English Literature* (Edinburgh: Edinburgh University Press, 2000).

Crawford, Robert, *Identifying Poets: Self and Territory in Twentieth Century Poetry.* Edinburgh: (Edinburgh University Press, 1993).

Devine, T. M., *Scotland's Empire 1600–1815* (London: Allen Lane, 2003).

Devine, T.M., *The Scottish Nation 1700–2000* (London: Penguin, 1999).

Gardiner, Michael, *The Cultural Roots of British Devolution* (Edinburgh: Edinburgh University Press, 2004).

Gifford, Douglas, *The Dear Green Place: the Novel in the West of Scotland* (Glasgow: Third Eye Centre, 1985).

Gifford, Douglas, Dunnigan, Sarah and MacGilvaray, *Scottish Literature in English and Scots* (Edinburgh: Edinburgh University Press, 2002).

Hagan, Annette, *Urban Scots Dialect Writing* (Bern: P. Lang, 2002).

Hart, Francis Russell, *The Scottish Novel: a Critical Survey* (London: J. Murray, 1978).

Haywood, Ian, *Working-class Fiction: from Chartism to Trainspotting* (Plymouth: Northcote House Publishers Ltd, 1997).

Kay, Billy, *Scots: the Mither Tongue* (London: Grafton, 1988).

McClure, J. Derick, *Language, Poetry and Nationhood: Scots as a Poetic Language from 1878 to the Present* (East Linton: Tuckwell Press, 2000).

McCrone, David, *Understanding Scotland: the Sociology of a Stateless Nation* (London: Routledge, 1992).

McIlvanney, Liam and Ray Ryan (eds), *Ireland and Scotland: Culture and Society, 1700–2000* (Dublin: Four Courts Press, 2005).

McIlvanney, William, *Surviving the Shipwreck* (Edinburgh: Mainstream, 1991).

Malzahn, Manfred, *Aspects of Identity: The Contemporary Scottish Novel* (Frankfurt am Main: P. Lang, 1984).

March, Christie, L., *Rewriting Scotland: Welsh, McLean, Warner, Banks, Galloway and Kennedy* (Manchester: Manchester University Press, 2002).

Muir, Edwin, *Scott and Scotland: the predicament of the Scottish writer* (Edinburgh: Polygon, 1982).

Murray, Isobel and Tait, Bob, *Ten Modern Scottish Novels* (Aberdeen Aberdeen University Press 1984).

Nairn, Tom, *After Britain: New Labour and the Return of Scotland* (London: Granta Books, 2000).

Nairn, Tom, *The Break-up of Britain: crisis and neo-nationalism* (London, NLB, 1977).

Sassi, Carla, *Why Scottish Literature Matters* (Edinburgh: The Saltire Society, 2005).

Schoene, Berthold, *Writing Men: literary masculinities from Frankenstein to the new* man (Edinburgh: Edinburgh University Press, 2000).

Smith, G. Gregory, *Scottish Literature: Character and Influence* (London: MacMillan, 1919).

Spring, Ian, *Phantom Village: The Myth of the New Glasgow* (Edinburgh: Polygon, 1990).

Thomson, Derick, *An Introduction to Gaelic Poetry* (London: Victor Gollanz Ltd, 1974).

Walker, Marshall, *Scottish Literature Since 1707* (Edinburgh: Addison Wesley Longman, 1996).

Whyte, Christopher, *Modern Scottish Poetry* (Edinburgh: Edinburgh University Press, 2004).

EDITED COLLECTIONS

Bell, Eleanor, and Gavin Miller (eds), *Scotland in Theory: Reflections on Literature and Culture* (Amsterdam: Rodopi, 2004).

Brown, Ian, Clancy, Tom, Manning, Susan and Pittock, Murray (eds), *Edinburgh History of Scottish Literature Vol 1–3* (Edinburgh: EDINBURGH UNIVERSITY PRESS, 2007).

Carruthers, Gerry, Goldie, David and Renfrew, Alastair (eds), *Beyond Scotland: New Contexts for Twentieth Century Scottish Literature* (Amsterdam: Rodopi, 2004).

Christianson, Aileen and Lumsden, Alison, *Contemporary Scottish Women Writers* (Edinburgh: Edinburgh University Press, 2000).

Craig, Cairns (ed.), *The History of Scottish Literature Vol 1–4* (Aberdeen: Aberdeen University Press, 1987).

Gifford, Douglas and McMillan, Dorothy (eds), *A History of Scottish Women's Writing* (Edinburgh: Edinburgh University Press, 1997).

Hagemann, Susanne (ed.), *Studies in Scottish Fiction: 1945 to the present* (Frankfurt am Main; New York: Peter Lang, 1996).

Hughes, Eamonn Longley, Edna and O'Rawe, Des (eds), *Ireland (Ulster) Scotland: concepts, contexts, comparisons* (Belfast: Cló Ollscoil na Banríona, 2003).

Kidd, H. (ed.) *Calemadonnas: Women and Scotland* (Dundee: Gairfish, 1994).

Norquay, Glenda and Smyth, Gerry (eds), *Across the Margins: cultural identity and change in the Atlantic Archipelago* (Manchester: Manchester University Press, 2002).

Schoene, Berthold (ed.), *The Edinburgh Companion to Contemporary Scottish Literature* (Edinburgh: Edinburgh University Press, 2007).

Schwend, Joachim and Drescher, H. W. (eds) *Studies in Scottish Fiction: Twentieth Century* (Frankfurt am Main; New York: P. Lang, 1990).

Stevenson, Randall and Wallace Gavin (eds), *The Scottish Novel Since the Seventies* (Edinburgh: Edinburgh University Press, 1993).

Stevenson, Randall and Wallace, Gavin, *Scottish Theatre Since the Seventies* (Edinburgh: Edinburgh University Press, 1996).

Whyte, Christopher (ed), *Gendering the Nation: Studies in Modern Scottish Literature* (Edinburgh: Edinburgh University Press, 1995).

POETRY AND PROSE ANTHOLOGIES

Byrne, Michel and McMillan, Dorothy (eds), *Modern Scottish Women Poets* (Edinburgh: Canongate, 2003).

Gifford, Douglas and Riach, Alan (eds), *Scotlands: Poets and the Nation* (Manchester: Carcarnet, 2004).

Kerrigan, Catherine (ed), *An Anthology of Scottish Women Poets* (Edinburgh: Edinburgh University Press, 1991).

Kravitz, Peter (ed) The Picador Book of Contemporary Scottish Fiction (London: Picador, 1997).

MacAulay, Donald (ed), *Modern Scottish Gaelic Poems* (Edinburgh: Canongate, 1995).

O'Rourke, Donny (ed), *Dream State: the New Scottish Poets* (Edinburgh: Polygon, 1994).

ARTICLES

Bell, Ian A., 'Imagine Living There: Form and Ideology in Contemporary Scottish Fiction' in S. Hagemann (ed), *Studies in Scottish Fiction: 1945 to the Present* (Frankfurt am Main; New York: Peter Lang, 1996), pp. 217–34.

Black, Ronald, 'Thunder, Renaissance and Flowers: Gaelic Poetry in the Twentieth Century' in Craig, Cairns (ed), *The History of Scottish Literature Vol 4* (Aberdeen: Aberdeen University Press, 1987).

Christianson, Aileen 'Gender and nation: debatable lands and passable boundaries' in G. Norquay and G. Smyth (eds), *Across the Margins: Cultural identity and change in the Atlantic archipelago* (Manchester: Manchester University Press, 2002), pp. 67–82.

Craig, Cairns, 'Beyond Reason – Hume, Seth, Macmurray and Scotland's Postmodernity' in Bell and Miller (2004), pp. 249–84.

Craig, Cairns, 'Postcolonial Hybridity in Scotland and Ireland' in Hughes, Longley and O'Rawe (2003), pp. 231–43.

Craig, Cairns, 'Scotland: Culture after Devolution' in Edna Longley, Eamonn Hughes, and Des O'Rawe (eds), *Ireland (Ulster) Scotland: concepts, contexts, comparisons* (Belfast: Cló Ollscoil na Banríona, 2003), pp. 231–44.

Crawford, Robert, 'Bakhtin and Scotlands' *Scotlands* 1 (1994), pp. 55–65.

Dixon, Keith 'Making Sense of Ourselves: Nation and Community in Modern Scottish Writing' *Forum for Modern Language Studies* 24:4 (1993), pp. 359–368.

Dunn, Douglas, 'Divergent Scottishness: William Boyd, Allan Massie, Ronald Frame' in Stevenson and Wallace (1993), pp. 149–69.

Dunn, Douglas 'The Representation of Women in Scottish Literature' in *Scotlands* 2 (1994), pp. 1–23.

Gardiner, Michael, 'Democracy and Scotland's Postcoloniality' in *Scotlands* 3.2 (1996), pp. 24–41.

Gardiner, Michael, 'Interdisciplinarity after Davie: Postcolonial Theory and Crises of Terminology in Scottish Cultural Studies', *Scottish Studies Review* 2:1 (2001), pp. 24–38.

Gifford, Douglas 'At Last – The Real Scottish Literary Renaissance?' in *Books in Scotland* 34 (1990), pp. 1–4.

Hagemann, Susan, 'From Carswell to Kay: Aspects of Gender, the Novel and the Drama' in Brown, Clancy, Manning, Pittock (2007), pp. 214–24.

Hendry, Joy, 'Twentieth-century Women's Writing: The Nest of Singing Birds' in Craig (1987), pp. 291–308.

Klaus, H. Gustav, '1984 Glasgow: Alasdair Gray, Tom Leonard, James Kelman', *Études Écossaises* 2 (1992), pp. 31–40.

Macleod M. and Wilson M., 'In the Shadow of the Bard: The Gaelic Short Story, Novel and Drama since the early Twentieth Century' in Brown, Clancy, Manning, Pittock (2007), pp. 273–82.

Maley, Willy, 'Ireland, versus, Scotland: crossing the (English) language barrier' in Glenda Norquay and Gerry Smyth (eds), *Across the margins: cultural identity and change in the Atlantic archipelago* (Manchester: Manchester University Press, 2002), pp. 13–31

McIlvanney, Liam, 'The Politics of Narrative in the Post-War Scottish Novel', in Z. Leader (ed), *On Modern British Fiction* (Oxford: Oxford University Press, 2002), pp. 181–201.

Massie, Alex, 'Sir Walter's Scoterati', *Scotland on Sunday* (16 June 2002), p. 1.

Monnickendam, Andrew, 'Literary Voices and the Projection of Cultural Failure in Modern Scottish Literature' in Maurice Burning and Ton Hoenselaars (eds), *English Literature and the Other Languages* (Amsterdam: Rodopi, 1999), pp. 231–42.

O'Hagan, Andrew, 'Scotland's fine mess', *Guardian*, Weekend Section (23 July 1994), p. 24.

O'Toole, Fintan, 'Imagining Scotland', *Granta* 56 (Winter 1996), pp. 70–1.

Pitchford, Nicola, 'How Late it Was for England: james Kelman's Scottish Booker Prize', *Contemporary Literature* 41:4 (Win 2000), pp. 693–725.

Reizbaum, Marilyn, 'Canonical Double Cross: Scottish and Irish Women's Writing' in K. R. Lawrence (ed), *Decolonizing Tradition: New Views of Twentieth-Century 'British' Literary Canons* (Chicago: University of Illinois Press, 1992), pp. 165–90.

Marilyn Reizbaum, 'Nationalism, Feminism and the Contemporary Literature of Scotland and Ireland' *Scotlands* 2 (1994), pp. 24–31.

Renfrew, Alastair 'Brief Encounters, Long Farewells: Bakhtin and Scottish Literature', *International Journal of Scottish Literature*, Issue 1: <http://www.ijsl.stir.ac.uk/issue1/renfrew.htm>

Schoene, Berthold, 'A Passage to Scotland: Scottish Literature and the British Postcolonial Condition' *Scotlands* 2:1 (1995), pp. 107–121.

Schoene, Berthold, '"Emerging as the others of our selves" – Scottish multi-culturalism and the challenge of the body in postcolonial representation', *Scottish Literary Journal*, 25:1 (May 1998), pp. 54–72.

Skinner, John, 'Contemporary Scottish Novelists and the Stepmother Tongue' in Maurice Burning and Ton Hoenselaars (eds), *English Literature and the Other Languages* (Amsterdam: Rodopi, 1999), pp. 211–20.

Stevenson, Randall, 'A Postmodern Scotland?' in Carruthers, Goldie and Renfrew (2004), pp. 209–28.

Whyte, Christopher, 'Imagining the City: The Glasgow Novel' in J. Schwend and H. W. Drescher (eds), *Studies in Scottish Fiction: Twentieth Century* (Frankfurt: Peter Lang, 1990), pp. 317–34.

Whyte, Christopher 'Gender and Nationality' in *Cencrastus* 42 (Winter 1991/1992), p. 46.

Whyte, Christopher, 'Masculinities in Contemporary Scottish Fiction', *Forum for Modern Language Studies* 34:2 (1998), pp. 274–85.

Whyte, Christopher, 'Masculinities In Contemporary Scottish Fiction' *Forum for Modern Language Studies* 34:3 (1998), pp. 274–285.

JANICE GALLOWAY

Burgess, Moira, 'Disturbing Words' in Kidd, H. (ed) *Calemadonnas: Women and Scotland* (Dundee: Gairfish, 1994).

Christianson, Aileen, 'Lies, notable silences and plastering the cracks: the fiction of A.L. Kennedy and Janice Galloway' in *Gender and Scottish Society: Politics, Policies and Participation* (report of conference held at University of Edinburgh, 31 October 1997), pp. 136–40.

Edinburgh Review Special Issue on Janice Galloway, vol. 113 (2004).

Galloway, Janice (ed), *Meantime: Looking Forward to the Millennium* (Edinburgh: Polygon, 1991).

Galloway, Janice, 'Different Oracles: Me and Alasdair Gray' in *Review of Contemporary Fiction* 15:2 (Summer 1995), pp. 193–6.

McGlynn, Mary 'Janice Galloway's Alienated Spaces' in *Scottish Studies Review* 4:2 (Aut 2003), pp. 82–97.

March, Christie, L.,'Interview with Janice Galloway', in *Edinburgh Review* 101 (1990), pp. 85–98.

Metzstein, Margery, 'Of Myths and Men: Aspects of Gender in the Fiction of Janice Galloway' in Stevenson and Wallace (1993), pp. 136–46.

Norquay, Glenda, 'The Fiction of Janice Galloway: "Weaving a Route through Chaos'" in G. Norquay and G. Smyth (eds), *Space and Place: the Geographies of Literature* (Liverpool: John Moores University Press, 1997), pp. 323–30.

Norquay, Glenda, 'Janice Galloway's Novels: Fraudulent Mooching' in Christianson and Lumsden (2000).

See also <http//:www.galloway.1to1.org>

ALASDAIR GRAY

Bernstein, Stephen, *Alasdair Gray* (London: Associated University Presses, 1999).

Bohnke, Dietmar, *Shades of Gray: science fiction, history and the problem of postmodernism in the work of Alasdair Gray* (Glienicke: Galda + Wilch, 2004).

Costa, Domonique, 'In the Scottish Tradition: Alasdair Gray's Lanark and *1982 Janine.' Literature of Region and Nation* 2:3 (1990), pp. 3–7

Costa, Dominique. 'Alasdair Gray.' *Post-War Literatures in English* 10 (1990), pp. 1–9.

Costa, Domonique, "Decadence and Apocalypse in Gray's Glasgow-*Lanark*: A Postmodernist Novel" *Scotia* vol. 18 (1994), pp. 22–34.

Craig, Cairns, 'Going Down to Hell is Easy: Lanark, Realism and The Limits of the Imagination' in Crawford and Nairn (1991), pp. 90–107.

Crawford, Robert and Nairn, Tom (eds), *The Arts of Alasdair Gray* (Edinburgh: Edinburgh University Press, 1991).

Gifford, Douglas, 'The Importance of Alasdair Gray's *Lanark' Studies in Scottish Literature* 18 (1983), pp. 210–252.

Gray, Alasdair, 'A Modest Proposal for By-Passing a Predicament', *Chapman* 35–6 (1983), pp. 7–9.

Gray, Alasdair, *Alasdair Gray* (Edinburgh: Saltire Self Portraits, 1988).

Kaczvinsky, Donald, 'Making Up for Lost Time: Scotland, Stories and Alasdair Gray's *Poor Things' Contemporary Literature* 42:4 (2001), pp. 775–99.

Lumsden, Alison, 'Innovation and Reaction in the Fiction of Alasdair Gray' in Stevenson and Wallace (1993), pp. 115–26.

Malpas, Simon, *The Postmodern* (London: Routledge, 2005).

Miller, Gavin, *Alasdair Gray: the Fiction of Communion* (Amsterdam: Rodopi, 2005).

Moores, Phil, *Alasdair Gray: Critical Appreciations and a Bibliography* (Boston Spa & London: the British Library, 2002).

Titinen, Joanna, *'Work as if you live in the early days of a better nation': history and politics in the works of Alasdair Gray* (Helsinki: Yliopistopaino (Helsinki University Printing House), 2004).

Williamson, Kevin, 'Under the Influence', in Moores (2002), pp. 165–87.

Witschi, Beat, *Glasgow urban writing and postmodernism: a study of Alasdair Gray's fiction* (Frankfurt am Main; New York: P. Lang, c1991).

JAMES KELMAN

Baker, Simon "Wee stories with a working-class theme": The Reimagining of Urban Realism in the Fiction of James Kelman' in J. Schwend and H. Drescher (eds), *Studies in Scottish Fiction: twentieth century* (Frankfurt am Main: P. Lang, 1990).

Bohnke, Deitmar, *Kelman Writes Back: literary politics in the work of a Scottish writer* (Cambridge: Galda and Wich, 1999).

Clarke, Alan, 'A Prize insult to the courage of Scotland's finest' *Mail on Sunday* (23 October 1994), p. 10.

Craig, Cairns, 'Resisting Arrest: James Kelman', in Randall Stevenson and Gavin Wallace (eds), *The Scottish Novel Since the Seventies* (Edinburgh: Edinburgh University Press, 1993), pp. 99–114.

Harrison, David, 'CURSES! WHAT THE ****'S GOING ON?' *The Observer* (16 October 1994) p. 9.

Jackson, Ellen-Raissa and Maley, Willy, 'Committing to Kelman: the Art of Integrity and the Politics of Dissent' in *Edinburgh Review* 108 (2001), pp. 22–7.

Kelman, James, *Some Recent Attacks: essays cultural and political* (Stirling: AK Press, 1992).

Kelman, James, 'Elitist slurs are racism by another name' *Scotland on Sunday*, (16 October 1994), Spectrum, p. 2.

Kelman, James, *'And the Judges Said…'* (London: Secker and Warburg, 2002).

Kovesi, Simon, *James Kelman* (Manchester: Manchester University Press, 2007).

Lockerbie, Catherine, 'Lighting up Kelman' *The Scotsman* (19 March 1994), Weekend, p. 2.

Maley, Willy, 'Swearing Blind: Kelman and the Curse of the Working Classes' *Edinburgh Review* 95 (1996), pp. 105–112.

McGlynn, Mary, '"Middle-Class Wankers" and Working-Class Texts: the Critics and James Kelman' *Contemporary Literature*43:1 (Spring 2002), pp. 50–84.

McLean, Duncan, 'Interview with James Kelman' in *Edinburgh Review* 71 (1985), pp. 66–79.

McMunnigall, Allan and Carruthers, Gerard, 'Locating Kelman: Glasgow, Scotland and the Commitment to Place' *Edinburgh Review* 108 (2001), pp. 56–68.

McNeill, Kirsty, 'Interview with James Kelman' in *Chapman* 57 (1989), pp. 2–10.

Milne, Drew, 'James Kelman: Dialectics of Urbanity' in J. Davies, ed, *Writing Region and Nation* (Swansea: University of Wales, 1994), pp. 393–407.

Milne, Drew, 'The Fiction of James Kelman and Irvine Welsh: Accents, Speech and Writing' in R. J. Lane, R. Mengham and P. Tew (eds), *Contemporary British Fiction* (Cambridge: Polity Press, 2003), pp. 158–73.

Neuberger, Julia, 'Cooking the Booker' in *Evening Standard* [London] (13 October 1994), p. 27.

Nicoll, Laurence, 'Gogol's Overcoat: Kelman Resartus' *Edinburgh Review* 108 (2001), pp. 116–24.

Nicoll, Laurence, 'This Is Not a Nationalist Position: James Kelman's Existential Voice' *Edinburgh Review* 103 (2000), pp. 79–84.

Spinks, Lee, 'In Juxtaposition to Which: Narrative, System and Subjectivity in the fiction of James Kelman' *Edinburgh Review* 108 (2001), pp. 90–101.

Toremans, Tom, 'An Interview with Alasdair Gray and James Kelman', *Contemporary Literature* 44:4 (2003), pp. 565–86.

Warner, Gerald, 'Time for a disaffection from literary slumming', *Sunday Times* (25 September 1994), p. 5.

Wavell, Stuart, 'Scots bewail 4,000-expletive blot on national character' *Sunday Times* (16 October 1994), p. 7

Wood, James, 'Books: In Defence Of Kelman', *The Guardian* (25 October 1994), p. 9.

A.L. KENNEDY

Bell, Eleanor, 'Scotland and Ethics in the Work of A.L. Kennedy', *Scotlands* 5:1 (1998), pp. 105–13.

Christainson, Aileen, 'Gender and Nation' in Norquay and Smyth (2000), pp. 67–82.

Christianson, Aileen, 'Lies, notable silences and plastering the cracks: the fiction of A.L. Kennedy and Janice Galloway', *Gender and Scottish Society: Politics, Policies and Participation* (Proceedings from a Conference at Edinburgh University, 1998), pp. 136–40.

Dunnigan, Sarah, 'A. L. Kennedy's Longer Fiction: Articulate Grace' in Christianson and Lumsdem (2000) pp. 144–55.

Kennedy, A.L., 'Not changing the world' in Ian A. Bell (ed.), *Peripheral Visions: Images of Nationhood in Contemporary British Fiction* (Cardiff: University of Wales Press, 1995), pp. 100–2.
March, Christie, 'Interview with A. L. Kennedy' in *Edinburgh Review* 101 (1999), pp. 99–19.

LIZ LOCHHEAD

Christianson, Aileen, 'Liz Lochhead's Poetry and Drama: Forging Ironies' in Christianson and Lumsden (2000), pp. 41–52.
Crawford, Robert (ed), *Liz Lochhead's Voices* (Edinburgh: Edinburgh University Press, 1993) Includes a complete secondary bibliography.
Folorunso, Femi, 'Scottish Drama and the Popular Tradition', in Stevenson and Wallace (1996), pp. 176–85.
McCulloch, Margery Palmer, *Liz Lochhead's Mary Queen of Scots Got Her Head Chopped Off* (Glasgow: ASLS, 2000).
Nicholson Colin, *Poem, Purpose and Place: Shaping Identity in Contemporary Scottish Verse* (Edinburgh: Polygon, 1992).
Todd, Emily, 'Interview with Liz Lochhead', in *Verse* 8.3/9.1 (Winter/Spring 1992), pp. 83–95.
Varty, Anne, 'The Mirror and the Vamp' in Gifford and McMillan (1997), pp. 641–58.
Wilson, Rebecca E. and Somerville-Arjat, Gillean, *Sleeping with Monsters: Conversations with Scottish and Irish Women Poets* (Edinburgh: Polygon, 1991).

MURIEL SPARK

Bold, Alan, *Muriel Spark* (London: Methuen, 1986).
Bold, Alan (ed.), *Muriel Spark: An Odd Capacity for Vision* (London: Barnes & Noble 1984).
Carruthers, Gerard, 'The Remarkable Fictions of Muriel Spark', Gifford and McMillan (1997), pp. 514–25.
Cheyette, Bryan, *Muriel Spark* (Devon: Northcote House, 2000).
Christianson, Aileen, 'Muriel Spark and Candia McWilliam' in Christianson and Lumsden (2000).
Edgecombe, R.S. *Vocation and Identity in the Fiction of Muriel Spark* (Columbia; London: University of Missouri Press, 1990).
Frankel, S., 'An Interview with Muriel Spark' *Partisan Review* 52: 3 (Summer 1987).
Kermode, Frank, *Modern Essays* (London: Fontana, 1990).
MacLachlan, C., 'Muriel Spark and the Gothic' in Hagemann (1996).
McCulloch, Margery Palmer, 'Calvinism and Narrative Discourse in Muriel Spark', in Neil McMillan and Kirsten Stirling (eds), *Odd Alliances: Scottish Studies in European Contexts* (Glasgow: Cruithne Press, 1999), pp. 90–9.
McQuillan, Martin (ed.), *Theorizing Muriel Spark* (Basingstoke: Palgrave McMillan, 2002). Contains complete secondary bibliography.
Massie, Allan, *Muriel Spark* (Edinburgh: Ramsey Head Press, 1979).
Page, N. *Muriel Spark* (Basingstoke: Macmillan, 1990).
Parrinder, Patrick, 'Muriel Spark and Her Critics' *Critical Quarterly* 25: 2 (Summer 1983).
Randisi, J. L. *On Her Way Rejoicing: the Fiction of Muriel Spark* (Washington, D.C.: Catholic University of America Press, 1991).
Rankin, Ian, 'Structure and Surface: Reading Muriel Spark's The Driver's Seat' *Journal of Narrative Technique* 15: 2 (Spring 1985).
Rankin, Ian, 'The Deliberate Cunning of Muriel Spark' in Stevenson and Wallace (1993), pp. 41–53.
Richmond, V. B., *Muriel Spark* (New York: Ungar, 1984).

Schiff, S., 'Cultural Pursuits: Muriel Spark between the Lines' *The New Yorker* (24 May 1993).

Sproxton, J., 'The Women of Muriel Spark' *New Blackfriars* 73, 863 (September 1992).

Stevenson, S., 'Poetry Deleted, Parody Added: Watergate, Spark's Style and Bakhtin's Stylistics' *Ariel* 24: 4 (October 1993).

Whittaker, Ruth, *The Faith and Fiction of Muriel Spark* (Macmillan: Basingstoke, 1982).

IRVINE WELSH

Finlay, Elspeth, 'The Bourgeois Values of Irvine Welsh' in *Cencrastus* (2003), pp. 5–7.

Freeman, Alan, 'Ourselves As Others' *Edinburgh Review* 95 (1996), pp. 135–141.

Freeman, Alan "Ghosts in Sunny Leith: Irvine Welsh's *Trainspotting*" in Hagemann (1997), pp. 251–62.

Gordon, Giles, 'Pandering the English view of Scotland the drugged' *The Scotsman* (13 June 1997), p. 4.

Grant, Iain, 'Dealing Out the Capital Punishement' *Sunday Times* (5 September 1993), p.14.

Horton, Patricia, '*Trainspotting*: A Topography of the Masculine Abject' *English* 50 (Autumn 2001), pp. 219–34.

Jackson, Ellen-Raïssa and Maley, Willy, 'Birds of a Feather?: A Postcolonial Reading of Irvine Welsh's "Marabou Stork Nightmares" (1995)' in *Revista Canaria de Estudios Ingleses*, special issue on *Contemporary Scottish Literature, 1970–2000* (ed.) Tomás Monterrey, 41 (November 2000), pp. 187–96.

Jamieson, Gill, 'Fixing the City' in Glenda Norquay and Gerry Smyth (eds), *Space and Place: The Geographies of Literature* (Liverpool: Liverpool University Press, 1998), pp. 217–26.

Kane, Pat, "Fatal Knowledge of Inescapable Masculinity" *Scotland on Sunday* (16 July 1995), p. 12.

Kelly, Aaron, 'In conversation with Irvine Welsh' *Edinburgh Review* 113 (2004), pp. 7–17.

Kelly, Aaron, *Irvine Welsh* (Manchester: Manchester University Press, 2005). Also contains a complete bibliography of Welsh's work.

Maley, Willy 'Subversion and squirrility in Irvine Welsh's shorter fiction' in Dermot Cavanagh and Tim Kirk (eds), *Subversion and Scurrility: Popular Discourse in Europe from 1500 to the Present* (Aldershot: Ashgate, 2000), pp. 190–204.

Maconie, Stuart, 'Fool Britannia' *Times* (26 December 1998), p. 24.

McMillan, Neil 'Junked Exiles, Exiled Junk' in Glenda Norquay and Gerry Smyth (eds), *Space and Place: The Geographies of Literature* (Liverpool: Liverpool University Press, 1998), pp. 239–56.

McKay, Ron 'Would the Real Irvine Welsh Shoot Up?' *Observer* (4 February 1996), p. 9.

Morace, Robert, *Trainspotting: A Readers Guide* (New York: Continuum, 2001).

O'Hagan, Andrew, "The Boys Are Back in Town" *Sight and Sound* 6:2 (1996).

Redhead, Steve, *Repetitive Beat Generation* (Edinburgh: Rebel Inc., 2000).

Self, Will, 'Carry On up the hypodermic' *The Observer* (11 February 1996), p. 6.

Walsh, John, "The Not to Shady Past of Irvine Welsh" *Independent* (15 April 1995), p. 25.

Williams, Nicholas, 'The Dialect of Authenticity: the case of Irvine Welsh' in, Maurice Burning and Ton Hoenselaars (eds), *English Literature and the Other Languages* (Amsterdam: Rodopi, 1999), pp. 221–30.

Young, Elizabeth, 'Blood on the tracks', *Guardian* (14 August 1993), p. 33.

Scotland on Sunday, Editorial, '*Trainspotting*'s Lessons For Middle Britain' (8 August 1993).

Index